GODLY REDEMPTION FROM
DISAPPOINTMENT, LOSS, AND COMBAT STRESS

Bread Crumbs
On Purpose

SANDY FULKERSON

TATE PUBLISHING
AND ENTERPRISES, LLC

Published by Tate Publishing & Enterprises, LLC
127 E. Trade Center Terrace | Mustang, Oklahoma 73064 USA
1.888.361.9473 | www.tatepublishing.com

Tate Publishing is committed to excellence in the publishing industry. The company reflects the philosophy established by the founders, based on Psalm 68:11,
"The Lord gave the word and great was the company of those who published it."

Book design copyright © 2013 by Tate Publishing, LLC. All rights reserved.
Cover design by Ronnel Luspoc
Interior design by Mary Jean Archival

Published in the United States of America
ISBN: 978-1-62295-365-3
1. Biography & Autobiography / Personal Memoirs
2. Biography & Autobiography / Religious
13.02.18

About the Title
Bread Crumbs on Purpose

In the classic fairy tale, Hansel and Gretel, bread crumbs were purposely left along the path so that those young children might safely find their way back home. As a child and thereafter, this author has always been captivated by the mental imagery of these two innocent children finding their way back to their safe haven by way of dropped bread crumbs after experiencing harmful, threatening encounters.

In this writer's case, bread crumbs, too, were laid along her life's pathway by God—her God knowing beforehand his plans for her as to why and where her travels would take her and what she would gain and amass from her life's experiences.

For her, these lifetime events would enlighten and provide the foundation upon which wisdom, knowledge, and faithful service would build. While all along her journey a reaching out ensued to many of those yearning for a friend, a kind shoulder, a compassionate support system on which to lean for a brief time, or perhaps an extended one.

A year ago this book's title came to mind—quickly replacing a military term upon which this book began. The importance and value of this "new" acquired name is as follows:

Throughout the life of this author (or into the life of anyone,) many different pathways are made available for us to undertake at countless times in our lives. God has granted each of us the permission, if you will, to make choices of our own. We are able to choose good, sound paths or perhaps passageways ultimately filled with peril. God has granted us the liberty, the freedom, of making our own missteps or our own victories!

However, he does always provide generous opportunities for growth along each choice and alongside all roads. Therefore, he will make available ample occasions for success when we choose to follow his lead and we earnestly seek his face.

For this writer, God was and has always been "present and accounted for." Each event, each circumstance, each broken occurrence, took place under God's gentle, loving care. He sheltered and protected the destiny of that initial small child and, thus, has continued to overshadow into her present life—this fulfilled and content grandmother of five lively grandchildren.

The many roads taken were chosen because of the *heavenly* bread crumbs lovingly laid "on purpose" upon those special trails—laid by a divine and blessed heavenly Father. However, as I learned early in life, not always will our way emerge sheltered, lit, and rise up to meet us in perfect harmony—it may be quite the opposite! But that is not to say that the *Bread Crumbs on Purpose* on a specific passageway was laid in error.

Our Lord has unique, divine plans for turning around our lives' negative settings into blessed joyous ones. Positive surroundings that will cause the recipient to marvel at the outcome of such set-apart phenomenon ("miracles")—blessed as we look back into those many years past, witnessing the holy hand of God ever *"present and accounted for."*

And just like our celebrated Hansel and Gretel, my own bread crumbs have led me safely "home." I now grasp and comprehend the "whys" and the "how comes." I recognize that I have always been cradled *in the palm of God's hand*—I have always been *protected beneath his wings!* I was designed for *this time* in my life— for this time of sharing my adventures and words of knowledge and hopefully bringing understanding, hope, wisdom, and peace into others' present circumstances.

"I know the plans I have for you," announces the Lord. "I want you to enjoy success. I do not plan to harm you. I will give you hope for the years to come."

Jeremiah 29:11 (NIRV)

"So do not fear, for I am with you: do not be dismayed, for I am your God. I will strengthen you and help you; I will uphold you with my righteous right hand."

Isaiah 41:10

"He fills my life with good things!"

Psalms 103:5 (TCB)

My quiet prayer and wish for you, the reader, is that you, too, will diligently search for the divine direction laid before you in the form of *your* bread crumbs! That special *"rabbit trail"* with spiritually visible bread crumbs is absolutely the blessed one—seek it and be inspired, honor it, and then follow it directly into your final home in heaven. Let it be the one that will train and equip you with the tools with which to reach those hearts that can only be touched and given hope through your reassurance and comfort. Share with others the encouragement and passion that only your spirit can provide!

Yes, you can make an eternal difference in your world—in the world of your loved ones, in the world beyond your comfort zone! There are many for whom your care will be inspiring—the sensitivity and hope that only your life, your path will bring to a humanity seeking a kind countenance and a joyful, generous heart!

Blessings to you and yours... Sandy Fulkerson

Acknowledgments

First and foremost, I must recognize my cherished, dear, kind-hearted husband, Dean Fulkerson. He has always been my very best friend. As in military slang, we have forever had each other's back—"each other's six." Regardless of circumstances and each of our histories, together my proud, tall marine and I have encountered the world and through God have achieved some miraculous feats. Dean, thank you for supporting me in my many *"wow moments"* and for being *so eager* to enter into various events requiring "off-the-wall" costumes, high energy, and a willingness to produce our own fun, while providing at all costs lots of fun for others! And without exception, thank you for granting both of us the permission to display a transparency in retelling the *"good, the bad, and the ugly moments"* of our PTSD-impaired marriage so that others may glean from our past difficulties, and by doing so, hopefully we will make a difference in the lives of young and old military families worldwide! Above anyone else, you have been my rock—my reason to "dance in the rain!"

Secondly, I must give homage to our fantastic three children. God knew without all of you, your father and I would not have survived the rigors of living decades under post-traumatic stress disorder conditions. Each one of you was the "wind beneath our wings." You inspired and gave us purpose and fulfillment. Thank you for loving us in spite of our "warts," in spite of the trauma and strain of living within a PTSD household. Continue to follow your God-laid path, your supernatural *"bread crumbs,"* and we will ultimately all gather together at our everlasting "home" in heaven. Always remember, the only journey worth initiating is the one that leads "home." (And thank you, Dawn, our "baby," for the consistent encouragement to document in print our life stories, as a legacy for those future generations.)

Thank you to our five grandchildren who make "getting up in the morning" worthwhile. How much you reward us for our having continued to live our God-given lives. Because your love is unconditional, when we look into your eyes, we see an honor, a respect, and an enthusiasm that does not exist elsewhere! How we have merited it, I do not know—but I do not want that look to ever end! As a family, the future looks bright and thrilling with you in it... To each of you, great, big bear hugs and sloppy, "smurkle" kisses!

To our pastors and the many men and women of God, thank you for the kindnesses, love, and the appreciation shown to us. Because of you and your steadfastness, your many sacrifices for the kingdom, Dean and I continue to stand in God and are "alive and well." You have honored us with an acknowledgment that has inspired much more than you will ever know. This book has become a reality only because of your teaching and your nurturing of what God has birthed and laid upon our hearts.

To the Veteran's Administration, the kind and knowledgeable personnel at the Houston, Texas, Vet Centers; the amazing Disabled American Veteran (DAV) organization; and to the many other organizations heralding the cause of the vet—thank you from the bottom of our hearts. Without your expertise, your counseling and group therapies, your professional medical advances, your disability application representatives and support systems—without your zeal and fervor for the American military and his/her family, your intense passion and dedication to making a difference for the veteran and to fighting "to the death" for veterans' rights, you are all "wow moments" in our lives, and without you, we would still be lost in the throes of post-traumatic stress disorder. We are above "the trench" complexities and challenges only because of your existence and dedication.

And last but never least, I honor and acclaim the multitudes of strong, courageous, and devoted women who treasure their marital vows and lovingly cherish their lifelong, war-weary servicemen, and who, all too often, compassionately become caregivers of severely disabled veterans. "Bravo!" to the adoring mothers and grandmothers of soldiers; to the spirited, dedicated women veterans; to the sisters, nieces, and cousins who have greatly and willingly sacrificed endearing family members to the security of our nation!

Without your favor and friendships, I would have been unable to rise above the weight and despair of Dean's war trauma. But because of all of you, I now stand on the other side of "the tunnel." I dwell in the glorious light, prevailing on two stable feet, planted in the assurance that "I'm okay. I am now _good_ until the end of my days!"

Thank you...to one and all...

> Friends have a way of speaking without words.
>
> —Anonymous

> To have a good friend is one of the greatest delights of life.
>
> —Ralph Waldo Emerson

> In the end, we will remember not the words of our enemies, but the supportive silence of our friends.
>
> —Martin Luther King, Jr.

May you and yours also reign victorious over the burdens of combat pain and suffering.

Contents

Preface

It was the summer of 1945. I was almost two years old; sadly, at this time my parents had made the dark and final decision to divorce. That year their divorce was to be one of the 500,000 American divorces as a result of America's participation in World War II. For my parents World War II was the straw added to an already tempestuous marital union. Little did I know, I was about to begin one of the loneliest phases of my childhood.

To that generation, children were seen and not heard, and my parents carried out that ruling to a T. Through my mother's eyes, I knew I would never be mature enough nor have enough experience to merit adulthood.

Therefore, living under these attitudes encouraged me to become even more shy and more isolated; I blended into the woodwork extremely well—*too well*—and for the most part became the perfect child. My mother's wrath went wild whenever I was brave enough to venture out of my restricted and understood place in our two-person family. I learned early on to smile a great deal and to be agreeable to just about anything, no questions asked; the loneliness had officially started.

My perception of my place in my parents' families made me feel like excess baggage, an afterthought, or perhaps just an inconvenience. After a few years, it became apparent that my role was that of a helper—an assistant—for my mother. I had value only when I obeyed completely, when I performed my varied chores perfectly, and when I babysat my two half brothers and half sister just as I had been instructed. Later on in our lives together, my life's function also included virtually everything else.

So as the accolades were handed down, I worked harder, and as I worked harder, the more accolades I received. Somehow I became wrongly convinced that this was a win-win situation; but in reality, unknowingly, I was having my childhood stripped from me, and I was in control of absolutely nothing and the loneliness and isolation grew.

I felt very much like an irregular piece in my family's puzzle because as much as I tried and desired to fit into my *father's* family, I continued to fail miserably and was left feeling empty. The more I tried to work for a place in my *mother's* family, internally I became more angry and then guilty because my mother would say repeatedly how she was doing the very best she could. And I believed her because I knew I had to; after all, she was all I had—she was my life preserver and with her at my side and with me in her good graces, I could survive life, or so I hoped.

But I also knew, indirectly, I had to become like her. Like my mother as much as possible for us to be unified and, therefore, for there to be peace in our midst. So we banded together to make this life work—to make *her* life work—and the aloneness continued.

At school, but only at school, I was the classic kid or, later on, the teenager, with few responsibilities and an airhead mentality. Each day I would turn on a mental, emotional, switch enabling me to change from a child with adult responsibilities to a kid living with few demands and expectations. This allowed me a freedom I did not, and could not, experience within my home.

I would become a kid at school, all the while trying my hardest to attain the best grades possible, but on the way home, I would transform once again into my responsible self. However, as much fun-loving and upbeat as I endeavored to become, my school friendships were limited and stifled, as I rarely was able to participate in after-school activities; nor was I always free on weekends.

I found my studying to be extremely demanding, even though I frequently made the necessary grades. While studying, I found myself "spacing out" or day dreaming, wanting so badly to be somewhere else—anywhere else—rather than the prison into which I had been born.

I was driven to achieve in school because by achieving, I concluded, it would bring me the attention, the affection, and the secure position for which I was so desperate within my families. But, as one can guess, it did not. I only created more anxiety and drove myself further into despair.

There were leading roles in Shakespeare plays and musicals, choral productions, regional spelling bee championships, merit awards, student body "favorites" nominations, etc. However, the hopeless sadness and the overwhelming confusion these all brought made me further wonder about the whole meaning of life.

Nevertheless, even at that age, I was still able to pick myself up over and over again to try one more time, to try to succeed at one more event—one more occasion.

Unfortunately when I was born into the role of enabling my mother's life and because we found ourselves in abject poverty, we both saw few other options. Sadly, my mother and I never observed life in the same way; however, in the end it did not really matter because through her reasoning, she was able to convince me and anyone else that the world was never round at all but rather completely square.

Her conservative political views, her strange fashion statements, her lofty moral issues, and her interior decorating selections were all transferred onto her children, and, yes, out of survival, we all desperately attempted to become carbon copies of her. Disagreeing with her choices only produced more of her endless instruction—and even more coaching only caused all four of us kids to become suicidal, no matter what our ages were at that moment in time.

You see, my mother grew up quite wealthy until the Great Depression of the late 1920s and early '30s engulfed our country. It was then her father lost most of his wealth and was never able to successfully regain it. After that loss, she found it difficult to hold her head up in their Southern Texas, small-town society. This added to her rebellious ways, which carried us, her children, threw years and years of muck, mire, and messes. But regardless, rich or not, she was going to do life all her way—and she did— with all four of us children in tow!

For many years, our small family subsisted on pasty oatmeal, diluted tuna fish, bland rice, watered-down pinto beans, and government commodities, such as powdered eggs, powdered milk, "fabricated" cheese and peanut butter; although, on occasion, we also enjoyed wonderful homemade rice and bread puddings. Looking back now, how I wish in those days there had been such luxuries as food stamps and Lone Star cards. In our world these "rich" stamps and cards would have equaled to living in paradise. As impoverished children, ultimately, we looked forward to eating something "special"; this infrequent occasion was the highlight of our month!

In the 1940s and 1950s a single, twice-divorced mother of four placed us in a rare category. At that time in our country, children from divorces were looked upon as *peculiar;* we were very much the minority, and we did not fit into society. Adequate government programs for families like ours were not in existence then; thus, we had to live on handouts and permanently borrowed money.

To continue bringing food to our table during even more extreme, dire circumstances, my mother began selling little items of value, such as some very old gold coins she had salvaged from her family's prominence. I remember in particular when she sold the last coin—how destitute we felt that day. It was viewed as the end of the end.

Never did our austere family know for how long we would have electricity, water, or gas. Even though we lived on the Texas Gulf Coast with its sweltering, prolonged heat, our various small, cramped houses only possessed at the most three box fans and for the winter, we shared two gas heaters. Without the extravagance of an electric hair dryer, I would dry my long hair for thirty minutes by laying it out on the lit gas oven's opened door—fluffing it every few minutes until dry.

Gas for our car was also strictly limited and severely rationed. Another financial hurdle and always in question was how soon we could pay out our bare-bones clothing from the thrift store layaway; we just hoped and prayed that the payout would be before we outgrew our bright and crisp new clothes.

Of course, all doctor and most dental visits went unknown in our household unless we experienced painful dental cavities. These cavities only meant that those special teeth were in need of pulling. This procedure was happily performed by a "ghetto" dentist on the poor west side of town—he pulled them for $5.00 each! Alone, I would ride a city bus to his dark, frightening home office; and soon thereafter, I would return home with a bloody, gauze-filled mouth and no pain killer.

Birthdays and Christmases were the very worst experiences—much more than just disappointing. They were hollow and cold, cruel, and destitute. Even after we began attending a poor, small church—not even then was the congregation made aware of the dreadful need for assistance by a single mother with four young children. This family's only request was for a holiday meal and a handful of inexpensive gifts. And our loneliness and isolation marched on!

Employment for me began early. I started to officially work at the age of fourteen. Before then I had been babysitting for strangers and bringing my hard-earned money home for small family-market necessities. However, it did not take me long to realize how little I liked other people's children, especially the older ones. By my middle school years I had become quite tired of kids—I seriously needed a substantial break from them that was not to come for a very long time.

A few close calls during my early babysitting career taught me that I must restrain my immature tongue; so in lieu of murder, and, thus, jail time, I opted to search for some other way of bringing money into the household "kitty." As a fourteen-year-old, this adult load had become gloomy, stressful, and already much heavier!

But living on the poor side of town, for someone my age, the only employment available was in telephone magazine sales! While there, I made all of five dollars for each subscription sold at a creepy phone bank. Many of the phone bank employees had special needs, which for a very young teenager added to an already difficult, grave atmosphere and circumstance.

In order to make these dreaded after-school sales calls, we were only provided our divided-into-sections local telephone directory. Without a doubt, I must have been an early pioneer for the *telemarketing industry*!

As you can imagine, this was not the best and preferred job for someone shy and browbeaten as I was then. However, I somewhat succeeded at my after-school job in spite of myself, simply because I could easily *turn on the switch*, just as I had become accustomed to doing in my relationships at school and outside our home. I could then become funny and charming! What we must do to make ends meet, even at fourteen years old! Kind of psycho, isn't it?

Before long I traded magazine sales in for sales at Woolworth's and JC Penney's. Now at last I could actually "see" the people I was selling to and discern how they were responding! How incredibly different (and challenging) this was because now, as I learned very quickly, I could also observe how upset and irate they could appear when something or someone perturbed them—someone like me!

Strangely enough, I must have had a giant *L* for *loser* on my forehead, as my job at Woolworth's for the longest time was to "pop" popcorn outside—yes, outside the air-conditioned building!

Woolworth's had placed a popcorn machine in a bricked-in stairwell between two dreary outside walls. For hours it was my job to man this station in the Texas, steamy, ninety-seven-plus degree heat, freshly popping my popcorn and luring Saturday shoppers to my stand by way of the *to-die-for* aroma. Through a fifteen-inch opening on both sides of my machine, I was able to take the customers' money, make change, and in return, pass the steaming, fragrant popcorn bag to each one!

Occasionally a cool breeze would find its way into my dungeon where there was a large upside-down ex-popcorn-butter bucket provided for sitting in between sales. Upon this bucket I would rest my 102-pound frame. However, after a hard, hot day's work, I was one greasy mess; but, hey, I was making all of $0.90 an hour, which helped keep my family's bodies and souls together.

You may ask, "Why did you continue working at Woolworth's after such lame treatment?" Well, for one, I was exceedingly aware of my mother's wrath if I did not consistently bring income into our household fund; in addition, I also knew from a participant's firsthand knowledge how poor and destitute we were; and, thirdly, I really had very little time to go looking for a replacement job.

That was until JC Penney's came into view! There I began working in air-conditioning, in the lingerie and children's departments! I was "uptown" now; I stayed clean and cool at my job—oh, yes, I was blessed!

God *had* blessed me; this I knew and had experienced since my family had started attending church. God had quickly become my all in all—oh, I was so in love with Christ! And then, a few years later, I also fell in love with my "one and only," and that latest love of mine happened to be attending the very same church.

However, he was new in our church's midst. When he was home from military school (sometimes in his uniform), he would bring his little ole' granny to our church services—services that could frequently consume six and seven nights of our week.

Over time, Dean became my very best (known to man or woman) friend! Soon I knew how much he cared and loved me when he patiently listened to my tales of family woes and gently kissed my tears away. He was definitely my Prince Charming. Where had he been all my life? Oh, yeah, my life had taken on some sparkle—my family's poverty was still very much present, but it did not seem as threatening any more. Now I believed I had a hope and a future!

Dating a year led to our engagement. There is an old family saying that states, "Anything that makes you giggle, smile, or laugh—either buy it or 'git the lead out' and marry it!" Well, that's exactly what occurred—I had already *bought* into Dean's laughter; now I was going to *marry* it! And, yahoo, life had just become the best!

I had previously gone to business college a year and was working while Dean was in school earning college credits. By the end of 1964, he shared with me how that he had already joined the U.S. Marine Corps. Among other valid reasons shared, he principally stated that it was our only way of beginning our lives apart from our families.

However, for any reason at all, I was very much in favor of leaving our town, but mostly I was in favor of leaving my mother and all the responsibilities of rearing three children that were not yet teenagers…*but the Marine Corps—really? Hmmm…*

We married in June of 1965 when Dean briefly returned to town after completing boot camp at M.C.R.D in California. The day after our wedding, packed with all our belongings crammed into our car, we headed to San Diego for Dean's Marine Corps Special Clearance Teletype/Radio Communications School. Our military life had officially begun for the next four lengthy years!

With my mother's blessing, we exited the great state of Texas, but only because she demanded and then scheduled our sending her $10 a week to assist her in the upkeep of *her* house and for the ongoing expenses of *her* remaining children, who were at that time ten, eleven, and twelve years old. In those days for my mother, $10 per week would buy a great deal, but for us, as a newlywed couple, it soon became an impossible, unattainable expense to budget.

Immediately upon arriving in San Diego, Dean applied for a married, dependent, off-base, living allowance. This allowance was all of $98.00 a month, paid directly to us by the United States Government! Wow! Needless to say, the marines must not have thought I was a necessary military item—after all, I certainly was not government issued and did not fit into a duffel bag!

Yes, I needed a job ASAP, and, fortunately, I was hired after just two weeks of daily searching and pounding those California streets. Thereafter, just like kids, we quickly discovered we were playing financial "catch up," and there was absolutely no money left to send home to our other family!

"God help us and keep us"—in all her glory, my mother's wrath hit the fan! Her fresh and boiling doses of anger traveled from South Texas all the way to Southern California; it was delivered by the US mail in letters that were smokin' from the time the stamp was licked and the envelope sealed. With great fear and trembling, we would hesitantly open her "bombs"... Thank God, she could not travel there, beat us up, and send us to *you know where*!

Her bitterness continued to "stew" until long after we were transferred to Havelock, North Carolina, where after a year Dean received his traveling orders for Vietnam. Back home to Texas we both flew, pulling all our meager possessions behind us in a four-by-six, two-wheeled trailer along with our pet, Punkin, and her four newborn puppies!

Then all too soon Dean left aboard ship, three weeks before the Christmas of 1966. I was unbelievably alone and frequently preferred to die! I sincerely doubted whether I could successfully bear this burden of grief.

For over thirteen months, I literally held my breath—only breathing when I received a letter or a cassette tape from my marine. I prayed until I hurt in the inner recesses of my head, in my tied-up-in-knots stomach and in my aching, broken heart. For well over a year, all too often I honestly thought I would break down, not believing I had the strength or the ability to endure month after month of separation.

Wreaking havoc, loneliness became a demon in my life. Naively, when I married, I believed my loneliness was replaced and gone forever, but instead, both insecurity and dread returned with it, and, oh, what a threatening trio they made!

I did not know where to turn for comfort and for a calming assurance that indeed God still had a future for us as a couple—because what if Dean died "in country"? What an awful thought! Oh, heavens, if that had happened, I know I would have disappeared in my grief!

My depression and fear consumed me; nevertheless, in spite of all the anxiety and often panic, I determined to hope against all odds and against all the horrid, bone-chilling, graphic national news commentaries and Vietnam on-location popular journalist reports.

I picked myself up again and again to try just one more time, both emotionally and physically, just as I had learned to do so well as a child. To attempt to succeed at one more challenge in my temporary life as a single.

However, all too soon this became a gut effort because, humanly, I was broken. On the other hand, I also knew beyond a doubt that even at this time in our lives, God was still present, and, of course, only because of him, there was still enormous hope!

With great rejoicing, Dean did return to the States to spend yet another year in the Marine Corps. For that one remaining year we were again stationed in California, before opting out of the service, but only after he was promised yet another tour (or two!) in Vietnam. Dean was a gung-ho marine, but he knew he would not return alive if he were sent back to fulfill yet another deployment.

Oh, yes, Dean returned home physically, but psychologically and emotionally, well...Dean was *never* to come back. The Dean I had known, the marine I knew and loved, remained eternally in the country of Vietnam—in a land of brown rivers and dense, lush vegetation.

He forever changed from the full-of-life personality he had once been: the caring and the tenderness we shared; his crazy sense of humor and this fun-loving guy with whom I fell in love; the patient and tolerant man I married and remembered so well. *That* marine was everlastingly seared in my heart and soul, but in the now, I had to discover how to manage a new life, *a new normal*, with this strange warrior who indeed had returned instead.

Back then I understood full well that it would take a little or even a lot of time for my husband to be able to return completely to our civilian life, both physically and emotionally. I fully agreed I needed to be patient, and I do believe I was much more than patient! And if I say so myself, I was indeed pretty awesome!

For whatever had gone missing in him and in our relationship, I just knew—I more than believed—our undying eternal love, our God-blessed union, would win out and would absolutely fill any gap or void.

Our love was better and greater than the jungles and rice paddies of Vietnam with its memories and its horror, and our love was much bigger than America with all her riots and wartime tribulations. After all, Dean and I had faith; we prayed; we believed in miracles; we had God; thus, we had hope. For in our heart of hearts, by golly, we knew the God of the universe!

So *where* was he? And *why* was Dean like *this*? Why was I still so alone *now* when I again had the love of my life next to me, walking beside me? However, Dean's new solid steel, combat-created shell was very much present—daunting, emotionally vacant, unshakable, and created of superman-iron strength!

In country, Dean had survived as "Rambo"; in our civilian home, he was to linger indefinitely in that role.

And the loneliness and isolation from just a few years gone by returned again to haunt and harass me; these demons unified and became my menacing, tormenting companions. Because my husband was no longer present, my sense of abandonment intensified as well!

I felt a grief-stricken loss, like something had been stolen... like I had been violated, but exactly *what* was taken, and *when* and *why*? It would take an additional thirty-six solitary years to learn the final answers to those grueling, empty questions.

Thirty-six years of both our lives were spent in a perplexed, secluded state, many times plagued and severed from others, but mostly severed from each other. These times were in addition to living through the rigors of raising three wonderful children; and often only for them, steadily striving at establishing a loving and protected home.

Yes, Dean and I remained together, but our loneliness, our individual brokenness unrelentingly persisted. And I questioned God's wisdom in placing his bread crumbs on this particular path because of the impending darkness and potential threat!

Home from War

Why the tears? How can I stop them? I hurt so badly—my stomach, my head, and my eyes; even my neck, shoulders, and back ache. And yes, of course, there are still more tears. I've been crying for what seems like hours. Without a clock, I do not know how long it's been.

I should remember that tears have never fixed anything in my life, but now they flow so quickly it seems that my tears have a mind of their own; they do not care what I think, what things I need to do. I have no reasoning and logical power any longer. They are right under the surface, ready to be shed at a moment's notice. And today was *another* moment's notice.

For a brief, senseless moment, I catch myself thinking back and remembering how desperately I had cried on that sultry summer night when I was nine years old. My mother was franticly screaming, "Run, Sandy, run! Go! You must get help now!"

In my bare feet, I had run out the front door of our farmhouse; down the dark, stony driveway; over the crab grass and weeds full of stickers; the rocks and gravel; and onto the still steamy Southern Texas dirt; finally arriving at the lonely rural, two-lane, black-topped road.

As a nine year old, I had never been farther out than that stretch of road and did not know if there was anyone in that unfamiliar direction who could help us.

In my panic and fear and through my uncontrollable sobs, I asked out loud, "Oh, no! Which way do I go? I don't know what to do, but I have to hurry before it's too late. Should I go to the right?"

And as I turned, fresh in my mind's eye was the vivid picture I had just left of my six-month, fourth-time, pregnant mother lying on her back on the living room couch! In her right hand she was brandishing a huge, sharp butcher knife poised at my 235-pound stepfather, who was at that moment on top of her—both of them screaming venom at one another!

So well I remember fearfully running down the very middle of that dark highway with the still warm pavement under my dirty feet. It was a clear night, about eleven, with a half moon partially lighting the way and the sky full of brilliant stars. As I glanced into the heavens of that late hour, I briefly wished I were doing anything else besides answering this mission's call. But there was no one else besides me to answer the need...just like so many other times!

Yes, for my age, I had gone for help far too many times. This was not my first trip. But it was my first down this road—this highway. We were *city* people—what did we know about being friendly *country* neighbors? And, therefore, up until now, we did not know a living soul anywhere close to our obscured, solitary farmhouse.

I ran crazily, with no rhyme or reason, for a mile or more, after making a spur-of-the-moment decision to pass by a dark, deserted-looking house simply because it sat at least three hundred feet off the highway. But now, there in front of me, about twenty feet off the pavement, was a little white house appearing out of the darkness on the right-hand side of this state farm road. As I slowed down and shook my head to refocus, I could see it clearly.

I do not remember much else after stumbling up the three or four old wooden steps to the door, banging and crying, to the shock of the two little old ladies who lived there and who must have called the police for me. They were both kind and tried their best to soothe both my emotions and panic.

Later on at midnight, I found myself back home where the police discovered my stepfather hiding in the barn with a deep, wide, bloody gash between his shoulder blades. As the authorities drove him away, I did what a nine-year-old could do for an upset, distraught, breathless mother who was slowly recovering in our house.

This was yet another day in my mother's world.

Tears came all too often in those early years, and tears are flowing all too often now, I thought as I lay on a makeshift soft pallet in one of our master bath's walk-in closets. This was Dean's and my dream house in the suburbs—much more expensive and grand than we could actually afford—but this dream house was ours... *for now.*

But instead of basking in our good fortune, our blessings, our miracles, here I lay on the floor, sobbing over my marriage of many years and beating myself up over not being good enough at anything, smart enough, pretty enough, sexy enough, a good enough wife, mother, daughter, cook, or even a good enough saint of God. I looked up and then around eyeing the strange underside of my clothing, hanging as neatly as I could manage with everything else stored and crowded in there. Visible are my two winter coats, several sweaters, church clothes and work clothes and leisure ones. All mine—not at all expensive by any means—but all mine nonetheless.

Why was this small, personal space the only place I felt was mine—the only place in our 2400-plus square-foot house with four bedrooms and two and a half baths where I could go, close myself in, and feel like I belonged? There must be something terribly wrong with me, I thought in my troubled, disturbed mind.

On that note and with serious anxiety, I soon returned to my endless crying, needing someone to comfort me and to loudly declare that I was okay and that things would get better all the while needing that someone to also build my confidence, my self-esteem, my hope and desire to experience yet another day!

I challenged myself: Why the tears? What was so wrong? What was it that was eating away at my will and ability to face tomorrow? What was it that was leaving my body depleted and broken—so broken I hardly recognized myself?

This current serious occasion was taking place on an early weekend afternoon—as many times before, the closet door was barely ajar, thereby allowing me to see well enough within the closet without using the bright overhead light. Some of the air conditioning could also find its way in . During the last year I had found much solace in this small, private space, and I had retreated there more times than I dared to admit.

Some nights after everyone was asleep and resting soundly, including Dean, I would spend the remainder of the night curled up on my mat like a cat taking a catnap . And though there was never sufficient padding, it did so much for my sanity that it was well worth the inconvenience and even the back and hip pain that I felt throughout the next day.

In the morning I would crawl out of my cocoon in time to visit with our children while preparing breakfast and getting ready for a full day's employment. Today, however, I did not feel too well. At that moment, my emotions seemed incredibly worse. I had cried much more than usual, and I was sure I looked a mess.

"Quiet! Shhhh! I hear someone coming... Don't move, don't make a sound!" I whispered . "Yes, I'll remain still, and they'll go away, leaving me time to get myself together."

"Mom? Are you in here? Mom? Mom?" our older daughter called rather hesitantly.

I could not answer! How would I ever explain how I look? How could I explain to her what's wrong, when I did not know myself? Lastly, how could I explain why I was exiting a dark closet? No, I had to be quiet and stay there a little longer. "I promise, sweet daughter, it'll just be a little bit longer." I again spoke softly to myself while begging silently for her understanding. "And then I'll fix my hair, put on a little bit of makeup, and pick up where we left off." It had worked before; surely it would work again.

"Oh, Dear Jesus, please, it has to work again—please, another time, God!"

"God, oh, God, give me your peace. Help me fix what's wrong with me because my marriage is falling apart more and more each day. How can I save it, God? How can I continue with the love of my life knowing all the while I'm losing myself? Reveal the answers I need to live, to grow. Help me, help me!"

And, yes, I did, once again, one more time; I picked myself up from off the floor, combed back my hair, and applied a little makeup. Into the family room I pressed on to assume my usual role with our children, even though I was running on empty and had reached an all-time emotional low.

As a new mother I determined early that I would give my children what I never had growing up. I would provide all of what they needed and as much as we could afford of what they wanted.

When it came to them, it was no longer about me; it had to be only about them and my husband; my husband whom I felt at times actually wanted and needed me, as much as I loved and desired him.

My extreme heartrending lows often came from Dean's disconnecting from me, disengaging from our lives together, from us as a family. So many times he would arrive home in the evenings, already entering the house angry without anything having been said, without knowing how our day had gone or even what had arrived in the mail.

By that time I would be in the kitchen preparing dinner, trying to make something out of nothing because of our slim to nonexistent finances.

Over the years, I had become quite proficient at instantly reading his face, mentally evaluating his hard set jaw, and I was able to make a final judgment call by briefly observing him while peeking out from under the cook-top's hood as he tiredly entered the breakfast room.

Generally it all translated to mean Dean's mood was foul and exhausted; he'd had it; his fuse was short—and we, as a family, must readjust and choose our times to speak to him, leaving us little hope of positively interacting for that evening.

Timing was critical during those many years—choosing our moments to introduce new or difficult issues was crucial. Of course, there were also those good times when all was well. It was during those special, healthy moments when we tried to keep anything negative from being discussed—after all, we did not want to spoil those occasional enjoyable days.

"Hi, babe," I would say, trying to sound upbeat and lighthearted and dreading to hear what could possibly have gone wrong. "How was your day? Is everything okay?"

More than likely, why he was upset was probably more car problems, another traffic ticket, or perhaps he had lost yet another job. Usually these newer negatives were not shared with me at the time they took place. I would be notified much later—if at all. I would be told only when he could better handle revealing the issues. Generally though, and often by accident, I would find the paperwork—and then my terrified heart would stop and the lump in my throat would grow even larger!

For us, any small, negative occurrences in those days translated into impossible, devastating, financially-dooming disasters—ones from which we were set back even further behind. There were nonsufficient-fund checks, warrants, and bondsmen. It was becoming harder and harder, oft times impossible, to financially recover.

There were also those grave evenings when upon entering the house, Dean would pass me with a fleeting grunt, mumble something to the kids watching television, and then continue to walk into our first-floor master bedroom, firmly closing the door behind him.

In our bedroom he would stay, pretending or, perhaps, actually trying to rest, until one of the children would call him for dinner.

At that time, he silently prepared himself a plate or would mutely reach out for the filled plate I handed him. He then settled down in front of the television set—alone. Knowing well the regimen of that period in our lives, our kids had already found refuge in their rooms. Our children could read their father's emotional state as well, if not better, than I could.

Trying to get close to Dean by touching or kissing him, I'd say "Hello," but it was not always well received or reciprocated. Many times the coldness and detachment implied were too cruel and damaging to my already overly sensitive emotions.

As the years persisted, it all became more exacting and less rewarding to "put myself out there" on a chance that this time Dean would respond romantically or at least meet me halfway in my physical advances.

After each strange and bizarre year passed, followed by each threatening episode of *walking on huge, fragile egg shells*, continuing time after time, I sadly and hopelessly discovered that out of pure survival, I, too, had become less affectionate and more distancing.

Many crushing rejections later and frequently crying myself to sleep; alas, I realized how anxious I was in approaching him. Through experience I already knew how abruptly and coldly Dean could resist my outward love, so I waited patiently for him to make the first move. Only then did I dare share my devotion – emotionally I had become too fragile to do anything otherwise. His undiagnosed, and therefore unmedicated, post-traumatic stress was winning.

Unfortunately we learned much later into our marriage—decades later—how this social disconnection, this coldness and the unbelievably well constructed shell of armored, shatter-proofed protection, were classic, frequent symptoms of post-traumatic stress disorder. Today the much shortened version of this disorder is better known within government facilities and disabled American veteran circles as PTSD.

The lack-of-communication problems that had become so rampant in our marriage, the lack of feelings, long-term isolation, and irritability, were very much associated with a mental health and emotional disorder that, in our case, was due to military combat trauma. War trauma that for hundreds of thousands would not be diagnosed, much less treated, by the Veterans Administration Agency until well into the 1980s and early 1990s.

All veterans and active-duty warriors have known during military service not to get close to those soldiers around them. Closeness is too arduous, too painful, when a friendship is lost to duty station transfers or worse—to death.

Regrettably, upon returning home from war zones, this same mentality, same state of mind and heart, carries over into intimate relationships. Our seasoned combat soldier knows firsthand how cruel and unsafe our world can be. He now has a fresh awareness of pain and death, a raw worldwide lack of trust; he is well acquainted with how quickly loved ones can be taken and relationships lost. Therefore, our warrior refuses to allow closeness with anyone, especially his wife, his children, his parents, or his extended family. His traumatized heart and spirit warn him to never let his guard down!

The vet/the warrior is programmed to stay "protected" from possible hurtful circumstances. This worked well while in war; however, in life in the U.S., it is the beginning of the damage that slowly kills all cherished emotional, life-long connections.

This is the "unseen" combat trauma injury—the mental and emotional cause of pain and suffering. With it, it brings confusion and seclusion into the serviceman's marriage and into his family unit—an entity, a part of himself that has already sacrificed far too much.

As Dean struggled with distressing combat memories, endured often daily flashbacks of combat episodes, lived through overnight nightmares of combat images and events, tolerated feelings of anxiousness and terror while shutting down emotionally and physically, our marital relationship and family unity labored and suffered immeasurably.

This pain, this unseen wound, is incredibly real—by many it is called a wounding of the soul. For this type of piercing wound, it will require "giving voice" to the sorrow, as in counseling; it will take acquiring knowledge on the subject of post-traumatic stress; and it will entail an empathetic, heavily involved, support system of family and friends.

Is there hope? Oh, yes—much hope—but patience must be paramount. It is vital and must reign supreme within the hearts and spirits of the soldier and his loved ones. For complete wholeness, we must wisely include belief in God's heavenly ability to restore, and thereafter, also include belief in prayer and the miraculous. There is an old adage which tells us that hope looks forward, but regret looks backward. Because in our future there's always a rainbow waiting…with godly persistence, there's eternal hope!

Dean's and my help would come much, much later…but for these immediate moments, the two of us, as well as our three children, were on our own to manage as best we could. With our human discernment it seemed that we were all alone without God's protection and care. But because our God is good—*all the time*—this limited observation could not have been farther from the truth, as will be shown later in our story.

No War-Trauma Support

When Dean was born on Valentine's Day, February 14, 1944, at a Gulf Coast hospital in Southern Texas, his father was not present. On that momentous occasion, his father was instead in our country's naval forces serving aboard ship during World War II. My father-in-law, during his war, was gone for over three years (thirty-seven months without a break, to be exact.) Among other disabilities, he, too, returned with post-traumatic stress disorder, which also went undiagnosed and untreated by the Veterans Administration for over thirty-nine years.

In World War II, post-traumatic stress disorder was still labeled *shell shock* and also *combat fatigue*, among other terminologies. By war's end, the army had admitted over a million "neuro-psychiatric" patients into its hospitals. By 1947, half of the beds in VA hospitals were occupied by men suffering with PTSD symptoms. However, during all those tormented decades, Dean's father suffered silently and worked hard at making an oft time's scanty living for Dean and his mother. As the long years passed, he became less and less capable of accomplishing even that small part of his head-of-household responsibility.

At last, during the middle of the 1980s, post-traumatic stress disorder was acknowledged in my father-in-law's life. By that time, his condition was termed *war neurosis*. Nevertheless, after many decades of patiently waiting, Dean's dad began receiving treatment by the VA and commenced collecting compensation for his severe service-connected war trauma and impairments.

However, after those prolonged thirty-nine years, he had already sacrificed thousands and thousands of hard-earned dollars in payments for often weekly civilian psychiatric visits. I would be interested to know exactly how many other servicemen must have had to do the very same thing in order to function in that day's American society and at their own meager work places.

My aggressive mother-in-law, on the other hand, became calloused and embittered due to her imposed bread winner's role. She was angry over the thirty-seven-month separation, giving birth to a child without its father present, plus with help from her parents, she bore the responsibility of raising that child in his early formative years without his father's physical and adequate material support.

When my war-ravaged father-in-law returned stateside, any form of emotional event would cause him to lose consciousness due to a damaged nerve overload. Once Dean was told by his dad that he and other of his fellow naval seamen had been given orders to go ashore as an escort for the marines—there they had witnessed the aftermath of the atom bombs on Hiroshima and Nagasaki! After those deadly, ongoing images of the effects of radiation upon humanity, the nightmares never stopped!

Therefore, when his ship docked and he disembarked to see for the first time his own three-and-a-half-year-old son, that reunion became one of his many emotionally, nerve-damaged episodes. There upon the boat dock, he trembled uncontrollably, lost consciousness, and fell to the ground in front of everyone!

Dean at Age 3 - "Waiting for Daddy"

My assertive mother-in-law was an extremely proud woman and had the drive and ambition to achieve very high levels in the business world—at all costs, if necessary! Having a husband that returned injured with unseen wounds was one of the most difficult and punishing obstacles in my mother-in-law's life. She never was fully able to accept her dismal fate and to lovingly respect and appreciate her "new" husband, in spite of his many daily challenges.

Nevertheless, she plowed ahead with him in tow. My in-laws both graduated from beauty and barber schools, respectively, and through the years shared businesses together and apart. Surprisingly, he was of more help with her beauty school studies than she was of help with his.

My father-in-law's occupation lasted a short twenty years until the day when he shakily nicked a client's throat while shaving him. Wisely he knew his time at this career was over, and soon thereafter, he took an early, well-deserved retirement.

From that day forward all the bread-winning and varied miscellaneous duties fell upon my mother-in-law's unwilling and soon to become weary shoulders.

For all the post-traumatic stress disorder issues in my life and Dean's, you would have thought that we would have had the best support in the world from the two people who had lived PTSD for decade upon decade. After all, my in-laws had been through much in their scarred married lives and had seen and bitterly tasted just about everything possible.

My mother-in-law could and should have been my mentor, someone to run to with my fears and distress. She could have provided a shoulder to lean on and, when necessary, one on which to cry! But she did not, even though she had pioneered other causes. Yes, she was of tremendous help to us in plenty of other ways, and she was also of support to others, but usually only when it benefited her. Every generous good deed had a motive behind it, a hidden agenda. There were chains attached to each financial assistance, each place to stay, or for whom she purchased "a little something."

She would have enormous expectations after aiding family members or friends, even business acquaintances. They owed her, and she would subtly or not so subtly remind us all, while producing at a moment's notice, the numerous cancelled checks she kept handy for such occasions.

These documents were proof of her "generosity," and similar to *Silas Marner*, she would systematically revisit and recount all the money she had invested in the lives of others. A lifetime of random acts of kindness was consistently, dependably stored for any future differences of recollection with a lengthy financial tally attached.

Neither was any private, personal information "sacred"; it was all subject to being shared with her large, extended family of mostly sisters, female cousins, and nieces.

Of course, by passing around how liberal she had been to us and others, she was setting herself up for praises and accolades from anyone listening. Her sacrificial, big-heartedness was well known to many and unless each assisted person saw through it for what it was, she was adored by all.

Dean's Parents during Better Times - 1948

You can only imagine, as in your worst nightmare, how well my mother and mother-in-law got along! Their relationship was unpredictable and damaging in so many ways. Throughout the decades of our marriage, never once was their relationship without stress and awkwardness. Even when civil, which was extremely rare, my mother's and my mother-in-law's fangs and claws were always poised or, at best, they were right under the surface. I remember on our wedding day, while running errands at noon, my mother-in-law tripped, breaking one of her toes, causing her to painfully hobble, in heels no less, throughout that evening's matrimonial ceremony.

I look back and seriously believe it was a blessed day. But not for the reasons one might think. My soon-to-become mother-in-law breaking her toe was a huge benevolent act from God himself. It was the miracle that caused Dean's mother to divert her focus to something else—pain.

With my mother-in-law somewhat out of the picture, my mom did not have the usual animosity staring her in the face, causing her to retaliate in private—or in public—whichever came first.

Our mothers were both rebels from the get-go. They were strong and opinionated to a fault, both pushy and doing life their way. Neither of them would back down on anything!

What a pair! Throughout our marriage, we had to keep them in their separate corners. There was never love lost between them!

Fortunately for me, my mother was more of a hermit, and in her latter years, she became more and more isolated from society. She was present at very few holiday occasions, which greatly assisted me, as my slim-to-none, let's-all-be-happy refereeing skills were limited at best...

After all, all I wanted in life was peace and love, and Dean could have cared less about refereeing skills. He was not about to begin teaching our parents anything amid the topics of long-suffering and group hugs. Dean figured our mothers were both on their own—*let the best "woman" win*—*or not!* He really did not care either way; after all, he was more than busy enough with his massive dose of PTSD.

In the long run, my mother-in-law sadly turned out not to be my "friend." For years and years I did not know this, even though my own mother had often forewarned me. I was terribly naïve, I was young and innocent; I was only smelling the fragrant rose petals along Dean's and my primrose path. My mother-in-law saw me coming and took many decades of unfair advantages.

My early home life had left such an unpleasant taste that, once I married, I was very much ready to move on and leave my mother and her life-long, daunting problems behind. I rationalized how I needed to think of myself for a change and that I should begin my own life now that I had the chance.

Sadly, that is just what I did. Most of the time in those newly married years, I only moved forward and was quite successful in seldom looking back. With this narrow mind-set, I focused on my husband's family instead of my own.

Dean being an only child and receiving all the attention was refreshing and new for me; I loved and welcomed it. I became the daughter my in-laws never had—or so they told me on numerous occasions!

Our son entered our world after many hours of labor, "twilight sleep," and my ob-gyn doctor's on-site nurse frequently slapping my hands if I touched anything! Never before nor since had so much attention been shown one child.

However, too soon after this joyous occasion, our child began suffering with severe colic and crying that quickly developed into an umbilical hernia. As a result, when sleeping he was carried around on a pillow; phones were disconnected; doors were locked or at least gently and quietly closed; whispered voices communicated in hushed tones, and everyone tiptoed while he slept—which was infrequently in those early months. Yes, everyone slept when he slept, and so it went, until one day, the colic had moved on. Angels sang, the world looked new, and it was a hallelujah moment!

From the time of his birth, he was the crown prince of the Fulkerson realm. Everything he did was the best, the cutest, and the funniest! He was paraded in front of beauty shop clients, grocery store and restaurant personnel, strangers on the street, as well as visiting extended family members. Thus, quite often between the time he was born and when he was three and a half years old, I relished the few hours a day I had my son at home.

Indirectly this helped me, I reassured myself! During her first year, our second child was plagued with acute diarrhea due to formula allergies. Day and night I was her only caregiver and soon it became a nonstop impossible struggle.

Dean was always absent or exhausted while attending college on the G-I Bill and somehow juggling three jobs to keep his growing family financially afloat.

My sole task was to care for the children—always alone—especially the newer one. Daily our daughter was ill with her bouts of formula intolerance, anemia, chronic ear infections and the accompanying high fevers.

Only after a year or so of our son being absent so much of the time did I begin questioning if possibly my mother-in-law was in competition with me over the love of my son—and that, in reality, she was not trying to "help" as she had so frequently said!

There were pictures taken of the children and all of us by the scores and scores—hundreds and hundreds; albums were filled and stored and then the snapshots overflowed into as many boxes. There was one set of photos developed for the in-laws' home and one set for our small family (just in case one of the sets became lost.)

I was not raised with cameras and developed pictures, so all of this *hoopla* was new for me. It seemed that flash bulbs were going off too often. We smiled, posed, and smiled once more—for years!

Kodak Moment: Dean, Sandy, Dean III - 1969

I was totally astounded by this; but, of course, I cooperated and joined in. And, yes, this came quite naturally, based upon my childhood—with no questions asked!

I made the best of my mother-in-law situation mainly because peace and love was vital to my new life. I had to have peace and love *at any cost!* Only later, as I matured, did I begin to recognize and to recount what that true cost had been. What I had paid dearly for this luxury and what harsh a price was paid by my three children, as well.

Unfortunately, I was so hungry for the *storybook ending*, I was desperate for the *happily ever after.* This need was vast and all encompassing, and it bordered on the bizarre. Including Dean, we all sacrificed to have our extended family birthday celebrations, our Easter-egg-candy affairs, and our tinseled Christmases.

In my subconscious, there must have been a life-or-death necessity to keep my in-laws as friends. However, I knew one thing for sure—I recognized how attached and dependent my husband was on them. Oftentimes during those many years, I felt like the odd-man out, from afar observing their relationships and wishing I had had that same support and interest from my own family!

Needless to say, it was not like I had anyone, anywhere, to consult for advice. My sisters were too young, I lived far away from my best cousin, and for me my mother's wisdom and emotional support did not exist!

I remember well the night Dean invited his parents to move to our very large city from the Texas coastal town in which they had lived for many years.

That night a huge red flag arose in my intellect, but quickly the premonition was dismissed, justifying their moving closer as being *good* for our kids and for Dean. They were in reality the only close grandparents our children could call their own. For difficult to understand reasons, my own mother and father were not considered present and available as grandparents.

And so, all too soon my in-laws did move—into our house for over four months! It was not but a few days of their "sharing" our house before I was anticipating and relishing leaving for work each day. It became a great excuse to be away, and I was even getting paid!

However, the weekends were extremely long and taxing. I was cooking far more than I could physically manage, but my mother-in-law had never chosen to become a cook. Remember, she was only a breadwinner and a career person, and she offered no excuses for not cooking at our house even though she was now retired. So I was the likely, knowledgeable candidate for the job. Surprisingly, I was also knowledgeable on cleaning up afterwards. When Dean's mother would reluctantly offer to assist in cooking, the huge amount of cleanup thereafter soon became an incentive for me to willingly volunteer for all the cooking and the cleaning involved.

The worst part of their ongoing visit was when I discovered that I was sharing my husband more and more as each forlorn week passed. As much as our relationship had suffered before my in-laws moved in, our marriage was seriously struggling then; however, I pondered if possibly I was the only one burdened and unhappy.

Thankfully, within three or four more weeks, Dean's parents had purchased a nice piece of land beside a small pond right across the gully, behind our back fence—a stone's throw away! By living so close, we were certainly looking at becoming cozy peas in a pod. They continued to possess a key to our house, enabling them to enter our dwelling at any time of the day or night. This his parents frequently did without notice or permission. Thus, our family had no privacy and remained on pins and needles in anticipation of yet another surprise visit.

As our children grew older, these unforeseen grandparent visits would send them racing at breakneck speed from our den to each of their rooms upstairs, leaving drinks, food, pets, a quickly turned-off television, and a rocking Lazy-Boy recliner as witnesses of their instantaneous departure! The house would become completely silent; none of them dared answer when a "Hello, anybody home?" was hollered up the stairs. It was hoped that surely our frequent family visitors would grow discouraged and readily return to their home instead.

Promptly, my in-laws contracted with a well-known builder to construct their house. This gave all of us something on which to focus, and, yes, there was a light at the end of the tunnel, even if it was only a wee, dimly flickering match!

We were becoming more impatient and eager as the days and weeks counted off. By then, not only was I suffering from colitis and diarrhea, but now there were also stomach-ulcer problems, as well.

"Will we ever have our house back—our privacy, less stress, less work?" I desperately begged while making crazy faces at myself in the mirror!

But, whoa and wahoo! At last the day came for Dean's parents to move out of our house and into theirs, and the angels sang. It was a banner day for the junior Fulkersons! Or so I thought.

Yes, the house returned to *normal*—but what also returned to our "dream house," in gigantic quantities, were Dean's dark moods and acute depression. With his parents elsewhere and no longer present 24/7, he did not feel the need or have the desire to pretend that all was well with him.

He would work and sleep—and sleep and work. Dean was working at night a lot those days. I would leave him asleep when I left for my job and find him asleep when I returned.

This continued year in and year out. However, for him, it was a good midnight/early morning schedule because now his nightmares and insomnia were not as devastating and debilitating.

Nevertheless, due to our sobering lack of adequate finances, Dean was required to babysit our youngest daughter during each school day. Somehow within those hours, he would also discover sufficient time to acquire some sleep.

In the course of those two years, daily our little one would beg him not to fall asleep. But his fatigue was so great, as was his depression, that her pleas fell on deaf ears. She needed for him to play with her; however, instead he found ways to check out for a short period of time in order to cope with life and its frightful circumstances.

When he was not working at night, he would be awake during the early morning hours between two and five o'clock. Most of the time his insomnia would be due to the terror caused by horrific nightmares, then followed by the tragic flashbacks that would haunt him during his waking hours, preventing him from ever fully resting. Perhaps, it was the dreadful stress he was under with little or no sleep attempting to maintain his employer's schedule of outside safety equipment sales and quotas. This degree of stress also caused his acute asthma to worsen and to not respond to over-the-counter pills and inhalers, medications we purchased with our already limited and dwindling grocery money.

Therefore, our toddler would play alone throughout each day, entertained mostly by the televised kids' programs. However, she did become very much accustomed to this timeline. How well she liked it we were soon to find out as her early preschool years arrived at last.

On the day she began pre-K, I was the lucky one chosen to take her to school. Luckier Dean, of course, was thanking God Almighty for opting out and remained home asleep.

Our Baby: Ready for Anything

With her strong-mannered streak visibly showing, our younger daughter pouted and fretted all the way to the private school that was part of the mega church for which I worked. We arrived at the school, and I promptly, but nicely, asked her to get out on her side of the car with her backpack, which was all loaded with the necessary school supplies.

However, she did not move but only looked more sullen and threatening moment by moment. I could almost hear the car clock ticking (and my office clock counting off time, as well). I knew, at this rate, I was going to be late for work!

From the time she was born, this baby-faced, little bundle of joy was a street fighter. She was birthed with her dukes up and with the stance of a wrestler! She was far more strong-minded and determined than I ever was or have been since!

While driving on that hot August morning, knowingly I said to myself in no uncertain, anxiety-ridden terms, "Oh, dear Sandy, you are in for a ride today. It is going to take all you have—a bag of chips and a load of oxen—to get this four-year-old out of this car!"

This was the same spoiled, strong-willed child that at eighteen months would repeatedly bang her head on our breakfast room and kitchen linoleum flooring, which without padding covered our house's concrete slab! After three, four or even five times of doing so, she would then yell, holler, and stomp her feet to prove her point! I was aghast as I stared horror-stricken—*how had that been birthed by me*, I questioned the heavenlies?

On this particular day I was already running slightly late for work, so I certainly did not have extra time for this type of scene. I got out after again ordering her, through my clenched teeth, to exit the car. When she did not, I slammed my car door and preceded in my three-inch heels to stomp around the back of the car over to her side, and hoping to intimidate her, I loudly banged on the trunk as I passed by. After pulling her car door open with a jerk, I grabbed her right arm and tried, against her powerful will, to pull her out of the car, but to no avail!

My adult mother's strength did little against her four-year-old determination! I tried again, but by that time, I was madder than a wet hen! However, this time, hooray, she was out with a jolt—hollering and stomping when I swatted her behind!

As my hand throbbed, I handed her the retrieved baby-girl backpack to carry in with her, but instead she threw it on the ground, scattering the #2 cutesy designed pencils, large-ruled tablets and basic-colored, great smelling crayons!

I took a long, deep breath, calmed myself and crammed them all back inside the bag with one hand while holding onto her with the other. This Oscar-winning performance was sadly leaving both the car doors ajar with my purse visibly in the front seat and all our valuable keys in the ignition. I had not even noticed .

I was so dreadfully upset—all those purse and key items really did not matter. I was hell-bent on getting this little person, at all costs, inside that school building, even if it killed me (and her!)

And from the looks of things, anyone witnessing this event would have placed high-dollar bets in my daughter's favor and called the coroner for me!

Sadly, I knew I had to carry this confrontation to its finality. I knew I had to win or I would never, ever, get her lasting attention again. So, after pulling and almost dragging her to the front door of her school—I suspended the backpack under one arm and held onto her with the other. I guess with my third arm, somehow I managed to pull open the heavy, awkward metal gray door. At this front door, she latched onto the doorframe but was not able to hang on very long and, thank God, we were at last inside the building! She continued her hollering and grunting, wanting to go back home and yelling in her toddler voice, "I don't want to go to school! I don't want to go to school! *I want my daddy!* No! No! No! You're mean!"

Thank goodness, no one else was in the entry, because by this time, we were late for school. As she was yelling, she was franticly grabbing at every notch and particle on the interior walls, and I was "patiently," one by one, prying her wee fingers from off each indentation.

Finally within a few more moments and some more determination, we had made it! We were at the office, and I knew, without a doubt, there was lots of help behind that final entry.

Like the Incredible Hulk, I threw open the door and once again, *my precious child* latched onto its frame with a steel grip; again patiently I pried each little finger off and pulled her as gently as possible into the administration office.

With that final heave, we both stumbled into that scholastic area with me and those infamous three-inch heels laboring to regain my footing in my most ladylike way.

What with my long hair in my face, sweating profusely, my once-pressed office clothes now heading in different directions, we both stood there panting and fuming! While blowing fire out my nostrils, I realized we stood frozen in front of five or six new parents with their children quietly and properly sitting, while watching our demonstration with horrified question marks on their faces!

We paused, got a grip and walked (or perhaps we dragged) over to a short, empty table where I dumped my little darling onto one of the small chairs.

"Stay!" I hissed like I was speaking to one of our pets.

Standing straight and quickly fixing my clothes, I walked to the front counter to get someone's attention—*actually I already had more than my share of attention*—but now I needed anyone's help and pity.

However, this wee little person of mine had bolted out of her chair and was following very closely behind with a semi-smile on her angelic face! This same scenario we repeated at least two more times until, to my utter surprise and overwhelming joy, the assistant principal walked out of his office. With a knowing smile and without uttering a word, he took my princess by her little hand and escorted her and her girly backpack out into the entryway, gently closing the door behind them!

Wow! At that moment, I owed this magnificent man my life, all the money I did not own, and all my future grandchildren! Yep! In a split second, he had become my BFF!

As he shared much later with me, Dean was on the borderline of suicide while he slept during the day after working all night, and trying to care for our third child. During those years of raising our children, I was not aware and discerning enough regarding the severity of those PTSD experiences, nor did I realize how close and how often we came to losing him! My awareness was tuned into his serious depression and resulting extreme fatigue, but my life's juggling act was working on overload. My plate was full and frequently overflowing.

Dean would stay up for hours—often four or five hours per night—because he could not sleep, because he was driven to stay "on patrol." Between midnight and five o'clock, these were the hours the Viet Cong (or the North Vietnamese) would attack and overrun our troops in the mountains and jungles of Vietnam. Those were the bewitching hours!

These were the hours to hunker down after having prepared in every way possible for an attack that would invariably occur again that night as it had every other night before—that is, if you happened to find yourself in those combat zones. Most of 'Nam and the countries adjacent were in those warfare regions!

We learned much later that not many Vietnam combat veterans can sleep during those nightly hours. The fear, the hyper-alertness, and supreme vigilance take over!

For years after returning home, nightly, combat military and veterans repeatedly check latches on doors, on windows, and then walk the perimeter of their property, at times with loaded weapons, inspecting and waiting for the unknown. These forever young servicemen are afraid of the possibility of someone breaking in to steal and kill those whom the soldier loves and has vowed to protect.

Our warriors have been programmed; they have been trained to react and to handle things themselves. They were schooled to not question orders; they always consider the safety of those around them before their own. Why? Because this is what soldiers do.

Yes, Dean returned home with his arms and legs intact, but he also returned home with malaria, with the effects of Agent Orange (as in neuropathy, which is a degenerative disease or disorder that affects the nervous system, and diabetes) with embedded shrapnel and cancerous melanoma; however, his unseen wounds caused by his war zone experiences were what brought him to his knees! Dean was home physically, but inside he waged a continuous war in his heart and soul.

He had invisible injuries and emotionally and spiritually, he became paralyzed—he had the thousand-mile stare. His personality and identity were modified according to the degree of the affects of war trauma. His "war" had come home with him... the war came home to us—to haunt us all for decades!

Dean went through the paces required for earning a living as best he could, just as his father had done before him. However, he was irritable and irrational both at home and on the job.

The majority of employers must only consider the financial bottom line. Very few of them choose or have the liberty to step beyond the profit margin to assist when they see something abnormal in an employee—as in a veteran staff member.

And due to a survival response, Dean protected himself at all times. He built a hard shell, an armored suit, and surrounded himself with it—while he searched for a mental and emotional hiding place—that evasive "safe place."

For Dean, survival and readiness became paramount at all costs! More often than not, we, as spouses, with our children, become those deafening, monumental costs. We become the U.S. military's collateral damage!

Foundation Deficiency

My mother indeed had taught me well. But in reality, her training could be said to have resembled something like the incessant, persistent water on a rock.

However, as a child, with all her coaching and indirect nurturing, she failed to inspire me; she did not encourage me to dance in life's storms, nor did she offer me the permission to dream and hope for better days. Instead, there was never-ending lecturing and instructions.

If my mom had only taken advantage of the numerous opportunities to see me for who I was becoming, she may possibly have been proud of me. Nevertheless, not once did I hear those words spoken—never was I to receive her blessing! I believe she was too damaged herself to provide that approval—that tool— for all her children.

I was quiet and reserved even as a young child. For my first seven years, I was an only child. My entire mother's teaching and requirements fell upon me with regards to her version of correct and proper social graces. I either learned rapidly or her teaching would begin again from square one. Heaven forbid that ever happening by choice!

I wanted to please her so badly that I chose to learn quickly because she was my whole world. Ninety-eight percent of the time, there was no one else in my life—not even my father. To me as a child, it seemed I only saw him on occasion.

It appeared to me we often lived from pillar to post. At last we landed in what used to be the officers' quarters of an army fort dating back to the pre-Civil War years. Along the Mexican border in those frontier days, army forts were necessary to protect against the warring American Indians and Mexican invasions.

The small houses had been nicely renovated and were being leased out to the public. We were fortunate enough to know somebody, who knew somebody, who put in a good word for us. While we lived there, I remember having two great, *real* birthdays. It seemed that everyone attended from our then little border town.

While my mother worked for Pan-American at an office job, I stayed at home with a live-in maid who only spoke Spanish. In this language, our maid and I communicated throughout our day together. In this way I learned Spanish by day and spoke English when my mother arrived home at night. At a young age, it became easy for me to learn and to have my needs understood in both languages.

Our live-in housekeeper and childcare provider was not at all expensive because Mexican citizens seeking any kind of employment crossed the border in droves. Occasionally, usually on an extended weekend, our housekeeper would take time off and walk across the Rio Grande River by way of the massive bridge separating our two countries; there she would travel further by bus into the interior of Mexico to visit her extended family.

We must have had several different inexpensive ($5.00 a week) maids during those couple of years. In reality, I now wonder how well cared for I truly was. When I was three years old, I was burned on my stomach and legs by boiling water left on the stove. Another time I ventured onto our back porch where I discovered the cutest small dog I had ever seen, and I wanted to get close and keep it as a pet. As I reached for him, he jumped and bit me from under my right eye to the upper right side of my mouth. I was bloody and terrified!

However, the most serious concern came from a young maid who had contracted tuberculosis. She and I shared the second bedroom. While sleeping on a roll-away bed each night, she suffered greatly as she continually coughed, spitting up blood clots and mucus onto a newspaper protecting the floor. Before long, she was gone, having been admitted to a tuberculosis sanitarium near the Mexican border.

When my mother was not working, she and I spent most of our spare time visiting her old school friends—friends with whom she had grown up and with whom she had attended dances and social events. These close friends had been my mom's bridesmaids and had shared in the awesomeness of her first wedding. Yes, I was always around adults; it was easy for me to act older and to blend while they had their adult conversations.

Sandy's Parents: Society's Wedding of the Year

From being told many times in private, I already knew my mom was extremely angry and bitter over her failed marriage with my (in her words) pathetic father. She spoke at great length about how badly she had been treated by him—how that he had frequently relished the company of other women while he attended college and she was miserably (her words) pregnant with me.

Therefore, I was born in a small college town while my dad was attending a military institution seeking to become a veterinarian. However, it was short lived in that my father chose to do instead some labor-intensive rough necking within the

East Texas oilfields; and, thus, his senior year in college was temporarily placed on hold—or so he thought! My dad was of small to average stature—never should he have worked in those hazardous oil-producing areas. Thankfully, no injury occurred.

However, it was wartime; how could he not have known better than to take himself out of higher education? Shortly after exiting college, he received a special delivery letter from Uncle Sam stating, "Congratulations…Uncle Sam needs you!" His dreaded draft notice had arrived for the army, World War II and Japan.

As a result, my father would never complete his schooling and enter his beloved career choice. Instead, after returning home from the war, he re-entered his family's 1912 restaurant business, which then provided his older brother the opportunity to attend college also.

Needless to say, that brother fulfilled his degree and eventually went on to teach school, earning for himself and his family a nice, steady salary, benefits, regular hours, and a comfortable retirement.

None of these advantages would ever belong to my work-worn father. He toiled away countless hours a day until his death from stroke complications at age seventy-nine. Nevertheless, he faithfully accomplished the development of the family café business along with successfully maintaining and nurturing his father's tradition and legacy.

In their own strange, stilted ways, I know my parents loved each other. To this day I have faded letters that surprisingly were preserved in an old steamer trunk. My amazingly handsome father was my mother's first love. This was obvious by the care with which she conserved his many army letters and other cherished possessions. These items were remarkably safeguarded in spite of the condition of her many storage areas, her numerous changes of address, her second marriage, and all the many, minuscule critters that lived and traveled among these priceless, precious remembrances.

Many years later, after she and my dad had each remarried, in her scratched old cherry wood stained dresser, in a special corner, she carefully stored jewelry my dad had given her during their courting days and the first years of their marriage—jewelry bearing both their names and a locket proudly displaying his college logo with their individual smiling pictures within.

However, instead she spoke with such ill will about my father. Many times as a child when this bitterness was revealed to me, it only left me perplexed and doubting to whom I should show allegiance.

She also often spoke harshly against my dad's parents, claiming that my grandfather had made unsolicited sexual advances. My grandmother, whom she claimed was not fond of her, had wanted my mom to perform some cleansing procedure after my birth that would have left her sterile and unable to have more children. Later the truth of this cleansing suggestion left my mother even angrier!

How true were these allegations? Who knows? All I knew was to be torn between families, and in the meantime, to store in my subconscious all those disturbing and alarming messages.

Instead, when my father would pick me up once a week for his six hours of visitation and would choose to promptly take me over to his parents' house to stay for the afternoon while he worked, I was nice and obedient, always displaying my learned manners and social graces. Whenever it was appropriate, I could also be amusing and enjoyable.

Never did I speak to anyone about my mother's hostile memories and accusations. In many ways, they frightened me, and in other ways, I was only secretly troubled by them. In her defense, I believe my mom sought to merely caution me against my father's parents. But what was a young child supposed to do with such information?

Looking back on those empty years, honestly, I was scared a great deal. Even when my mother would go into the grocery store or into the Sears and Roebuck department store and would leave me in the unlocked car on the parking lot or parked at the curb, I hid on the floorboard trying to become as flat as I possibly could. With no air-conditioning available, the heat in the summer was quite intolerable in spite of the open windows. In my young mind, it seemed as though she was gone for hours—and I was left feeling abandoned to protect and fend for myself.

Once I became worried during a visit with my father. I remember riding in the backseat of my dad's car while resting my chin on the front bench seat. I can only suspect that we were again traveling to my grandparents' house for me to spend the afternoon with them and my very-close-in-age cousin. We had been driving for a while; he had been carrying on this discussion, most of which I do not recall now.

What I do recall is the small part of that conversation in which he was revealing how he had remarried and that they had decided I was to call my stepmother, his new wife, *Aunt Mary*. I was confused—I did not know what all this meant. I did not know how to act nor how to respond.

However, I knew at that moment that this was something to which I should comply. Yes, this topic was big-time important, but I had not been given a choice in the matter.

On that day the title *Aunt Mary* was chosen for me and agreed upon, and it was thus so, for the rest of our lives.

At the time of this remembrance, in age I must have been no more than four years old...

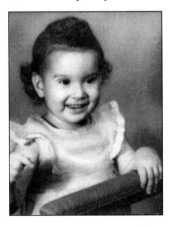

Sandy at Age 3: Full of Life

Another memory of mine was when my mother once had an opportunity to marry a nice-looking physician from Mexico named *Felipe*. She came very close to accepting that proposal, and I am sure there were probably many others of which I was not aware because she truly was a beautiful woman.

However, the proposal she finally did accept was from a friend of a friend with whom she double-dated.

My stepfather-to-be worked in close proximity to where we were living at that time. He had served in World War II, fighting at Midway, etc., within the Pacific Theater. He was a marine, and I am sure, due to his combat history, he, too, as a veteran must have suffered from post-traumatic stress disorder. Of course, most of those mental health and emotional injuries were not spoken of then; they were a well-kept secret, or so, our government thought and hoped.

Even though a seemingly heavy drinker, he still had managed to keep a pretty good job working for a prominent dairy. He had never married, had no children, and was ten years younger than my mother! It all sounded so good, and very soon the marriage plans were on!

I was aged seven when my mother and stepfather married and all of eight years old when I welcomed my first baby brother into our world. Yes, I was tired of being an only child. I was tired of being lonely and thought, in my childish way, that now I would have company and someone with whom to share my problems.

What was I thinking! He cried and cried and cried some more! It became crazy at our house. But for sure I was no longer lonely!

Thank goodness, because we still lived on the border, we were able to afford a live-in maid! Therefore, at this time I was not being worked to death...as yet. Those days would arrive within the next two to three years.

For instance, let's reminisce about the summer when <u>our</u> three kids were three, two, and one—and all three were in diapers. Not

Pampers, but cloth diapers! The kind you have to soak in a yucky diaper pail and slosh around in the bathtub in bleach! Then you continue to wash all of the diapers in the washing machine, and hang all of them outside to dry in the fresh air and sunlight. The odor being released and shared with the world could and would have stopped a train!

I was just ten years old when I was drafted by my mom to watch the three kids for that summer while she and my stepfather worked their outside jobs. Regularly I would overhear her speaking on the phone to her lifelong, dear friends, bragging about how wonderful I was. "*Sandita* is doing such a great job! She's wonderful—what would I ever do without her?" she said over and over again to everyone in town, and she knew everyone in our still tiny town.

She had a habit of calling me *Sandita*—both privately and to her friends. How I hated that nickname! It sounded so pitiful and lame. But she never asked how I felt about it, and I guess it must have been for me her term of endearment. No one else has ever called me that before nor since, except maybe Dean when he's feeling cute!

During that summer, you will not believe how hard I worked for those three long months! I changed cloth diapers all day long. Within our household it seemed that no one else present was potty trained besides me!

Then there were the baby bottles—*millions* of them! These bottles were not only filled with dry formula mixed with water—no! You had to also fill them with rice cereal, oatmeal cereal, or maybe even barley cereal—and finally drop in a large spoonful of baby food, the meat formula kind. The holes in the nipples had to be enlarged to accommodate the five-course meal coursing through! My younger brute of a brother, the middle child of the three, weighed well over ten pounds when he was born and walked into his world! No way would he settle for an ordinary kind of baby bottle with "normal," healthy formula.

Nowadays, they tell us we have to worry about dozens of allergies and food complications. But not in those years. All we cared about was how to hush up the baby! So that my younger brother would sleep through the night, we gave him whatever he wanted and lots of it—that made everybody happy! Not only did I take care of children that infamous summer, but I also polished furniture, vacuumed carpets, mopped and waxed linoleum, cleaned the bathroom, washed our other, regular clothes and hung them all outside to dry along with the cloth diapers, put the kids down for naps, and even had time to think about dinner. And my mother bragged and bragged—and I worked and worked! Somehow a great combination—one made in heaven, right?

Just before I turned twelve, we moved to a city approximately three hours away. I was entering the sixth grade and was very unhappy with the whole idea of moving. We were relocating because my now stepfather had received a promotion—which meant more money. Yes, more money was great, but I was leaving all my school friends!

With our moving so far away, my own father's legal, weekly visitation rights became two weeks in the summer. To facilitate this transfer, I would hop on a Greyhound bus and ride it to my old hometown. Upon my arrival, I would be picked up by him or by another relative.

Those all too short, fantastic summer vacations were so much fun, especially during the years when I was caring for my brothers and sister or I was employed, holding down a part-time job—full time in the summer.

During those summer holidays I felt like a celebrity—what lasting fond memories I have of those trips!

For those two weeks, I was no longer Cinderella; instead, I had temporarily become a beautiful, middle-class princess! During my vacation, no longer did I consume poverty food; instead I had "special" food. At that time my father's family owned two food establishments, and while I was visiting *anything I wanted to eat* was available. Having anything I wanted to eat was in itself reason to enthusiastically visit. No one within that family ever knew how truly destitute I lived the rest of the year.

I could hardly wait from year to year to participate in this transition. As I temporarily lived a different lifestyle, I felt rich and privileged! There is an anonymous saying that goes something like, "Never deprive someone of hope—it may be all they have." I was that someone. Hope was all I had and I refused to let it go!

Because of my father's family's status in this quickly expanding border town, I felt proud and valued as I walked downtown or visited with their friends. Here, my family was recognized and influential. However, the rest of the year I lived in my real world, where we were destitute and felt very small in relation to the outside world.

Nevertheless, the enormous element that seemed to be missing for me during these visits with my dad was my insatiable need of either genuine love or a greater demonstration of affection. To this day I am still confused and not sure which it was. As I think back on those four years until I turned sixteen and my father's legal financial obligation ended, plus including the dozen or so years prior, I do not take away much in the way of memories of genuinely expressed love towards me by my father, my stepmother, nor my grandmother (my paternal grandfather for most of my growing up years was ill and nonresponsive to me).

Perhaps my presence was difficult. Divorce was not a popular, well-accepted circumstance among that community's Catholic families. With me being the by-product of a marriage gone wrong and a frequent weekly, or later yearly, reminder, how could anyone affected in my family move on with their lives?

And though I had become quite accustomed to not being loved *outwardly* (or perhaps even *inwardly*) by my mother, with my grandmother I had noticed the difference demonstrated between the welcoming warmth shown by her for my favorite cousin and the lack of her emotion reserved for me.

However, regardless, at this time I must give voice and praise to how my paternal grandmother did physically care for me all those many years of weekly Sunday afternoon visits, followed by weeks of summer stays!

I can only imagine how arduous this arrangement must have been for Granny, along with her never-ending, care-giving role of serving my ailing grandfather. God bless her for walking that extra mile—for the many kindnesses shown a little lost and lonely girl trying haltingly to find her way!

As fate would have it, after eight years into her second marriage, my mother was divorcing again! There were numerous times when my mom would bitterly inform all of us children that she had made only two mistakes in her life—these were her marriages to our two no-good (her words) fathers!

However, unfortunately for all of us, this time around she was responsible for four children—ages fourteen, six, five, and four. Her occupation was that of a secretary, earning a few meager dollars over $200.00 a month! No longer did we have that live-in housekeeper of many ages ago. During the time period of this second divorce, we now also did not have a house—it had been swiftly foreclosed on and our car had been stolen through repossession by strange men as we secretively watched. However, we found an affordable, fairly cute rental house and began our existence without the usual, reassuring cash flow of two monthly adult salaries.

Without the luxury of a car, my mother would ride a set of public-transportation buses to her employment each day. At the location where she transferred from one non-air-conditioned bus to the next, there was a ghetto-type grocery store nearby. At that dreadful store, she would purchase our sparse groceries for that evening, followed by transporting the heavy bags from the bus's drop-off point to our rental house three blocks away. During the winter, the coastal wind was cruel, blowing through her thin clothing, and the frequent rain made for wretched, humbling conditions.

Most of the time, as we grew older, we always had a pet, especially during the times when we had a fenced-in backyard. Needless to say, this pet of sorts served us more as a security watchdog. However, as nice as this all seemed on the surface, we truly could not afford a pet. Not once did our pets visit a veterinarian—never were they protected with any inoculations or heartworm additives. They were loved and fed as best as we could provide; they lived just like we kids did—with very little in the way of special services.

One day our small mixed-bred dog, Sugar, had yet another litter of puppies. At that time we were feeding her oatmeal—that was our daily staple—so very soon it also became hers. However, with Sugar, Mother had yet another mouth to feed. Mother was not doing too well emotionally, trying hard to keep us all from living on the streets or having to divide us up permanently among willing relatives.

Too often, in her awkward, immature way, she would remind us children as to how she could easily leave us on somebody's doorstep, but instead she was choosing to continue to provide for us as best she could, for as long as she could. Our future together was always ominous, and money was not often present—there were no extras—not even for our poor beloved dog that now required extra food (oatmeal) to supply milk for her babies.

One day my distraught mother tragically informed me, "I'm going to have to *kill* Sugar's puppies. There is no money to feed them, and I know of no one who will take them all right now." I was mortified and could not imagine such an atrocious act so I just nodded my troubled head like I always did, hoping against hope that something else would present itself to prevent that appalling scene from taking place at our house!

A few days later, as I entered the kitchen to begin washing dishes, my eyes fell upon my mother's back as she knelt in our makeshift, enclosed back porch where Sugar stayed with her new family.

Over her shoulder I saw her place yet another tiny, helpless, one-and-a-half-week-old puppy into a plastic bag while holding it tightly until that puppy with unopened eyes and ears stopped breathing. Then she removed it and laid it next to the other lifeless one. For this litter, Sugar had given birth to three or four babies, so it must not have taken long. Horror-struck, I chose not to stay to watch any further—the hot tears and cruel astonishment were too great!

I was deadly sick. I felt hopeless and useless. I was ashamed that we were reverting to such depths of depravity! I was sad for the state we were in, and I was so angry because I knew I did not have the power to make my mother stop this mercy killing! How could I? What with school, I was already working as much as I could possibly handle…and so was she! My goodness, how my mother must have felt!

How awful for us to live like this. Surely a brighter day, a better tomorrow was coming where we could be a normal family and not be so wrenchingly poor!

But that brighter day I so fervently prayed for did not come for us right away. Instead there was first the day when my mother made the desperate decision to commit suicide. Her detailed plan, as she tearfully described it to me, was to take the older car and to run it off one of the city bluffs into the deep waters of the Gulf of Mexico. At the time that car was at least twelve years old.

By leaving me with the newer car, I would be able to continue working at my full-time job, and I could raise the children by myself! By myself—what was she thinking? How insane was that? How would I ever be able to accomplish that?

The younger kids and I were in hysterics! We were still living far away from our extended family; at best we were isolated and disconnected in our relationships with them. Thus, there was no relative close by to intervene; so almost immediately in our desperation, our simple-minded and insensitive church pastor was called.

Upon arriving, he made a joke of it all while making my distressed mother feel all the more foolish, immature, and faithless for thinking such thoughts and making such ridiculous plans! All too soon, he chuckled his way back out the door!

We were numb with despair! During that infamous visit financial assistance was never offered, no comfort or words of wisdom were shared, no scripture was quoted, nor did our pastor suggest arranging a mental-health day for my work-stressed and wearied mom. Yes, that day her suicide was averted, but we never called for this "man of the cloth" to return to our house again for anything.

Unlike the way it sounds, there were many funny times in our growing up years at my mother's house. Perhaps they were not so funny then, but in hindsight, we children hee-haw at the memories. One of those times was when we began attending a breath-taking camp meeting held in a town neighboring the Louisiana-Texas border. For an average person, the drive from where we lived would have taken no more than five or six hours, but we were above average, so for us, it took all of eight, if not ten hours to drive 275 miles! Our ten-year-old car would only go forty miles an hour; plus, we also stopped regularly for one unknown reason or another.

This camp meeting was not only our vacation each year, but it was our "I can hardly wait" obsession! We were going to a spiritual Mecca and having fun, too—what a combo! So after the first year, like so many others, we were hooked and became regulars each year thereafter.

We would take our bedrolls, our pillows, our bath towels and planned in detail our scanty wardrobe. At first while the three kids were still small, all five of us stayed together in the women's dorm, which was a very large, open, barn-like building filled with row after row of dozens of dark olive green, miserable sleeping (even for a teenager) army cots. Electric fans were present throughout, and to the side there was a pale green dorm-type restroom area equipped with many, cramped stalls, showers and numerous sinks to accommodate all the women and their small children who were housed there.

The camp meeting cafeteria had a set menu, and the food served there was extraordinarily good. This was special food, and we feasted! However, I had never seen so many miniature bowls of purple-looking, round, mushy, seeded balls encased in syrup. I very soon learned these were prunes—they were being served frequently to keep all of us campers regular in our bathroom habits! In my prim and proper way I was aghast and deeply embarrassed, but I have to admit, they were delicious, and I secretly looked forward to them each morning...a lot...which made me a "regular" camper, I guess!

The second year we attended the camp meeting, a young man from our church inquired if he could hitch a ride with us and offered some money accordingly. Oh, hallelujah! "Yes, of course," we quickly answered, probably a wee bit too anxious. "Doesn't he know we do not have air-conditioning and it feels like 110 degrees in the shade?" we asked each other, but none of us volunteered a discouraging word!

So into our small, forest green 1955 Nash Rambler complete with four *new* retread tires, we were going to pile the five of us, plus our young man, along with our entire luggage for that long and glorious week.

Boy, oh, boy, was our young man in for a real *treat*—traveling at forty miles per hour with the five of us! It's a ten-hour trip with no cool refrigerated air, in Texas, in the month of August! By now we had become accustomed to hanging out the windows, but was he willing to do that, too?

We securely packed our Nash Rambler with luggage, attaching it safely to the roof of the car; stored our lunch and dinner items—consisting of potted meat, Vienna sausages, tuna fish, and saltine crackers—in cubby holes, nooks, and crannies throughout the vehicle; then we waited patiently for the exterminator to arrive at our house to fumigate our resident roaches.

"After all, a lot of roaches will die in our house during our absence for a week! We are using our money wisely—yes, of course, it all makes sense, right?" And we all nodded our heads "yes," like obedient children.

The poor bug man pulled up to our house, unloaded his trusty, well-worn, heavy equipment, and inquired, "Is the house ready to be locked? Does anyone need to re-enter for any reason, because once I start spraying and fogging, no one will be able to go back in," he instructed us in a deep, businesslike, almost military tone.

All our heads nodded, indicating, "Yes, it is ready, sir. Charge ahead as ordered!" Which he promptly did, as we all waited and watched anxiously while standing on the driveway...until, to our wild-eyed astonishment, the vapor started billowing out of the open front window that we had overlooked!

Oh, my, oh, my! When my mother witnessed the swirling fumes exiting the house, her arms started flailing, and she began at once to yell and run around our small front yard attempting to gain the attention of the bug man inside. Within seconds, he came flying out the front door just ahead of the dense haze that was following close behind, while slamming the front door behind him!

My mom yelled; she argued; she begged, cried, and pleaded, never giving up, until she convinced this man, against his better judgment and against his years of experience, to go back in to shut the open window!

This was unbelievable, I thought to myself, rolling my eyes toward heaven! I truly believe even God was impressed and surprised by her and then awed by this buggy man's decision!

Would you believe he re-entered that *pit of doom?* We knew he had conquered it when we heard the window's miraculous closing thud!

Seconds later he appeared before our stunned, shocked faces—gagging, crying, retching, choking, spitting, and frothing at the mouth! To our amazement and wonder with his bugged eyes tearing profusely, he stumbled over to our front yard's eighteen-inch-over-the-ground water faucet, and like a wild man he frantically fought to cover his head, shoulders and chest in water—arms everywhere, knees bent, legs spread apart! And then out of sympathy, honor and utter respect, we all turned our heads, unable to watch this graphic scene any longer!

This saturated, dripping, red-faced man grunted something unknown to my mother as he bypassed her, literally threw his equipment into the bed of his old truck, and peeled out in disgust. At that precise moment, we all bowed our heads and comforted ourselves knowing our lousy, dreadful roaches were definitely, without question, in dedicated hands!

Immediately into our old but faithful Nash all six of us hopped, we threw it into reverse, took one last look, and off we went—because now, we were officially on vacation!

If only someone could have seen us, he would have agreed how we resembled the Beverly Hillbillies (only from Texas), because beautifully suspended on top of our old, beat up luggage and bulging, black garbage bags was our brand new, blue sparkling ironing board, ready for service!

Oh, yeah, we were all set as we quickly hung out the windows with the sun-drenched, sweltering breeze blowing through our hair—until it rained; saturating the luggage, and the windows hastily went up!

A Place to Call My Own

Dean and I were married on a South Texas summer evening, June 12, 1965. Every member of our modest, mostly low-income church family received a pulpit-announced invitation, plus formal invitations were mailed to a few other close friends, coworkers, and relatives—for a grand total of about two hundred. With standing room only, it became an extremely well attended, large wedding for there being so little money spent and few assets available.

My mother and I had been working on different wedding projects during the four months Dean spent in boot camp in San Diego. Mother had made all the from-scratch artificial bridesmaid bouquets, as well as my wedding bouquet. It was much cheaper that way; unfortunately, very cheap was in that year and low-cost was not!

We chose a McCall's pattern and requested the bridesmaids to have their dresses made accordingly. The pattern appeared very attractive on paper. However, once the girls were in the dresses, I was secretly disappointed. I had a total of four attendants along with my two sisters as a sophisticated junior bridesmaid and a cute flower girl. My colors were lavender and white.

To select my once-in-a-lifetime special dress, together my mother and I visited an inexpensive downtown dress shop, which surprisingly also carried wedding dresses. After sorting through several, I settled on one dress displaying long sleeves, simple puffy shoulders with a fitted, dropped waist, and a very wide, iridescent layer-draped and crispy ruffled skirt. Throughout the dress, there were dozens of shimmering sequins on the skirt, causing it to sparkle with every movement. Therefore, with resolve and a crisp

$5.00 bill, I proudly placed my wedding dress on layaway. I had spent a grand total of $50.00!

My wedding shoes were pearlized white and high heeled. The special bridal tiara I discovered in a crowded downtown shop in a dusty, hazy glass case while I was waiting to catch a bus home after work. Mother designed my homemade veil with glued-on glitzy sequins to match those on the wedding dress. From the princess tiara, the veil cascaded down to elbow length. The look was stunning!

My hair I wore as I always did—midback length and curled up (my father once shared how he thought I looked very much like Linda Darnell, a popular movie star from the 1950s). It would have been amazing if my new mother-in-law could have been available to style my hair for that special day, but instead she was overwhelmed with her foot injury.

I did not indulge in the usual manicure or pedicure regimen, but I did wear a little blush and mascara, with no lipstick. There were no earrings, but, yes, a costume jewelry pearl necklace was spotlighted. (We were becoming husband and wife in a very strict Pentecostal church; therefore, lipstick, eye shadow, and earrings were seriously frowned upon!)

My mother and I rented two large white ivy-decorated candelabras to match a gigantic heart she had created, forming it essentially of thick wire and placing it on a homemade stand. To the molded frame she somehow attached yards and yards of puffed netting around the edge, pulled it tightly into the middle, producing a giant explosion of tulle. The final touch was to sparingly decorate the heart creation with fake lavender flowers and greenery.

Our remaining wedding party consisted of several family members—a brother was a groomsman, two other brothers lit the candelabras, and my baby brother was the ring bearer. Dean's proud-as-punch best man was his own father.

In the late afternoon rushing in on all of two wheels, my father arrived with his three children and my stepmother. He brought with him a load of leftover, multi-colored finger sandwiches from one of his restaurant's catering jobs. My mother was outraged but not because they were leftovers! Apparently the fury was over the sandwiches not being in pastel colors to match the lavender/white theme! However, the colors of *orange, yellow, brown, black,* etc., really did not matter—no one else cared; they were promptly devoured in no time—and later we heard they were delicious! (FYI: Because most of our church was low income or *no* income, many of the families attending our momentous occasion had arrived quite hungry!) The multi-layered wedding cake my mother-in-law ordered was devoured also; plus the extra white-sugared Mexican wedding cookies my father brought were consumed; the pastel mints and bowls of peanuts were demolished as well, and the very large amount of non-alcoholic punch was all gulped down in a flash. But this was to be my only wedding, and I did not really care who ate what nor how much of it.

Beginning of a Bright Future - 1965

Earlier on that humid wedding day, unfortunately by myself, I spent most of the morning filling rice bags for the traditional throwing of good luck. Considering all the labor and time involved, I seriously questioned during those long morning hours if these rice bags were all that necessary. "How much 'good luck' does a couple really need?" I asked myself while wiping my brow; however, I dutifully continued filling bag after bag until they were beautifully completed and ready for use.

Amazingly, but not completely surprising, a month before my wedding day, I faithfully began taking my birth control pills, just as I was directed to do by my doctor—exactly one month ahead! He was my first gynecologist ever and, thus, I asked no questions—just nodded my head like I knew what I was doing.

Unfortunately, I did not, and there were no timely instructions or advice regarding this process issued by my mother. By this time, she was much too busy designing the wedding décor and the seven-foot heart-shaped backdrop. However, in reality, she probably would not have known much about those pills anyway; these were very high-tech and new to us. My virginity had not prepared me for any of this.

Consequently, at our wedding rehearsal on that Friday evening, I did not feel well. I mentioned my worsening dilemma to my matron of honor, who quietly informed me that taking a few extra pills would not have harmed me and would have taken my upcoming menstrual cycle into the next week. But now, for me, it was too late...*I began my period the morning of my wedding!* Often that day I came close to doubling over with severe cramps and a weakness I had never felt before using these unknown pills.

Therefore, that evening during the wedding procession as our guests stood in anticipation and reverence and as my father and I walked down the aisle to the altar, I was subdued and feeling frail. My father's misunderstanding of my physical struggles seriously slowed us down, and as he gently looked at me with concern, he gave me a side whisper, asking, "Are you okay? Is this what you really want to do?"

I sent him back a flimsy smile and replied, "Yes, I'm okay. Everything is okay!"

With that said, we continued down the aisle that led to my prince—that someone I loved with an endless, unconditional love!

Certainly and absolutely on that church's aisle were sparkling, God-inspired bread crumbs leading to the brightest of futures.

The evening was a grand success and at last our lives began as a couple! I felt like I had just been granted a pardon and been liberated from my mother's domineering, steel grasp. No longer was I in a prison—Dean had stolen me away!

Little did I know then, and really only until recently after decades of marriage, has Dean shared how seriously the evening before our wedding he had considered not marrying me! He declares he felt ill-prepared and feared his military future and what that could mean for us during wartime. Wow! What a crock that would have been! I am sure, without a doubt, my mother would have killed him in stages, and I would have croaked from a broken heart. Even to this day, it hurts to my core to dwell on that possibility!

However, Dean did follow through and during a quick stop in San Antonio, we visited the Alamo for my first time. Scratching that off our "bucket list," we continued to Southern California, where he had military orders.

From the very beginning, Dean and I were just like two bugs in a rug. We were best friends and had so much fun together—we thought and played and laughed alike! Much of the time, we were in stitches—like kids on a playground! We could talk for hours regarding our varied thoughts about life as a whole and, of course, about our many gigantic, unrealistic future plans and dreams.

For the first time in my life, I belonged somewhere. I had a place of equality beside someone I loved very much. A place I did not have to create anew each day and then worry and fret over emotional isolation if I did something wrong or did not perform just right an expected duty or errand. I had my very own spot, and I was being allowed to make some important choices and decisions.

I was free to be my own person—whoever that person was! However, I promptly discovered that first I would have to find her, because Sandy did not readily exist—from childhood, she had not been encouraged to develop into anyone…she had never surfaced!

However, with the strength and determination of the beautiful lotus flower, Sandy indeed was working her way through the mud and the murky river bottom of her past, reaching for the sun, a new day, and preparing to blossom.

Thus, with all the commitment I was capable of, I faithfully knew beyond a doubt that Dean's love and devotion would never be withdrawn by this awesome, one-of-a-kind person with whom I had become best friends and married. At last I could fully relax and rest in the knowledge and assurance that I was loved forever unconditionally.

Dean thought I was beautiful and smart and skilled. He inspired me. I loved him more than life itself and like no one I have ever loved before or since. And I knew Dean loved me; absolutely nothing could enter and sabotage our lives! And I felt a comfort, a gentle peace, and an ease of living.

In California as we settled into married life, I began working as a secretary at an import company while Dean was on base attending communications school. We had rented a small efficiency apartment on a tropical bluff in Old-Town San Diego overlooking the Marine Corps Recruiting Depot where Dean had served his time in boot camp and was now learning communications skills.

But this furnished small, efficiency apartment had no bed, only an old couch that made out into a bed. And when it was extended, it came within ten inches of slamming into the front door. Honestly, we could literally stand on the (couch) bed and partially open our only door without setting one foot on the floor! But, nevertheless, this was our safe, special home…in all its glory and blessings!

Everywhere outside, throughout the entire small complex, courtyard-like area, were dozens of gorgeous tropical plants with flowers blooming in all colors and many lush vines freely draping themselves. In the evenings, night-blooming jasmines would fill the air with an aroma like nothing we had ever smelled! This was a paradise, our paradise, and we were more than content within it!

On a Saturday after exactly one blissful month of marriage, we had our first, heated argument. My mother had sent me yet another one of her lethal, smokin' letters, and Dean had had it with us—he had reached his limit with my tears, feelings of empathy, and family responsibility!

Fuming, he left our apartment to collect our stored suitcases, hauled them in, and literally threw them all onto the living room floor. I was ordered to pack and go back home immediately. However, instead of doing as ordered, crying I left the apartment and walked a short distance to a park to which Dean later drove and found me.

I knew in my heart of hearts I could never go back to my mom's house, not now that I had tasted freedom! If I ever set foot to live in my mother's home again, I would remain there until the day she died—continuing to help her with her life and forever losing mine.

From that time forward, my mother's control on me was severed. I had truly been liberated! I had been away long enough to know that I could find a decent job and make it on my own. Oh, yes, I would be scared, but I was much more fearful of returning to my mom's dominance!

To this day, I am always amazed at how many people take over other peoples' lives seemingly without a thought that it may be wrong and harmful to do such a thing. And they justify it by convincing themselves that it is for the unique betterment of the person they are absorbing and overpowering.

I recall my father once asking me, "What do you want to study in college? I'll pay for as much as I can." Or, "Why don't you go into modeling? That would work so well for you." For a few suspenseful seconds, I was only able to stare at him with my mouth open, not knowing how to respond. Then, I gently acknowledged what he was saying—but I knew, all too well, that where I lived, no one in my house dared dream of having such lofty ambitions and toying with such impossibilities!

To this day I do not think my father fully understood (or perhaps he chose not to know too much) how into dire survival my mother's small family was living and how far into the realm of poverty we had entered. I know I never told him—personally this true reality was too damaging and humbling for me. It was my secret, and by keeping it my secret, I enabled my dear mother to continue doing life her way.

Therefore instead, as prearranged, I dutifully enrolled in business classes; I lived close enough to walk to the junior college. This decision was made totally by my mom. Yes, she had determined I was to become a secretary just like her, and I was to begin earning money promptly. Furthermore, I was also instructed that for the first year, I would work part-time (which I did, catching two buses to my job each day after class) followed by full-time employment in order to bring in as much money as possible. All my salary was destined to be deposited into the household fund; my wallet remained empty!

We never discussed it, but now in thinking back, I believe there was a weird understanding that this arrangement would take place for the rest of my life or hers, whichever came first!

Much of my life had been prearranged from the moment of birth. Seemingly, I had had no real choices. I made absolutely no plans of my own. My days and experiences were designed to occur only by the person in charge—my dear mother. So, it went, year after year—until I was able to consider marriage.

Needless to say, there were other suitors besides Dean, but, thankfully, I was wise enough and had enough foresight to know not to fall for just anybody. As desperate and dire as my circumstances appeared, I chose not to marry just to get away from my problems, as others I knew had done.

And, surprisingly, my mother did allow me to date. My dating in my teenage years assisted me in coping with the heaviness, the doom and gloom that hovered within our house.

One year as a result of our attending our yearly camp meeting on the Texas-Louisiana border, I met and dated this young man who was incredibly good looking, a Christian, and who played his guitar at this camp-meeting church. I was overwhelmed and felt very special for having gained his attention!

In short order we were engaged, and I was sporting an impressive, shimmering engagement ring. This from-afar courtship continued for a while until his letters slowly stopped arriving. I was disappointed and right away became worried sick! Having met him on a visit, my church family members would later ask about my fiancée, and then they would promptly add, "No news is good news," but I knew better. In my life, things did not work that simply and turn out that well. There was trouble brewing somewhere. I could feel it in the pit of my stomach.

At that particular time in our lives, I was very good friends with Dean. We would spend time together at Pick's, a little drive-in teenage soda joint where we would order steak fingers and French fries (special food)! It was like today's Sonic Drive-in, but in those days, you were considered the in-crowd by being seen there with a date. Of course, there were carhops, and all the latest and most popular songs were pulsing from blaring, massive, outside speakers. Yes, the two of us were there but not on a date; after all, we were only friends.

Dean would patiently listen to my anguish over my seemingly soured engagement. I would bounce ideas off him, my needing to make decisions as to what I should do to get my boyfriend and my life back on track. He would listen tenderly and openly advise me as I struggled to hang on to what I had found in my fiancée and for whom I thought I loved.

Finally one night, he generously volunteered by saying, "Sandy, let me write him a letter and seriously remind him how wonderful and beautiful you are. I think I can talk some sense into him."

It sounded great! It was definitely the answer, and Dean assured me this would be done by the very next day or at least very, very soon. What an awesome friend to do this for me! Profusely I thanked him and God. My problem was fixed; it was solved, just like that. This was amazing!

And then I waited and waited for a letter to come from my loving husband-to-be stating his undying love and how he had missed writing to me. But nothing came! I spoke to Dean again while at Pick's Drive-in. "Just have patience," he advised. "A letter is probably on its way. 'No news is good news!'" Sure it is!

But it was not good news because the letter never came! After sending my fiancée numerous mushy letters questioning our relationship and receiving nothing in return, I wisely concluded that our engagement was over.

After locating a medium-sized box, into it I gently placed every one of my fiancée's priceless letters, included anything else my sweetheart had given me and on top of its contents, in a small box of its own, I added my remarkable engagement ring. I remained brokenhearted!

The box containing my perceived future went into the mail uninsured. Never again was I to speak to my first love—not even when my family once more attended my last camp meeting.

Yes, there on the platform in all his splendor was my ex-fiancée, playing his guitar and as good looking as ever. However, thereafter, he was seen sitting beside his small, pale, churchy girlfriend and future wife-to-be!

To myself I could not help but wonder if she was wearing *my ring*. Because of my humiliation, I had not dared look at her ring finger. Right then, my world had ended! I had been replaced! Where was my awesome God now?

For me, this camp meeting became a lonely, dismal week; thank goodness, it was my last trip. The appeal and attraction was no longer there.

It was only much later into our married lives that Dean shared with me the whole truth to this story. Never did he write his letter to the jerk I was engaged to. Never did he intend to write the jerk I was engaged to. How could he? He was in love with me himself! Writing a letter to my ex would have been counterproductive and was something he could not bring himself to do. Oh, God bless him!

It would take some heartrending private time to move ahead and to fall in love with Dean instead. However, this path lined with those bread crumbs on purpose was God's way of answering my nightly prayers asking for love, hope, and His perfect will in my life! Sometimes we must walk through excruciating pain before we can witness the true plan of God unfold. This became one of those times.

Now quickly flashing back to Southern California where we lived soon after our marriage…

Thankfully, Dean and I stayed together after that first fight. I was not going anywhere (like I had anywhere to go)! We set up housekeeping, and because of having little money, we found inexpensive things to do and places to go. Lots of things! We attended church and met some very nice friends who, unlike us, were not in the military. I was enjoying our life and was excited about being in California. Thank God, it was far away from Texas and my previous life there!

I had been given two or three cookbooks at a bridal shower; thus, I busied myself trying new and frugal recipes. Remember, Dean had spent two and a half years in military school; plus, his mother did not cook, and his grandmother fixed turnip greens, red beets, *polk* salad, etc; therefore, anything I prepared, he bragged on. Well, we already know what happens when I am bragged on! And so I cooked and cooked each and every day—all kinds of risky stuff!

As I cooked our special food, my grateful mind could not help but go back to those years of poverty when at my mother's house, we barely kept our bodies and souls together. I especially reminisced over the many Saturdays when my mother would capture all four of us kids, forcing us to form a solid assembly line. Set in front of us were way too many pots sitting ready with the seasoned meat taken from boiling a hog's head and other unspeakable body parts, along with the prepared corn meal and lots of tin foil. Sometimes there were those expensive delicious raisins thrown in, as well.

Yes, you guessed it—we were lined up to prepare Mexican tamales...but not the tamales that the general population would make. Tamales that only our house knew how to create! In conversation sometimes people will say how poor they were growing up—nope. *We were poor!*

We would begin early in the morning. We were instructed to spread the corn meal (masa) on the tin foil, throw in some meat, tightly roll it up, and seal the edges. Sounds easy enough, right? However, on these special weekends, our mother was talking to kids and some of us were really little kids who did not want to be involved in any of these extracurricular, exclusive-event affairs, except when it came to hunger and dinner!

So at the beginning, in the early morning, while we were still asleep, we made some pretty "normal" tamales. They looked good and were the appropriate size.

But toward the middle and into the end of the day, our tamales became larger and larger, closer to the size of massive bricks!

Hour after hour, more masa, less meat, each one was wrapped in foil, down the assembly line it went to the last kid who threw them all into the refrigerator's freezer; efficiently becoming a more rapid process!

Nevertheless, the purpose for the tamales succeeded; it kept us fed and altogether, as did the to-die-for bread pudding that was made from all the "tails" of week-old bread and, of course, Mom's awesome rice pudding. We probably were not healthy, but in those days, neither were we always hungry. Mission accomplished!

Now as I sat in our California kitchen, I counted my many vast blessings. Dean and I did not have much money, but we were rich in everything else.

As much as I like tamales today, not once in my life have I chosen to reenact those momentous scenes from years gone by. However, when my siblings and I get together, we laugh until our sides hurt—we overflow, and we are on the floor—recreating those incredible memories of our tamale-making days!

All of us remember how we would toss those tamale bricks across the room like footballs. Once frozen, our tamales became *lethal weapons.* We could have sold them to the military as missiles; what a missed, Reynold's wrap opportunity!

The Call of Vietnam

Overall, I loved and thoroughly enjoyed our military days spent in the United States. We had purpose, proud, patriotic employment, and we were together (two peas in a pod, right?).

Not long after we had settled into my new job and San Diego in general, we received further orders to relocate to Havelock, North Carolina, to the Marine Corps Air Wing there. For twenty-five dollars, we purchased our four-by-six, two-wheeled hauling trailer that was well used, weather-beaten as all get-out, and had definitely seen better days. But to us it showed great potential. We loaded our king-size wooden rocking chair, filled the trailer full, and off we went in search of more, new adventures.

Both of us were eager, ready to take in all America had to offer. Along our way, we visited the Grand Canyon and the Painted Desert; thought we would witness the Petrified Forest all standing green, straight, and tall, while reaching for the sky, only to find, to our amazement, these brown rocks lying on the ground! We briefly dropped down into Northern Texas and then visited anew great sights in Arkansas and Tennessee while continuing into the gorgeous Smokey Mountains. Every day, we were in amazement as we traveled from West Coast to East Coast. The sights took our breaths away. As a child growing up, I had only traveled once, so this was all magnificent to me.

On this particular transfer, we were in route during the fall season; the trees with their changing leaves were radiant. Never in my life in South Texas had I ever seen trees like these, many with huge, perfectly formed pinecones, and all the waterfalls and brooks, the cottages and mountainside homes. We were experiencing so much, so quickly. In no way had my past allowed me to anticipate such encounters. I could not believe this was happening to me—to us.

As soon as we arrived in Havelock, North Carolina, we began looking for a place to live. Base housing at the Cherry Point Marine Corps Air Station had a long, daunting waiting list, so for us with little money, waiting was out of the question.

In an adjacent tiny town, we found a furnished rent house for a reasonable price; but still I would need to find work quickly. The wee house came complete with three rooms; the living room's focal point was a large black pot-bellied heater and flue. Promptly my new job came through in yet another small town, but this one was located directly on the Atlantic Coast. There I worked five and a half days a week, traveling fifteen miles each way.

From our little house Dean traveled in the opposite direction to the marine base. With only one car, we tackled serious issues in managing our schedules.

My job was in the Loan Department of the only bank in town. I accepted payments, took dictation for correspondence from both loan officers, balanced my money drawer at the end of each day, and gave out very strict credit reports. It was not great, but it helped pay the bills, and I was willingly hanging in there. I brought home almost $195.00 a month and was thankful to accomplish that.

On our way each day, we would pass acres and acres, farm after farm, of these beautiful, healthy tobacco plants.

It was in North Carolina where we experienced our first trip through the tobacco fields, dirt-track stock car races, and our first high-school-gym donkey basketball game. They were each a *hoot* and worth every penny we spent. One morning we woke up to everything covered in snow. I was hysterical—this was my first snow ever!

During the year we spent in Havelock, we moved three times. However, we spent our first married Christmas in our first little rent house. On that Christmas morning, without a tree or presents, we immediately realized that overnight our uninsulated house with linoleum floors had become terribly cold.

Our landlord swiftly educated us on butane tanks and how they needed to be maintained, which translated meant filled with butane gas every so often as money was available; something we had not done and now had little money to do so!

Being Christmas Day, in the middle of nowhere, the one butane store in town was not open. Therefore, we managed to spend our day under our electric blanket, a timely and much appreciated wedding present. For another eight months, our next furnished rental unit was an attic apartment above the home of an elderly widower. It came with two bedrooms and throughout was lined in gorgeous, glossy knotty-pine paneling. Our new landlord was a dear man who obviously missed his deceased wife.

However, within eleven months of patiently waiting, our request for Marine Corps base housing became a reality. We gave our kind landlord our notice and moved into a duplex with more room, for less money, and it meant less travel for Dean. This lasted all of two weeks, at which time we were informed that our legendary orders for Vietnam had also become a reality. We began repacking all we had just unpacked, and I gave notice at my employment.

Sadness and fear had not had opportunity to take hold— we were both too busy. But when at last we were on the road back home to Texas with all our things once again secured in our 4x6, two-wheeled trailer, and our dog, Punkin, with her four new puppies all bedded down in a corner of the backseat, we had ample time to evaluate what this certainty meant to our lives. At that time, we had been married all of one year and three months.

While driving over and around the beautiful rolling hills of Alabama on a busy, narrow, two-lane highway, the tongue of our hauling trailer became worn through and through, breaking away from the trailer hitch. It could have rolled into heavy, oncoming, five o'clock, eighteen-wheeler truck traffic, but instead it plowed into a ditch full of wild grass at least seven to eight feet tall!

Dean safely came to a stop and backed us all the way to where the trailer had left the road. As hard as we tried, through the extremely high grass and deep ravine we could barely see the trailer or any part of our belongings.

To say we were scared to death barely touches our then true feelings. We quickly realized what the other possibility, the other scenario, could have meant and visually imagined the many, many cars and eighteen-wheelers in one major, mass vehicle accident. The mental picture had an enormously sobering effect! How indebted and thankful we were to our many guardian angels encamped around about us.

That evening became dusky almost immediately, making it impossible to consider salvaging any of our personal effects that night. Driving back to the closest town, Dean checked me into a sleazy motel while he and the pets secured the accident site.

Very early the next morning we were shoulder to shoulder in the high grass and tall, razor-sharp weeds in what was an impossible situation. Over the hours, we retrieved as many of our possessions as we could find, even if they had not survived the impact. As we pushed the trailer out of the ditch, not once did we consider the possibility of snakes and other critters; instead we continued salvaging our property piece by piece out of that gully with the resolve of bringing them all home to Texas.

However, while continuing our search for what seemed without end, every so often I would look up to the edge of the ravine, wishing I could pass this unpleasant task on to someone else. So many of our wedding presents were ruined, and though I knew that, I could not part with them—not there in Alabama. I could not leave our special gifts in a strange place! For us, the Vietnam experience was going to be strange enough.

When we arrived at last at Dean's parents' house, we were exhausted while trying hard not to be completely defeated. Our lives seemed in shambles. Even our dog and her family were stressed and seemed relieved to be somewhere permanent for a while. Now we had four weeks to prepare for our lives apart and to find a secure place for me to live; relocating once again what remained.

Bingo! For rent across the side street from my in-laws was a convenient upstairs garage apartment. It served the purpose and was safe. Being upstairs, I did not have to worry about peeping Toms. Dean bought me a pink flocked, three-foot Christmas tree; reluctantly left Texas on a commercial airplane; received additional intensive training at Camp Pendleton in California; boarded a seaworthy military troop carrier; and left from California for parts unknown in route to Vietnam—three weeks before Christmas. The trip would take four weeks for fifteen hundred marines to arrive in country and onto Vietnam soil.

I wanted so badly to stop living; nothing in my life thus far had prepared me for this. I could not pray it away; I could not stop it; I could not fix it; I could not scream loud enough or get angry enough. I was helplessly left behind, and I was hopelessly sad. I truly did not think I could live through this, and it scared me because I was not even sure if I wanted to live through it!

How could this have happened to us when we were doing everything right? While in Havelock, we had been truly dedicated volunteer youth pastors at our small country church; by golly, I sang solos during church services; we gave our offerings; we were living right before God...

"God, how could you allow this," I cried and yelled in muffled tones while hopelessly alone in my apartment, and in my complaining I felt like the psalmist David. "Do something to help me! *Where* are you, God? I need to know how I can stop hurting so badly. I'm going to wither and pass away from sorrow. Oh, dear God, you know I am going to die of a broken heart!" And I sobbed and sobbed alone for hours, for days, for months— grieving *as unto death*!

It was several drawn-out weeks before I received a long-awaited letter from Dean by way of the San Francisco Armed Services Post Office. I lived to get my mail, holding my breath from one tender letter to the next. In my mind, a letter meant Dean was still alive as of that postmarked date. And so it went, from one postmark onto another, week after week.

I reasoned that if it took five days for me to receive Dean's letter, then I would breathlessly count back and proclaim, "Okay, as of last Monday, he was still alive. I only have to worry about the last five days." Somehow that made sense to me, and I would begin to hold my breath again until the next time and the next affectionate, thrilling letter.

I forced myself to watch the national news every evening even though with misgivings I dreaded it. The channels would showcase correspondents, Peter Jennings and Dan Rather among others, being filmed with our military troops during firefights in the jungles and vegetation of Vietnam.

They would film the ever-present rice paddies, the brown-water riverboats, our Huey helicopters, the wounded, and the wounded...and sometimes, even the dying and the dead—the prisoners and the lifeless Viet Cong and/or North Vietnamese.

I had to make myself watch the news each day so that I would know, as first hand as possible, what price my husband was paying. I did not want to bury my head and pretend that all was well or even a little bit well. I had fearfully watched these same journalists while Dean was in boot camp, and I fully intended to know the high price that was being paid not only by him but by the many others! And then I prayed and tried with all my strength to believe for his safety.

The readily available exposure of this war gave America a reality view of the true price for freedom that was being sacrificed by servicemen and women in blood, finances, and personal loss. However, it also further incensed the antiwar demonstrators and gave them more ammunition—more fuel and momentum—to use in their protests; a new weekly lifeline; a fresh impetus with recent up-to-the-minute stats.

Our world in that day was *upside down*! There was an extreme restlessness, a rebellion, and agitation like no other time in our history. Our society was reaching outside the box and experiencing it all with absolutely no limitations.

Returning to America crippled, broken outwardly and inwardly, many soldiers proudly wearing their uniforms (even though they all had been advised not to); our military servicemen were profanely screamed at and spit upon; their duffel bags angrily thrown into the deep waters after disembarking their returning troop carriers, or while thumbing a ride home along America's rural roads or major highways, they were pelted with beer bottles, tomatoes, anything and everything available—only because they were *guilty* of having sacrificially served their country during an unpopular war. These young men either enlisted, were commissioned, or they responded to their draft notices and did not frantically run for the safety of the Canadian borders.

However, on the other hand, many of these same servicemen and women experienced the presence of *angels—angels who humanly administered assistance, appreciation, and kindnesses that only could have been sent from God Himself.*

Unlike World War II, America provided no parades—no thank-you's for our military—no welcome home announcements, no celebrations and merriment for a job well done.

Instead there was only silence from relatives or condemnation from neighbors, previous friends, and town people. Our soldiers shut down out of survival and self-preservation; hanging their heads in undeserved shame. Isolation physically and emotionally became necessary—and then in time, it also became comfortable.

Even for me it was difficult to believe in our country, and I was not self-medicating unlike so many others. I did not do alcohol or drugs or sleep around; and, yet, even I found it troublesome to live in this society while still trying fiercely to believe in our politicians and in the speeches coming out of Washington because their actions and their dialogue did not ring true! They were all too quick to talk the talk but obviously did not walk the walk. Examples our politicians were not!

In my life thus far, I had always been incredibly patriotic, almost to a fault. But now that this act of patriotism was hitting so close to home, I was finding myself questioning everything our country declared and failed to stand for.

For many, it probably did not matter how truthful our officials were being with us regarding the status of this war—the Vietnam War—but for me, my whole life and my future was deployed overseas!

Therefore, I cared; it mattered to me. I was past playing games with the lives of our finest and our best—our young American men and women. I could not have cared less about our leaders' political or military careers. From hour to hour, day to day, my husband could have been dying in a foreign country and my life would have been over.

While beating their drums with their propaganda, how dared our politicians and military brass advisors treat the lives of our youth as though they were nothing but pawns in a chess game! Using them up and spitting them out, our young, as though they were dispensable and then nonchalantly sending them back home to us in boxes draped with American flags soaked with their blood; or returning so scarred mentally, emotionally, and/or physically that we no longer recognized our children or our spouses!

As parents, instead we gladly welcome our sons and our daughters, our loved ones, back onto our shores; with open arms we determine to care for them. We become caregivers to our husbands whom we love with an undying adoration regardless of their injuries or the understood, daunting lifelong challenges and commitments. And we forge ahead willingly, making life work for our soldiers and for our offspring!

Yes, move over politicians and military officials; we as families have a work to do with what war has created and brought into our lives. However, with God's help, we will persevere for we are American wives, mothers and grandmothers. During Vietnam our government often stood in front of this nation's populace— our grand hierarchy complete with big heads, and with big and vast career advancement agendas! And I screamed in my pain as they made flawed decisions that directly affected the outcome of our personal lives and that of our country.

I was so terribly close to hitting rock bottom. My insides were at war with each other as I tried unsuccessfully to mentally, emotionally, survive and work through these in-depth issues of my heart and soul.

My upbringing, my temperament, is to fix things, so thereafter I can rest and relax knowing I have done my part in contributing to the stability around me. I prefer not to wait to mend things in my life; therefore, procrastination is the worst decision for me to live under.

I was successfully conditioned in my early years to work at making good things happen for the betterment of those I lived with. There was always a life-and-death urgency then; the need was continually too huge to wait for precious time to pass.

In my family growing up, any hardship had to be addressed and attacked with expediency for us to continue, for us all to survive. I was required to be willing to sacrifice anything and everything in me—to die, if necessary, in order for those I loved to endure and to be able to live and have more than I ever did.

But I could not fix this. I grieved and travailed, but I had no means, no contacts. I was sick in my heart and soul; depression became my partner as I went to work each day and as I managed to function each weekend.

So how did I do it, you ask? That question is so simple to answer. I just turned on "the switch"—the same faithful switch that I still had access to from my childhood. The one I used during those years while I attended elementary school, etc., when I could become funny and charming, a friendly companion to my school friends.

My switch still worked for me—society demanded it of me. My family and in-laws demanded it of me. There were no other alternatives.

"Oh, God," I pleaded, "I *hurt*, God, I hurt so deeply and so vastly that I have no idea where my hurt begins and where it ends! I feel that I am bleeding out and no one sees or acknowledges the wound—not even my husband! But I cannot—I will not—burden him with my distress. He must only focus on self-preservation and the military business at hand. Honestly though, God, I have earnestly looked around, and there is absolutely no one available who understands this pain. *Indeed, I am alone—with You, God—but humanly alone.*"

And almost immediately a *heavenly peace* descended and *filled the room...*

Unfortunately, not my mother-in-law nor my mother, both having lived through World War II and having had husbands overseas, were of any comfort or encouragement to me. Sadly for me; that was just the way it was. I believe my mother must have been too self-absorbed with all her ongoing problems, and I think my mother-in-law must have felt that I had it easy—that I had it made just having to endure a short thirteen-month tour with no child to care for, unlike what she had had to endure those many years past.

Somehow I continued to live and breathe, but that was all I did during my phase of war—my Vietnam.

Nevertheless, in my own right, during that year-long-plus experience, I grew both mentally, spiritually, and overall, down to my very core. There was a growing up inside, and I emerged with the heart of a champion—a warrior of sorts, just like my husband. While drawing from all my past experiences and training, I became tough within—insecure and at times shy—but nevertheless tough.

My growing up and maturing was like building blocks. The building blocks started when I was a toddler, when it was just me and my mother scratching out a life for ourselves. But each year, as my responsibilities within my family grew to adult levels, the blocks became wider and thicker. My base became more secure, and the blocks began to reach towering heights, virtually unseen while rising into the billowing, elevated clouds.

I did not have my direction yet, but, by golly, I knew internally that once I gained more footing, I would and could do great and mighty things. I was destined to do things that only God could have planned for me—just for me and no one else!

Yes, my bread-crumbs-on-purpose moments were already laid just for me and my future.

Surviving the Moment

Within reason, there were times when the thirteen months Dean was away passed quickly. I did my best to stay busy. For one, I took Dean's grandmother, Granny, to the neighborhood grocery store most Saturday mornings where she would spend no more than $17.00—this in reality was a large portion of her small monthly Social Security check. Spending all of $17.00 would worry her deeply, and she would frequently complain about how high and quickly the store prices were escalating. Secondly, I would spend Friday nights with my mother's children—my two brothers and sister—who were then in their preteens and early teenage years respectively.

On those Friday evenings, I would bring my siblings over to my apartment where we would fix popcorn, have soft drinks, and munch on nuts and candy. We would watch television and just spend quality time together, while giving them a break from the extreme poverty in which they still lived.

These two brothers were already working odd jobs and bringing home money that my mother swore was required to make ends meet. Nevertheless, no matter how much they earned, there was *never* enough to go around to satisfy her insatiable demands.

During Dean's entire thirteen-month tour overseas, our US Government was issuing what was termed "combat pay." This allotment was paid to everyone serving in an American War Zone. Dean was generously sending this monthly combat pay of one hundred dollars directly to my mother's address. Never did we benefit from a penny of it.

Rick's Surprise Visit - 'Nam 1967

For the longest time, I did not know about this additional payment being made available to us. During those months, I did not hear about it from my mother. "Mum" was the word; plus, she also managed to overlook thanking us or acting grateful for this financial aid. More than likely, she felt we owed it to her, and we were merely catching up for all the past, unpaid money that we had been compelled to send her from our time in California and North Carolina, but had been unable to do so. We all know paybacks are hard!

About the time that Dean was already discharged from Vietnam, my brothers began working at a hotel restaurant bussing tables and washing dishes. This hotel was very well known—part of a chain—and at least a mile from their house.

Even though there was a family car available, our mother required them to walk to work for each of their shifts—shifts they sought to have booked together for that very reason. Most of these shifts did not end until after midnight—depending on the volume served that particular day or weekend.

After working long, dismally hard hours, they faced yet another walk home in the early morning hours, sometimes each one walking alone, only to get up later that morning and attend school at the normal time, while feeling fresh and ready to learn.

Currently, as a mother and grandmother myself, I have no idea how my mother could have justified this behavior. From my childhood her favorite comment to me was to say that I was "nothing more than a snotty-nosed kid that knows nothing about life!" I may not have known much about life at that early age, but because of her and her life, I was indeed learning rapidly. Something was seriously and pitifully wrong with my mother's childrearing skills!

My heart aches for the hardships placed on those three innocent children—my two brothers and sister. And there is a guilt that I still carry because I left them to fend for themselves after my knowing full well what my mother was capable of doing. They suffered mightily under our mother's severe authority and dictatorship!

A few examples of my mom's parenting skills are as follows:

1) After I married and left home, apparently finances became even more dire. In my mother's house, we had a pantry of sorts where nonperishable items were kept. In order to control our two developing preteen boys from eating the food that was purchased for the use of entire meals, my mother secured the pantry with a padlock! In this desperate move, she guaranteed what was still available for mealtime. When I was still there for those countless years, we went hungry many times; we did have a measure of food to curb our appetites, but it just did not stretch far enough.

   With my mother I remember standing at the checkout counter numerous times and spending fifteen dollars for our weekly groceries for five—and even then, not having enough money to completely pay the pending bill. Therefore, at the grocery counter with many people standing in line behind us and eyeing us with disdain, we would have to sort out items in order to reduce the total to the amount we had in our pockets! My younger siblings grew up under those circumstances; humiliation was a daily dose, and, for all of us, our self-esteem and self-worth remained afar and unclaimed.

2) Where we lived determined how our family's dirty clothes were processed. In our last home, we loaded clothes onto a child's wagon—enough to fill fifteen washers at a washateria located three blocks away. There we would take over the facility, wash and dry, and then walk the folded loads back to our home.

I heard later that once I was married, this regimen continued but with one less person to assist. The three kids would load those same washers unmercifully in order to save the few extra quarters needed for buying their readily available vending machine candy and chewing gum. This delegated duty would all occur while my mother remained at home, resting; however, the duty had to be done in a timely manner and according to her specifications or else they would be unmercifully chastised and emotionally isolated.

3) Grocery purchasing was another assigned duty. I would be instructed to purchase X amount of items for an X price. A list and the grocery store sales paper would be provided, and, God help me, if in any way I deviated from the assigned plan.

I began buying the weekly groceries at age twelve. I would walk to the grocery store, whether it was six blocks or 3/4 of a mile—in the heat, the cold, or the rain. I would push the overly loaded grocery cart across busy streets or over rocks, dirt, ruts, and mud. Upon my return home, the groceries would be scrutinized, checked for errors in judgment, which all determined whether I had done as ordered, or if I needed more instruction and the consequential wrath.

Two of my siblings repeatedly ran away from home, only to be brought back by well-meaning police officers, or reluctantly sent home from friends' houses because of our mom's continuous calling, harassment, and legal threats. Many times, in all kinds of weather, the younger two of them slept under bushes, bridges or overpasses, and beside the garage apartment behind our mother's house. In essence, these children desperately felt, and were shouting to society, that our mom's house was not home for them. The very next day they would attend school unbathed and in filthy clothes, as though they were leading normal lives. This never-ending trauma caused my young sister to choose to quit school in the eleventh grade and move away with her boyfriend to Colorado, where he had more family.

Proudly, my older brother joined the military service of his choice, only to be discharged in short order due to my mother's letters and phone calls to his commanding officer, and then onto the CO's superiors, claiming hardship and poverty reasons.

None of the dreams and desires of these children were heard, nor did they ring true in the heart of our mother. Though I was not always emotionally able to enact what I learned under my mom's rule, I did discover how *not* to live and how *not* to transfer my pain onto the lives of my children. God has prepared a unique design and new bread crumbs for each of our children and grandchildren who deserve to begin unsullied lives of their own. We must do all we can to halt the generational abuse and endow our future generations with positive role models and pure hearts.

After serving for seven months in Vietnam along with his original 1,500 other marines, Dean qualified for a week of R&R or *Rest and Recuperation*. This event was a "stand down," which referred to the brief period a soldier leaves an active combat area in order to rest and regain strength.

The two of us were to meet in Hawaii, where each one of us traveling the direction necessary was to arrive on the same day.

Detailed plans were made and communicated. The projected date was taking place during the last few days of June in 1967, and into the Fourth of July.

I did not learn until much later that Dean almost had to cancel his R&R due to a possible change in orders. As many of us know, the military is not required to go by most of society's standards—they have the option of making their own—and all of Dean's plans, as well, were subject to changes.

I was so enthusiastic and excited that I included in my packing some clothes my mother-in-law on one of her good days purchased for me way ahead of time—most of them had been on sale due to earlier winter clearances.

At last, the day arrived! For over a week my job was not to be my responsibility; it had been reassigned. I eagerly boarded the plane to take me first to Dallas, then to Los Angeles, and finally to Hawaii.

I am *not* a good traveler and never have been. I have issues, *b-i-g issues*, with motion sickness! In preparing for this trip, all I found available for motion sickness was Dramamine—a sedative for me that makes me so terribly dizzy, nauseous, and pretty much knocks me out. Nevertheless, knowing this, I purchased it anyway and endured the twilight-zone trip across the ocean and into Hawaii.

Another issue on that once-in-a-lifetime trip was my clothing. Based upon my mother-in-law's *sound* recommendation, I was wearing, during this hot summer month and headed into a tropical paradise, a wool, celery-colored, two-piece suit with a long-sleeved matching blouse beneath.

Why would I do such a crazy thing? Because I was gullible and easy to convince, of course! I also was wearing some good-looking, oyster-colored high heels. It is obvious that in this way, I could suffer mightily as I traveled from airport gate to airport gate—and terminal to terminal!

But that was not the worst part. On the top of my head, sitting like a nest in search of a bright colored bird was a pillbox-type hat, celery-colored to match, complete with a hat stickpin encrusted with lime-green rhinestones; never did I take the hat off. I did not think I could get it back on in the right place over my mother-in-law's 1960s French-twist creation! So, I remained the whole trip stiff-necked and sitting/sleeping in a straight-backed position—from South Texas into Oahu! But after all, in my defense, without instructions, I certainly could not let my hat get lopsided or drop too much to the front or to the back. It remained perfectly positioned for hours and hours, and for what seemed like days! So, there the pillbox was, like a beacon for the entire world to see.

When we finally arrived, I disembarked the plane on the tarmac, hesitantly wandered into the terminal, and I am pretty sure I looked like I owned the place—a princess or something. As I was walking into a more congested area, I saw my loving husband of now two years. In his arms, he was carrying a bouquet of flowers and had a colorful lei around his neck.

But then, to my sheer surprise and utter dismay, he walked within three feet of me and continued on, never acknowledging or showing any recognition. And without interruption, he continued walking as I turned and stood there bewildered. Heavens! It had only been seven months. How could he forget what I looked like? I recognized him. What could possibly be wrong? Had he forgotten me already?

I softly called to him by his nickname, "Spike?" Immediately, he turned around. With a crazy, questioning look, he stared for several seconds and swiftly made his way back. And then he started to giggle, and giggle, and heehaw, pointing to my magnificent pillbox, which, for him, had been the thing of confusion! Needless to say, never, did I wear that outlandish, get-up-and-go hat again. Instead, I conveniently left it in Hawaii for someone else to enjoy!

Being active-duty military, we had the best time possible in Waikiki because, for us, everything was discounted. On the island, we stayed at Fort DeRussy in officers' housing for which we paid all of seven dollars a night! The Fort's accommodations were right on its own private beach with a personal view of the ocean just like the many surrounding exclusive hotels.

All week I did not cook, even though we had a complete kitchen. And with several military discounts, we also had enough money to lease a plum-colored, 1965 Ford Mustang. Yahoo! We were on top of the world and having a blast! Hawaii was truly a beautiful paradise, just as advertised.

That fleeting week went by way too fast. Nevertheless, we managed to squeeze in a multi-course Luau—an all-afternoon limo-driven private tour of the island, complete with pineapple fields and delicious samples. We saw the Tiny Bubbles man, Don Ho, at a Polynesian affair. We swam and we shopped, ate out every meal, and even enjoyed a Pearl Harbor tour on the tourist boat, *Leilani.*

However, because of my motion-sickness issues, this Pearl Harbor Tour became super-duper memorable, and one on which I thoroughly embarrassed myself by throwing up all over the blue, interior deck—yes, in front of God and everyone! But then, all too suddenly, it came time for me to return to Texas and for Dean to return for the balance of his Vietnam tour. My departing flight was scheduled for midnight; his departure was to be soon thereafter.

We counted the hours as they clicked by, demanding for them to last longer than sixty minutes. We found our way to the island airport and waited. We said our good-byes like two newlyweds, and I unhappily boarded the plane destined for Los Angeles.

Despondently, I waited for the plane to taxi, as I begged and pleaded to God, just as I had promised Dean I would. *But my plane did not crash upon take-off!* I felt God was not present and had chosen not to listen that night.

Without a doubt I knew that if my plane crashed upon take-off, I would be able to stay a while longer with Dean—at least until they found another plane. Dean, on the other hand, would not have been able to stay with me. Vietnam was patiently calling him, as were his superiors there, but my heart did not think in those war terms. I was leaving my whole world behind and returning to Texas to absolutely nothing!

Departing at midnight aboard a plane usually means everyone sleeps, and my fellow passengers were no exception. Because I had had my mind seriously involved on saying my good-byes and then planning and praying for the crashing of the plane, I had forgotten to take my motion sickness pills...*oops!*

At approximately 6:30 a.m., we arrived in Los Angeles—California time. I was hungry enough to have a small pastry and a cold drink. When the time arrived to board again, I soon realized I was on a *puddle jumper* for the whole distance. Already, I was not feeling too well, but, "Hush, you'll be okay, don't be a baby," I whispered to myself.

Our first descent was into Phoenix—it was then that I began getting more and more nauseous. Each ascent and descent was unbearable, and there were several of these.

The flight attendants did their best to aid my distress, but nothing they provided made a difference. At last into San Antonio, Texas, we descended to transfer planes. As I wobbled down the gangplank, I was cautiously asked if I needed assistance; even though I was able to mutter "No, thank you," I knew I could not physically nor emotionally manage any more air travel. I was done!

After placing a call to my in-laws, for several hours I slept in a restroom on top of my small carry-on. The next thing I knew, I was traveling home in the backseat of my in-laws' car. At home I was placed on medication and slept for several days; however, my grief and anguish were not over. Dean and I still had six more months of war and separation.

It was during the second half of Dean's Vietnam tour when he started volunteering for more dangerous military assignments, which were entitled, "In-Field Patrols." By this time in his deployment, Dean did not feel he was doing enough for America and for the overall war effort. Therefore, he asked to be placed on more missions. As noble and courageous as this humbling request sounds, looking back now and at our future years of marriage, this was where heavy-duty PTSD hitched a ride home and came to dwell between the two of us and then later amidst our three children.

Battle Buddies have "Your Six"

During the time we spent in Hawaii, just two months before this volunteering petition, most of the old, clever Dean was still present. However, that original Dean would never leave the war zone—out of duty and survival, he changed and returned to me thirteen months later empty, angry, and isolated.

Already through military school and then military service, Dean's teenage innocence had been taken and replaced with maturity and reality. Early on, he had lost a portion of his childhood innocence while in boot camp. During ITR—further intensive Marine Corps training—he lost another piece. Thirty days aboard a troop carrier, while it inched its path across the world to an unpopular war, brought yet another loss of youth and early manhood.

Cruel and brutal war trauma in Vietnam produced the passing away of the final segment. Now the world was viewed differently through Dean's eyes; he had become a true marine and now shouldered, along with all other marines, a responsibility to uphold the mission statement of the U.S. Marine Corps. (Please refer to the last chapter to view in more detail what the honorable Marine Corps ethics, values, and motto stand for.)

Several months later, Dean experienced his most lethal, crowning dose of post-traumatic stress disorder. It occurred when he and one other soldier were barely left alive on the top of a mountain following a midnight—and then again a two o'clock early morning *overrun.* Dean was the radio/communications man during those two to three hours while the VC systematically destroyed the command post and the generator, which took with it the lighting and all communications. Dean and his unit started out that evening with dozens of marines accounted for, well fortified and prepared for anything, or so they had planned.

However, after 1,200 North Vietnamese were victorious in running over the top of them, having two men left alive in any capacity should have been called *a miracle!* However, later that morning, when the sergeant in charge arrived by helicopter to view the carnage, he did not call it a miracle—he called them both cowardly, scrutinizing them with indignation for not having died with the rest! This was the beginning of Dean's survivor's guilt, as he stood on that mountaintop covered in mud and saturated with blood—his own and that of many others.

How close Dean, too, came to being decapitated. Instead, after the explosions, God caused the on-fire military tank under which Dean partially found himself, to spew out some of its internal heat, causing the enemy standing over him to release his grip on Dean's helmet and to move on in his determined march of death and destruction.

Soon after Dean's arrival back at the DaNang Air Station, he developed "the shakes" and was sent on to the Philippines for a short recovery—only to return soon after back to his unit and his duties there. (Of course, none of this was shared with me back home!)

There was once an explanation given about PTSD and how it is an anxiety disorder—and a disorder of the heart. The explanation explains how war injures the soul, confuses the mind, and ruins the soldier's identity.

PTSD is a severe emotional and behavioral disturbance—a powerful version of the stress response that may occur after exposure to an exceptionally stressful, threatening, or catastrophic event or events.

Combat trauma PTSD occurs in those who have been exposed to a traumatic combat-related event (or series of events) that involved actual or threatened death or serious injury and caused an emotional reaction involving intense fear, panic, helplessness, or horror. (More information is available in the Resource section.)

When his full thirteen-month tour was completed, Dean departed for the States aboard a commercial airline—alone. During that war, that was how most of the servicemen were being sent back home to America. Vietnam was set up as a rotation, which meant that new troops were being rotated into Vietnam, and seasoned, experienced soldiers were being returned to the States. This made for strange bedfellows, and cherished friendships were difficult to achieve when unfamiliar, new warriors were continuously arriving in country, replacing the well-known and well-worn, tested and true ones.

Dean's return to the States and home was a celebration for us. We could have cut the relief and de-stressing with a knife. However, the first indication of PTSD was within two nights of his homecoming. I had already given up my apartment so we were staying temporarily at his parents' house until it was time to journey back to California and our new duty station.

That second night, we had been asleep for some time when Dean awoke suddenly in a cold sweat, calling out in an anxious tone and loudly asking if I had heard the rockets? Had I heard gunfire? It puzzled and concerned me, and I answered, "No, I did not hear anything—are you okay?" Without answering, Dean turned over and was off again into a restless, shallow sleep.

I knew this threatening nightmare was something new to our relationship; I also knew I needed to be worried about his mental and emotional state. Needless to say, I stayed awake for a while before going back to sleep myself, just to be sure he was not going to wake up again and be terrified.

The frequent nightmares had begun. The images, the reenactments, the fear and terror, the panic, the horror, and the gore returned time after time. They eagerly joined the *Jungle Rot* that menacingly appeared on Dean's ankles and feet—Jungle Rot from staying wet and hot, and then cold for days, weeks on end, in rice paddies, during monsoon seasons, and sleeping in deep and muddy, military-tank-tread impressions—in addition, there were the effects of malaria, gruesome rats, along with the embedded shrapnel, and, finally, last but not least, cancerous melanoma.

Dean's "fight or flight" adrenaline would take over time and time again. When this occurred, he would attempt watching midnight television to occupy his mind, trying to steer it away from those intrusive memories, those invasive nightmares. At any cost, his need for survival was paramount! However, he was systematically drowning in confusion and distress, in fatigue and survivor's guilt!

The U.S. Marine Corps had trained and retrained, conditioned and, thus, produced a warrior in my husband. Dean had become a sharp-shooting, well-oiled combat machine that reacted and was ready to fight at a moment's notice—with no forethought, absolutely no questions asked. Though this warrior, this Rambo, was no longer in the war zone where this type of mentality, effort, and response are rewarded with medals, ribbons, and rank, it did not matter. The well-created combat machine remained keen and ready to take action, to quickly take charge of any situation.

The military had installed "the switch" but had failed to either remove it or to at least deactivate it through counseling or therapy.

But truly in reality, how does anyone accomplish this deactivation in men that are asked by our society to prevail, to triumph as men, and to take responsibility? We ask of them to be mature and to provide for their families—to protect those they love, or those who are defenseless, ill, and in need?

But then upon their return home, we ask our servicemen <u>not</u> to be warriors; we require them to de-activate this mentality and emotional conditioning themselves because it has the enormous potential of being inconvenient and problematic in our everyday society!

"*They must conform,*" we say—there are laws and jails; heaven forbid, there are mental hospitals for those who have issues and are troubled. "Get yourself together, please," we beseech and plead. "Get your rest, so that tomorrow, with a good attitude, you can 'punch a clock' and put in a full day's work; you must provide for the mortgage, the car payment, the utilities, put food on the table!" That's our American way of life with Chevrolet, Mom, and Apple Pie; and out of desperation, we continually shout out this reality and grocery list of needs and requirements.

Thus, our dear, loving husbands and life-long partners try and try again. After the two World Wars, Korea, Vietnam, they tried! And after the Gulf War, Iraq, Afghanistan, again they have tried! But all the while, they have full-blown post-traumatic stress disorder camped out on their shoulders and emotions, and in their minds they have traumatic brain injuries (TBIs.) Each day the injuries and traumas are there until who knows when.

In those distant, post Vietnam years, early each morning our active-duty military and veterans pulled themselves out of bed, after having either slept fitfully through the night…or, perhaps, they were up and alert from 2:00 a.m. until 5:00 a.m. while on patrol, hyper-vigilant, walking their property lines, many equipped with frightening weapons, securing their homes for the remaining hours of darkness.

Or, perhaps, they are just plain scared to sleep, afraid to become subjective to those atrocious, evil dreams—those nightmares that will rob them of their confidence and fortitude. For these many warriors, it's no wonder there was then, and there still is today, extreme irritability and irrational behavior!

I found myself becoming irritable and irrational just writing this piece! Wouldn't everyone? Haven't we all lost our cool due to lack of sleep or peace, security or financial stability, and most of us do not have the debilitating mental/emotional disorder of post-traumatic stress, plus other incapacitating disabilities.

No wonder our servicemen and veterans have self-medicated throughout history. How could they not, after our patriotic general public has ushered them home, patted them on the back and said in no uncertain terms, "You're back now, put that ole' war behind you and move on. Get out there and find a job; after all, you've got babies to feed!"

And they did…find a job. Many of the Vietnam veterans found a job between the bouts of alcohol and the euphoria of drugs. Yes, they worked those jobs, because they had to—not because they felt adequate and capable in their fatigue and lost identities.

Nevertheless, in today's world, they rest beneath bridges and overpasses or beside abandoned storefronts because they are broken physically and inwardly. They are tired and worn and defeated. All they ask from us is a few coins and a dose of respect.

There were those who chose to use the historic G-I Bill and in so doing, they decided upon some hurried career goal. Or perhaps they went from job to job, never settling on anything, never building up necessary retirement—always laboring under that cash flow problem, year after year. With PTSD (and TBIs), the person must live for the moment. Nothing else matters; *just that one moment!* Each one is an achievement, and if he or she can be lucky enough to add a day to that one moment, they have done well and have been successful!

Thus, when we are young and busy enough working and raising our families, and can emotionally run fast enough to stay ahead of the war demons, then our nightmares will not find us until we are well into our fifties or sixties. The goal is to preoccupy our minds with anything, to not think about war experiences and the dead we left behind!

PTSD is no different now than it was in World War II, Korea, Vietnam, or in today's Iraq and Afghanistan, nor will it be any different in the wars to come. It has always been a "common response" to an "uncommon event."

The wars, years, and circumstances change; the faces, ages, and locations change, but as long as we remain human, we will have this normal reaction of PTSD to horror and gore. Left untreated, it can take years in recovery.

Our vet is not weird, odd, different, or moody; he has been wounded. He is injured just as though he suffers from missing an arm or leg or an obvious brain injury.

Just like missing a limb would not be considered his fault, so it is that this disorder, this behavior, is not his fault. But as spouses and partners, neither is it our fault.

A large percentage of pressures Dean and I experienced as a couple were caused directly by his wartime trauma. Dean entered combat and did not return the same as when he left for war; his life's coping mechanisms were compromised.

However, that said, I am here to shout that love and hope are weapons PTSD cannot defeat, because they are virtually invincible! They have made the difference in marriage after marriage (our marriage), in spite of the overpowering and disheartening divorce statistics of Vietnam, Iraq, Afghanistan, and the many wars before and in between.

Therefore, be inspired; survival and then success can be achieved as long as both parties are determined to strive for their relationship, followed by thriving in life. There are times when we must remind ourselves that those blessed bread crumbs released along our paths will always lead us to positive places—guaranteed!

Seeking God's Design

O n this, our last trip to an assigned duty station, Dean and I were on a military deadline. In short, by a certain time on a certain day, Dean was required to report to his new company administrative office for his final year in the Marine Corps. No exceptions and no excuses! If he did not, he would have been termed *AWOL*. That label could have cost him rank, a monetary fine and probable military jail time.

To date, Dean had progressed admirably with his rank advancement. As a teenager, those two and a half years of training at a military institute had served him well. Because of his previous conditioning, he arrived in Vietnam with the rank of Lance Corporal but quickly earned corporal and then advanced to Sergeant E-5, both while "in country" within thirteen months. Losing any of those hard-earned stripes was not something we took lightly. Now we were on our way to California with our belongings, once again being pulled behind us in our dependable trailer—the same one that had traveled across the United States and witnessed with us many spectacular sights; the same one that ran head-on into that Alabama ravine; the one that waited patiently while we served in Vietnam. Punkin, our friendly mutt, now well over a year older, was quite at home in the roomy backseat.

We were making great time, did not have too many cares in this world except the few aforementioned. We were sure about having several days to spare to settle into an adequate apartment before reporting to the El Toro Marine Corps Air Station in Santa Ana, California. It was dusk and we were still on the road choosing to travel to just one more town. In West Texas, it can be quite hilly, and we had just topped the peak of a large hill when we saw something below in the middle of the highway right in our path. "What is that?" we both asked out loud as we crested the hill, with an overloaded trailer shoving us ahead and our vehicle gaining momentum.

In seconds, as we grew closer, our eyes became like saucers when we realized the thrust was sending us barreling toward a cow in the middle of the interstate! To the left of the road, Dean swerved as gently as possible, but the solid, dark brown cow moved backward to our left. Again, Dean swerved, but this time to the right; once again, our cow moved forward to our right. Its eyes were transfixed on us—like a deer in headlights—but this deer was not standing still!

With squealing, smoking tires, we broadsided her and sent her flying at least fifteen feet farther down the highway. For us, this downhill experience was similar to crashing into a brick wall traveling sixty miles an hour. With no seatbelts, both Dean and I collided with the steering wheel and dashboard respectively.

Upon impact, and flying at us from the backseat, was Punkin, our medium-sized dog. She went airborne, hitting me, the dashboard, and then falling in a heap onto my floorboard. As we opened our doors, we took some time to calm our frenzied, anxious dog while dodging the spewing liquid and vapor escaping from under the hood of our car.

Our family-sized car's front end was buckled in half and fairly close by was this huge cow on her side, seemingly dead on this busy Texas Interstate!

How did I know what gender she was? Well, simply, because... we had managed to hit a *pregnant, mother-to-be cow!* That was what made her very big. In what seemed like a few moments, a variety of cars and eighteen-wheelers had appeared out of *nowhere*—similar to where we found ourselves—*absolutely in nowhere.* We stood there in shock, without noticing that it had quickly become very dark out there in ranch land.

As we waited for the locals to discuss and finally resolve to whom this special cow belonged, this January evening had become much cooler. After determining the cow belonged to a Mr. Erwin, we learned the way this was decided was by the cockleburs on our cow's tail. The said Mr. Erwin was, of course, not a happy camper, nor was he taking any responsibility for the broken fence through which the cow had escaped. He tried for the next six weeks to make no amends for the harm and damage done!

The helpful sheriff transported the three of us to the one motel in town. I vaguely noticed I had begun suffering a migraine. The next day, Dean's parents drove out to assist us until it was settled that the car repairs would be held up for more time than Dean and I had to spare.

We lingered until the order was placed for the required parts that would return our car to its former self.

We thankfully traded cars with Dean's parents, had a trailer hitch installed on their car, and departed once again with California in our sights.

Alas, the infamous Mr. Erwin hired an attorney, who just so happened to also be the county judge. Needless to say, not a penny was paid by this man for our damages.

This time as we resumed our travel to California, both of us were quiet and nontalkative. Physically, we were not feeling well—the accident had rattled things loose that were not created to become unhinged and to stand alone!

After the accident, neither one of us saw a doctor; we were in too big a hurry to get back on the road leading to our designated duty station.

In reality, however, we were very banged up about the neck and shoulders, chest and lower back. I would have difficulties with my head and upper body for six months into our tour in California; Dean was no better off.

Mile after mile of not chatting gave me plenty of time to think back on all the possibilities that could have taken place on that country highway. How fortunate—how blessed—we were to have walked away! Once again, we had angels surrounding us! *It was another one of those Bread Crumb moments.*

As the monotonous wintery landscape passed by, giving way to more of the very same, I made myself comfortable, laid my head back and allowed my idle mind to wander. It began taking me into the past to my younger days of growing up on the Mexican border and how, even at that early age, my tender heart had been turned toward God. As a minor, I felt a longing, a hunger, for a godly presence.

My mother's father had built one of the oldest Presbyterian churches in our hometown and in the area known as The Valley. In his prime, he was an influential man—a man of means; he had earned his fortune by becoming a regional, wholesale grocer.

At one time he held the public position of city assessor and collector. His life's information was listed in a publication of prominent, wealthy state of Texas businessmen called *The International Blue Book*, copyrighted 1912.

My mother often persisted in her love of telling us hard-to-believe stories about her life growing up in a wealthy household. The following are two of those incredible stories:

At one time, her wealthy, well-known father owned a bullfighting ring across the Rio Grande River in one of Old Mexico's border towns. Enthusiastically, she would inform us that many of the most famous bullfighters would come to compete there in my grandfather's business. (For those who are not aware, this very long, often not so wide river is the deciding boundary between Texas and Mexico.)

My mom would describe in detail the dreadful, without-mercy-abused life of the many horses that were used to fight the bulls; how often they were gored, disemboweled, hastily sewn up, and quickly returned into the bullring. In those early years, there were no animal advocates to picket this business.

As the story goes, at some point during this bizarre business ownership, my grandfather had loaned the Mexican government a sizeable amount of money, which ultimately they could not repay. Instead, as retaliation for his requesting payment, the high government officials ordered the burning to the ground of his profitable bullfighting ring. It would never be rebuilt.

There was even talk that the yearly pilgrimages my grandfather and his large family made down to their summer house in Monterrey, Mexico, were cover-ups for the smuggling of arms to the Mexican Bandito, *Pancho Villa and the Resistance!* The story tells how the weapons and ammunition were hidden among the volumes of family clothing and packed household possessions. He was never caught by the authorities on either side of the border, so who knows the true validity of that story.

In his eccentric way, my grandfather was a religious man of conscience and principles. However, he was also remote and distant to those surrounding him. My mother liked to describe his stance as proud and reserved, but, from my childlike estimation, he was cold and indifferent.

All six of my maternal grandfather's children wrestled with their own emotional stability and displayed limited abilities at showing true sentiments toward each other and to their own intimate relationships. Regardless, in time, each one married, became district attorneys, county judges, a minister, a prestigious university language professor, and a registered nurse. My mother, however, was the black sheep and family rebel, with no college education and no career. The six of those siblings produced a total of eleven children.

During a seasonal, customary vacation to their summerhouse, my mother's mother died of pneumonia in Monterrey, Mexico, barely reaching her late twenties. Due to the deadly illness, her fifth child was delivered prematurely and my grandmother passed away soon thereafter.

My aunt, the fifth child, was born black in color as a result of the infection and high fever of my grandmother's sickness. She was born four months premature. As a freckled redhead, she always appeared frail and sickly; nevertheless, she surprised everyone and managed to live into her eighties.

My dear mother was five years old when her mother passed away. Soon, a spinster aunt came to live with the family for the sole purpose of caring for the children. She remained in their house even after my grandfather, who was into his forties, remarried. His new wife was a young lady, aged eighteen or nineteen. In reality, my uncles were close to the same age as their new mother. Together, my grandfather and his new wife had a daughter, who became the princess of the house, my mother would resentfully express.

Out of sheer, desperate loneliness, my mom retreated into books—lots of books. Without hesitation, she missed her mother deeply and did not fit in any shape or form into the new family grouping. Therefore, she checked out and read until her teenage years, at which time she started exhibiting her rebellious and in-your-face attitudes.

In those early years, my mom was the blonde in the family who desperately desired curly hair so badly that when she was told by her friends that if she shaved her head backwards and would do the same for her eyebrows, then the returning hair would grow back in curly and thick! Of course, she liked what she heard and she did just that; she shaved both, backward!

For months and months, she wore different scarves while her hair grew and finally most of it returned, but nothing grew in curly or thick and her eyebrows never did return at all! From that time forward, she penciled in her eyebrows and faithfully continued with the purchasing of *Tony and Lilt* Home Permanents to achieve the curls she fancied.

I am certainly not an expert, but I believe my mom labored her whole teenage and adult life with responsibility issues. From my vantage point in the family, and as I became an adult myself, I worriedly sensed she was lacking in logic and emotional development. There were times in her helplessness and severe battles at decision making that her maturity seemed maxed out at possibly sixteen years of age. It was as though she had stagnated in her youth and failed to progress into the adult process of reasonableness and discretion.

As an example: I was about five years old when she and her next-in-age baby sister decided to take their father to court and to sue him for their inheritance. Needless to say, they fell short on accepting the fact that there was not much inheritance left after America's Great Depression of the late 1920s and early 1930s! However, somehow they won the lawsuit—each one of them receiving approximately $7,000.

How my aunt spent her birthright I do not know, but my flamboyant mother bought with her inheritance this ugly, camel-haired coat and also began a children's daycare business, complete with multi-leveled playground equipment. Within the year, the business was a thing of the past; however, the unattractive, bulletproof coat lived on for years! At her father's death, my mom received a check for one dollar as her final portion of his legacy. She was angry—madder than I had seen her in a while! Because of miscellaneous small properties, she surmised that her siblings had received much more than $7,000 each. This wedge drove the family division deeper and we children found ourselves even more isolated.

For a few more hours, I watched the endless California-bound miles pass—the trees, the fences, and the ranches with sheep, cattle, and horses. As I continued to reflect back to those early days, especially to when I was eight years old, I pondered my driving desire/my deep insatiable hunger to know more about God himself; about his church; and what he had to say about me. When I was six we lived across the street from an Episcopalian minister and his family. For three years, I played with these children, especially the twin daughters, who were more my age. During our summers, I attended their church's Vacation Bible

School. I was like a sponge; I loved my time in those cherished morning services.

However, no one in my family attended church—neither before nor after my stepfather came to live with us. Seldom did we go to the church my grandfather built; on occasion, we attended the church of my aunt—the Spanish-speaking female Presbyterian minister; and on other occasions, we attended an older Presbyterian church not too far from our home. The few times we attended there were mainly because the two new babies in my family needed to be baptized.

There were instances when I visited the Catholic church with my cousin; as a baby I was baptized Catholic because of my father's family's faith. My mother clearly did not care either way and wanted only to please him. However, soon after their divorce, my Catholic days were over.

Nevertheless, as a child, I was so eager to become a part of any church that I somehow convinced my mom to allow me to attend church by myself. I was no more than eight years old.

As young as I was, I managed to dress myself each Sunday morning. After walking three blocks to a main thoroughfare, I would wait on the correct side of the street for the city bus. Not always knowing the bus schedule could cause a lengthy wait.

Those experiences were not as difficult and overwhelming as one might think—because by this time I had four close *imaginary friends*. They were always by my side when I felt overwhelmed with life's struggles and isolations. My friends' names were Barbara, Margaret, Dick, and Bob. They knew how to encourage and how to assure me in my limited abilities.

Each week when the bus reached the corner of the church, I (and my friends) promptly stepped off the bus, ventured into this large, decades-old Presbyterian church and together we would find my Sunday school classroom.

I only attended the hour-long Sunday school class, but on occasion while waiting for the main service to begin, I would peek into the sanctuary because I enjoyed watching the families as they sat together. After a few moments of observation, I and my make-believe friends would cross over to the other side of the street and would wait once again for the returning bus to pick us up, while carrying on our animated conversations.

I kept this schedule until we moved out to the farm—by that time I was nine years old. However, I remember that at this church, as in any church thereafter, I was painfully shy. No one there seemed to know who I was, and sadly no one asked if they could assist me in any way. Once again, I blended into the woodwork; I was disposable and I knew it. How did I know it? Because I was receiving the same message from many varied directions.

There were other times, as I became a teenager, where I would pray to this unknown God, way up there—somewhere! I would barter with God by asking him to grant me a miserable time at a friend's party or a junior high school dance just to ensure that my mother and stepfather would not have a brawl back at home while I was gone. I felt guilty leaving them to their own devices and not staying around to monitor their actions—just in case I once again was needed to run to a neighbor's to call the police.

It was during one of these fights that my stepfather was beaten by my mother about the head and shoulders with one of the old granite-type, invincible telephones to the point of breaking the receiver over his head. In the struggle my frightened little sister was gashed over her eye and scarred by that same phone.

However, this small amount of interaction with the God of the universe was a staying power in my life; without that connection, I suspect I could have taken a dangerous, love-starved path into prostitution and points beyond. Standing alone, it was God's continuing presence that kept me centered, desiring to make healthy choices instead of seeking attention in all the wrong places! He had dropped those bread crumbs on purpose, just for me. Yes, God often answered those bartering prayers that I naively dispatched into heaven. God, knowing my thirst for

His love, saw to it that for me there was no fun to be had on those "specific prayer nights," and in exchange, as requested, at my home He made sure my parents behaved themselves until I returned!

With these spiritual baby steps, my faith and trust grew, as I continued to seek and find my way to this supreme heavenly being I knew so little about. My pathway continued as did my celestial bread crumb moments.

I was fifteen years old when I became a Christian. By this time in my life, I was not as interested in church as I had been even two years before. Miraculously, I was being allowed to wear makeup and to date. Oh! I loved movies and dances, rock 'n' roll, and Elvis Presley.

However, my divorced mom had started attending a Pentecostal church with our neighbors. Our neighbors and their children were very *churchy* and had all kinds of restrictions on how to live. Many of those do's and don'ts had to do with makeup, movies, television, dancing, jewelry, slacks, and co-ed swimming!

I had barely started to have some fun in my life; how could I be asked and expected to give up so much for God? Therefore, I began dragging my feet and, initially, so did my mom—thank God! So we each took turns answering the telephone each Sunday morning when our faithful and godly neighbors would persistently call, asking if we were going to church that morning because they were ready and able to give us a ride! Month in and month out, they called. Almost each time, we had a great excuse. At the beginning, our good excuses rocked, but toward the end, they became quite lame after a year. My mother gave in first and became a born-again saint of God. Wow!

I have to admit though it was much easier living with her after her faithful church attendance and conversion. God certainly was making a difference in her life. But me? I was not ready and quickly thought I probably never would be. After all, I was a kid—a teenager. Rock 'n' roll was still alive and so was Elvis!

I lingered while my mother and the kids attended church many nights a week. It was lonely, but I was coping and convinced that God understood.

All this was going great until the Sunday I mistakenly agreed and said, "Okay! I'll go." Oh, my, I must have been one hardened sinner, because over an extended period of time, it took me at least ten trips to the altar of salvation to become a child of God! Needless to say, never once have I looked back; God has had my life from that moment on. How blessed I have been to live in His presence, protection, and affection because even in the sinister times, His divine hand has been ever present!

Therefore, at this time in our married lives, Dean and I had a known God—One who had spared us, not only in Vietnam but now in the States, and because of His care and His blessings, we were now again on the road—a road delivering us to California. Upon arriving in Santa Ana, we moved into a huge, white stucco apartment complex that covered several city blocks. At least 90 percent of it was inhabited by marines with their families—all stationed at the El Toro Marine Corps Air Station. Several of the family units were populated with countless children whose toys, bikes, and big wheels were scattered throughout the apartment courtyards. No longer did any landscaping exist. Nothing green was left in those open spaces, due to dozens of pounding little feet trampling everything in sight.

Thank God, Dean was able to check in onto the base with a day to spare. For the first month or two I did not work until we grimly concluded we needed some extra cash flow to last us until his next monthly paycheck.

Because Dean was paid once a month, there was plenty of opportunity for feast or famine. To earn money I looked for something to do and discovered Avon.

Within a couple of months, we recognized the need to purchase some inexpensive furniture to replace the tattered and worn furnishings in our second floor, one-bedroom unit. Each day or night there were frequent ambulances and first-responders hastening up and down the streets of this marine complex. If we were sound asleep and the recurrent, urgent sirens began blasting, immediately Dean would hit the floor in a panic, a cold sweat would appear, and a look of terror would cover his face! While on the floor, reliving in live, vivid detail the momentary flashback, without delay he would scramble, hopelessly endeavoring to find cover.

This PTSD fear and panic-filled alarm was forever present and ready to activate—all that was needed was *the trigger*—and all American sirens could successfully produce the required trigger.

Dean painfully explained to me how they sounded exactly like the sirens when the bombings would begin at the DaNang Air Base in Vietnam. There the Viet Cong (or North Vietnamese) would "walk the bombs in" in hopes of destroying many, if not all, of the parked Phantoms on the airstrip, as well as the stacked bomb dumps. In particular, he would divulge that when these stored bombs received a hit, the explosion was similar to an atom bomb.

For that year in Santa Ana, we lived with various degrees of dread, never knowing when another emergency would bring one more ambulance, or perhaps police cars with sirens, into our immediate neighborhood.

Within the first month or two during our final year in California, I started my small Avon business. Once again, I was in sales. I would dress up a little and walk over two blocks to my new Avon territory located in an adjacent, large apartment development.

Once arriving there, I would take a large deep breath to settle my nerves, and while smiling and acting upbeat I began knocking on doors. However, the poverty level present in those units was troubling for me and highly defeating at times.

The children's lack of care, the mothers' lack of hygiene, the empty conditions of the living quarters and scruffy surroundings was shocking even to me, who had not too long ago come out of poverty myself! Yes, I would sell and place their Avon orders, but many times I felt guilty by doing so.

A week or two later, I would return with their merchandise and seek to have a future order in place—or sadly, I would make trip after trip attempting to deliver the order, only to find instead an empty apartment—address unknown.

Looking back with a little more awareness, I see now what terrible dangers many of those circumstances provided for me. For instance, I recollect several times being ushered into a very sparse, dirty apartment filled with numerous minority men, all drinking, laughing, and joking in their language, possibly at my expense. Yes, they would oftentimes purchase Avon, but I now can appreciate how truly blessed I was to have had God's protection.

I knew at the time to be cautious and vigilant, but when I would return with those men's products, I would again receive another order. Only now do I see how perilous that situation was; however, because I paid our bills often unfamiliar to Dean, I also knew we required quite a bit of extra money!

Thank God, Christ was there with me in my ignorance and innocence—and Jesus was present also in our marriage's acute financial hardships. Nevertheless, Dean never knew the potential danger involved in selling my Avon; I could not share that with him because we desperately benefitted from the profits.

Within a short period of our arrival in Santa Ana, Dean began drinking and going out with other marines when their communication center shift was over. Some nights he barely came home, and, when he did, he would only be there to sleep a little, somewhat sober up, and prepare for the next swing shift.

This continued for most of the year. Thus, I remained by myself, while keeping the apartment clean, the laundry done, and Dean's fatigues (daily uniforms) starched crisp and ironed. I kept the food ready for when he would be there, and I watched a great deal of television.

Oftentimes, I would stay on alert throughout the lonely nights waiting up for him. There were a few occasions in the early morning hours, I found I could not stand the apprehension and I would call his mother to, I guess, also worry her! I had no one else to call; no one knew about our circumstances and challenges, certainly not our remote church family. In my grief and solitude, I would sob and agonize, call out to God again in desperation and sometimes in anger, literally making myself sick with anxiety.

All this unusual behavior was new to our marriage; before Vietnam, this sad commentary would never have occurred. In those earlier years, Dean was predictable, reliable. He used to want to come home because I was there, because I was vital and important to him.

However, while in Santa Ana, I did not know then that alcohol and drugs are ways of self-medicating the monsters of war; self-medicating ways to significantly drown out the nightmares, flashbacks and survivor's guilt. Then each time more and more of the medicating substance is required and the progression never ends.

Needless to say, my being his significant other and our enjoying each other's company were no longer fundamental in our marriage, and I did not comprehend how to respond to this latest conduct. At first, I became mad; I felt insulted. I would fume and cry in my isolation and brokenness.

Then, at last, the light bulb dawned for Sandy; I grasped the crystal-clear realization that it did not matter how I felt or what I thought; this was not about me at all! I either endured this lifestyle, or I could go back home! Well, I knew how home was. For me home was an oppressive and all consuming dead-end road!

Instead I remained in California, but over and over I would ask myself, "What is happening here? What has changed? Is this something I can mend?" Alas, everything I had tried, failed. The longer I stayed and suffered, the more I was aware I did not possess what was required to repair or improve anything regarding my husband!

However, there was more to this story than just the out-of-hand alcohol problem, because now, present within Dean, was an aloofness, bordering on indifference and alienation with serious mood swings. I tried to ignore it, to justify it, to pretend it was my imagination; however, I just knew my intuition was right on. Overall, I discerned we were in deep trouble. Our exceptional marriage of just two and a half years was in serious, dreadful trouble.

Dean was emotionally disconnected, unplugged from our marriage and from me.

I knew Dean loved me, but most of the time the body armor, the shielding and protective covering that had become a large part of him after returning home, separated us. There was no getting past it; there was no forcing my way in. When I would try to press the issue, the reaction was severe. I learned to readily back away, recognizing how wrong the timing had been.

In one of the combat experiences Dean had, he found himself in a vulnerable, gut-wrenching position overrun by swarming North Vietnamese, which brought with it a condition of intense terror and, in the natural, one with a hopeless, fatal ending! It had been life or death/annihilation; he had to kill to remain alive and came close to failing the task.

However, now in the shadow of American freedom, he continued shielding and safeguarding himself with the same fierce determination of never again finding himself defenseless. He would not let anyone beyond his emotional armor; no one, including me, would hold his unprotected heart and do with it what they pleased.

I would have to wait for him to let his guard down—wait for him to be willing to be a part of us at that moment, on that day. This was new to our relationship; it was on-the-job training for me. Many of my mistakes were colossal, as I navigated through uncharted territory.

The alcohol reliance made matters worse and caused my resentment to grow. During those years, if only I had had an understanding, compassionate friend, I and our fragile union would have better weathered the post-traumatic stress condition.

Because I loved Dean completely and I knew firsthand how he was before this PTSD tyrant arrived on our doorstep, that memory of him carried me through many hours of dread and loss.

Our heavy alcohol drinking concern was expensive at its best. Numerous times, my tiny Avon business supplied what we needed when there was not enough money. I provided as best I could, making our lives work.

Nevertheless, there was yet another way I was able to make money. On numerous occasions through our church's connections, I was called upon to sing at funerals. Our pastor's wife would accompany me on the piano or organ. I never knew the deceased for whom I sang, but that did not matter, I told myself. I was providing a service and the family was assisting me by paying the sum of five dollars. Five dollars does not sound like much today, but at that time, it added up nicely.

By October first of that year at the Santa Ana, El Toro Air Station, Dean had already visited an urologist to see why we were not becoming pregnant. By now, we had been married over three years and I thought I was ready for a baby. (To be honest, I was secretly unsure as to how we could provide for one).

On that memorable visit, as standard procedure, the urologist ran the customary sperm count testing and later regrettably informed Dean that there was no way—*absolutely no way*—that he could father a child! What? This was not what we had expected to hear. Vietnam and the infamous thousands of barrels and frequent spraying of Agent Orange had dealt us yet another blow!

Miraculously, after receiving that disheartening and dismal report, within the next two weeks, I was able to joyfully declare to Dean that I was pregnant and had been since September!

Thank God, Dean knew without a shadow of a doubt that he was the father! It would have been an additional crushing setback for our relationship if he had suspected unfaithfulness based upon the military specialist's documented low-sperm-count urologist's report. Is not God good, all of the time? Promptly, we sent out Western Union telegrams to all our new baby's to-be-grandparents, announcing the latest and greatest news. I was so excited, and I prepared mentally and emotionally to give life to a little one that would be a part of me and a part of the one person in this world whom I cherished with all my heart!

New Stress, New Pain

With much ado we completed our year in Santa Ana and our four years in the Marine Corps! As a result of his E-5 rank, the military was willing to pay for the packing and moving of our personal effects back onto Texas soil. I was four and a half months pregnant and was grateful for having the packing and heavy lifting taken care of.

Into this new phase of marriage, we no longer needed our extraordinary hauling trailer; we had outgrown it! We now had a bigger load of inexpensive furniture.

We took our time driving to Texas. The route had become quite familiar through the years. In our relatively short time, we knew the regimen and had become seasoned military travelers!

Upon our arrival, Dean's parents spoke of a house they had in mind for us to buy. It was a two-bedroom, one bath arrangement with a bricked-in carport and a huge fenced-in backyard. It was not too expensive, not in need of immediate repair; plus, it was located in a well-established neighborhood.

Within a short time, papers were signed, and we moved in. We were in a whirlwind of activity. We could not believe we were homeowners with a baby on its way during the month of June.

However, as life would have it, we were made aware of the monumental hurdles we still had to climb—all within a brief amount of time.

While Dean was serving in Vietnam and during the same firefight that cemented his post-traumatic stress disorder, he had been cut over his left ear by the Viet Cong, desiring to entirely remove it as a souvenir of prowess. Thank God, the ear was not removed. Instead, because of that previously described military tank distraction, that VC then moved on to someone else.

135

However, that cut had caused what appeared to be an elongated, blackish blood blister above Dean's left ear.

If Dean's ear as a trophy was not the reason for this initial cut, then this meant that his throat certainly would have been slit from ear to ear. That night, many of the killed marines had their throats cut as a final assurance to the Viet Cong that everyone was dead. How close he came to death or mutilation—only God's intervention and purpose can be our explanation.

After returning home to Texas, Dean's mother rode his case over this injury. Thankfully she did, seeing as how I had been unsuccessful in convincing him to have his ear examined while still in the military in Santa Ana.

Expeditiously Dean's appointment was made with a well-respected surgeon who without delay made hospital arrangements to have the blister removed. In no time we were in surgery, praying like the dickens. This was in the month of April, following the January of our military exodus.

During surgery, the biopsy returned as *melanoma*—the deadliest form of skin cancer. With that information documented, our surgeon proceeded to remove an even larger section, followed by taking a skin graft from Dean's thigh and grafting it in for cosmetic purposes.

Dean's recovery took several days. By the end of his hospital stay and follow-up, we were assured by our doctor that he had removed all the cancer and had gone even further into the healthy surrounding flesh. However, our doctor also understood if we had valid reservations and, to be sure, recommended our consulting with the Houston VA Medical Center to ease any additional concerns—such as, the cancer possibly having spread down into the neck glands and lymph nodes.

Without a doubt, we felt confident about our surgeon's expertise; plus, we had little to no money to go any distance into checking further into this prognosis.

Through Dean's original marine recruiter's friendship and who was now a county service officer, Dean not only was provided a Service-Connected Veterans Administration Card, but his case for this deadly melanoma surgery was turned in for payment to the government as a service-connected issue.

Thank God—another miracle! This was certainly a wonder in the making, because I know none of this makes any sense—not even to us! We were not out any money—someway, somehow, it was paid in full, even though Dean had a rushed military discharge without this cancer-producing wound officially recorded on his medical release papers!

One day something bizarre occurred not long after we moved from California into our house. We had decided to paint our master bedroom to give it a fresher look. Dean's family had always used Sears' paints, so off to Sears and Roebuck we eagerly headed.

While at the store, we chose our color and purchased one gallon of Select paint. At home, we already had our paint pan, brush, and roller, so we deducted we were complete in our purchase.

The next day, as Dean applied this one-coat paint, we agreed it was not covering very well. He would apply still more paint, but the previous color was again bleeding through. Over a small area he then applied a third coat, but still had the same frustrating problem!

Consequently, Dean gathered his emotions together and returned to the store—*alone*—(big, huge mistake!) He located the older gentleman who had sold us this "awesome" paint in the first place. At the time of the sale, this salesman had spouted off the paint's properties and coverage benefits. But, now standing in front of him was an irate and furious six-foot-seven, 230-pound, young man …and immediately he was backstroking and stuttering a bit, as I was later told in great detail.

The salesman's comeback remark was, "Oh! Of course, I know! The problem must be that you did not purchase with this paint, a Sears-recommended paint brush and paint roller!"

Oh, my gravy, that was all it took! Our resident and combustible PTSD triggered, took over, and Dean lost his cool! In his perpetual anger and rage, he grabbed the older man by his shirt's collar and pinned that man's pudgy self to the wall in the middle of the paint department of Sears and Roebuck!

Needless to say, we were gladly given more and better paint, and, for obvious reasons, the poor man left the store immediately to change his complete set of clothes!

When Dean proudly arrived home and hesitantly shared the story as to how he was able to acquire expensive paint and more of it, I was not only pregnant but was mortified and scared spitless!

But, nevertheless, I am pleased to announce that no police authority ever came to our front door with arresting orders. Just in case, however, through closed blinds we kept a watchful lookout for several weeks thereafter.

Another immediate hurdle was ahead of us when Dean registered for college using his G-I Bill. He was taking four classes that first semester and failed out of three of them. In previous years, prior to Vietnam, he had done well during the military with all the classes necessary for his *MOS* (a military term for "job classification") and teletype secret clearances. His memorization and comprehension skills of the materials presented were not ever a problem.

However, after Vietnam, he was incapable of grasping, retaining, and succeeding in English, history, psychology and biology. His concentration abilities had been compromised.

We have since learned that when the brain is damaged by trauma (in our case, war trauma), it goes from a learning brain into a surviving one. As it focuses on survival and only survival, it struggles to process information and to deliver it in an understandable format. Therefore, memorization, concentration, and retention become difficult, if not impossible, and college classes are defeating taskmasters.

He did not register for the second semester; instead, he began a job. (So many vets do this exact same thing when PTSD leaves them unable to function in college classes—unable to use the very benefits for which they sacrificed at least four years of military duty and often life and limb.)

Dean had a couple of jobs during this period, one of which was managing a bread route. The bakery was very close to our home and early each morning, everyone in the vicinity could smell the bread baking at the plant. It was like heaven to us—although it was no longer wonderful to Dean and the others that worked there. Needless to say, he worked very hard at his position and would have been promoted if it had not meant our relocating. Relocating was out of the question and we chose not to take the promotion.

During hurricane season and with an impending hurricane on its way, bread sales did extremely well. During the year he worked for the bakery, we had a mega-sized hurricane, even for the old-timers! That afternoon, Dean stayed at work far too long. By the time he drove home, he was driving over live, downed power lines; already at our house, the electricity providing urgent TV weather alerts was out and our TV remained silent. I had never been so scared and alone during a hurricane! As the storm came ashore, it was not long before a portion of our roof went with it, while busting out one of our bedroom windows, as well.

Our son, who was thirteen months old and barely walking, was intent instead on crawling over the soaked carpet full of broken glass. Hoping to prevent further damage, Dean considered it necessary to go outside to secure the broken window by way of a large piece of plywood, a hammer, and a bag of nails. During the height of the storm Dean and I were screaming at each other and doing hand motions through the broken window—our hearing and understanding totally affected.

That hurricane did more damage than anyone anywhere had forecast. All the secured yachts and shrimp boats along the coast had always weathered other big storms, but this time they were piled like match sticks along the shoreline's concrete edge.

It was reported the winds had been clocked at over 200 miles an hour and that we had averted a tidal wave! Once again, we had been rescued! What did all this mean to us? It meant another miracle, because we lived, as did my mother, within eight blocks from the shoreline, while Dean's parents were living within two blocks from the same coast! A tidal wave of any size would have wiped us all off the map!

Counselors and therapists are not always made aware regarding the private moments in a marriage. Possibly the veteran does not remember those times, or, to protect himself, his subconscious chooses not to retain moments too painful to recall. Unusual, strange behavior and outward aggression can express themselves fully behind closed doors in the personal, obscured lives of a couple.

They did in our house, more times than I wish to remember. I wanted so much to believe I was cared about and was desired for all the utmost reasons. I chose to file away these negative occurrences once again—and I remained in our relationship.

There were many occasions when my husband was spending much of his free evenings and/or early mornings away from home, but this time he was drinking heavily with college friends. They, too, were married but did not have a child like we did, and, somehow, they had more money to blow. In addition, they were not claiming to be Christians and churchgoers.

I would stay up until 2:00 – 3:00 a.m., pacing the floor, weeping and praying while wringing my hands with doubt and worry, knowing full well, Dean's absence was not a good sign. Already, I would have been alone all that day taking care of our little one, except, of course, for the hours that our son spent with his grandparents.

For whatever reason, there came a time when a blond, blue-eyed, very young woman entered our lives and became Dean's *person of interest*. During that time in our lives, we had a 1969, Dodge Charger hardtop with bucket seats, a white top, sky-blue body, and a white, leather interior. It truly was a handsome, expensive looking car, but a difficult one for a family with a new baby.

I was puzzled when I started noticing long, blond hairs caught on the buttons of the leather upholstery—mainly visible on the passenger's side. But I kept my questions to myself because what good would it have done to say anything? What, another argument for me to lose? Another reason to beat myself up for not being good enough, sexy enough, pretty enough, loving enough, or more setbacks for being a goody-two-shoes? My heart would pound at triple time strength as I worried about our relationship and our future.

Many times, I loathed myself for being so wholesome and naïve! This particular goodness, since Vietnam, had become a problem, and it seemed to have been wasted and lost on the man that returned from war. This man, I no longer knew, nor did I know how best to live with him. I was facing a death and could not prevent it from occurring! It was just God and me facing each difficulty, each event, and each crying spell, with no end in sight!

Not only did the war come home with him, but it entered our four walls, nonchalantly dwelling in the middle of our marriage!

It was the PTSD demon; it was the elephant in the middle of the room—all the rooms—all our decisions and our life's occasions were affected by this unknown phenomenon. And at any given point, whatever happened in our relationship that would cause it to turn sour always seemed to be my fault! Something was desperately wrong; and, yes, Dean would look to me to correct it; or, worse still, *he would not look at me at all!*

I am emotionally dying. I thought to myself and then said out loud, "My God, I can't cope with this new problem; however, I'm sure there are others that can and because of those coping skills that I don't possess, I must be an undiluted *low life*! You created a deficient, damaged human being, God, by breathing existence into me! I should have been aborted because I am not worthy to be married, to have children, and to handle life; I daily search and then know without question, how worthless I am! I am so terribly sorry, God. I am so sorry for disappointing you and so many others!"

There is a proverb that says, "The mind believes what it sees, and then sees what it believes."

Through my childhood and teenage years, I was molded by my family's responses and interaction to only believe what I saw outside myself. Now, in marriage, I was being shown the same mind pictures as I had then, and I sincerely assumed I had no value, no giftings and talents to share with this world. Once again, I had become insignificant!

Then there was that one-of-a-kind day when I found myself in an adjacent small town, at the home of my husband's new interest. Dean and I had driven there; the trip was a blur and must not have been mentally acknowledged because the wounding had entered so deeply. Thus, I was only going through the motions.

Dean exited the car and then I saw her, his new love, for the first time, and I was startled at how homely she was–even to being somewhat overweight. (Up until then, my husband had made me to believe that being even slightly overweight was not acceptable; therefore, I had worked hard at returning to a slim figure soon after childbirth.)

As she approached the car, I observed, cradled in her arms, a baby, who must have been four months old! At that moment, emotionally, I was beating myself up for foolishly requesting to be introduced and to spend time with her. Goodness, was I going crazy?

What had I thought I would accomplish through this encounter? However, in my immaturity I did know I was going to plead my best case in hopes that Dean's girlfriend would have some remorse and would give my husband back!

Also, I knew I did not want to drive her around while trying to maintain a civil conversation—so, I suggested she drive our 1969 Dodge Charger while I held her sleeping baby; and, all too quickly, she agreed!

There was definitely something wrong with this picture! However, with this arrangement, I was given sufficient time to study my new friend, all the while swallowing with great difficulty my crushed feelings. So, for the next hour and a half, she drove the three of us—me, herself, and her baby—throughout the small town and into the rural areas.

In my own spirit, I questioned what this young woman had that I did not, and in that short interlude, I became bitter to a considerably new level.

During our time together, I learned she was quite young and living with her parents. Besides being overweight, I saw she was lacking in fashion sense; and it was obvious, she was also lacking in finances. Her baby girl was wrapped in stained, secondhand clothing and blankets, and she was not well cared for. Nonetheless, this baby was sweet and precious, as all babies are enchanting and gifts from above.

I am afraid to report that not much was accomplished that day. It only made me look and feel more foolish and desperate, more insanely dim-witted, to myself and probably to everyone else, Dean included.

Later on, I ventured out and bravely asked Dean why he felt so drawn to this young girl. What was it about her? His simple answer: "Because she *needs* me." *And evidently, I did not!* Within myself, I was not able to answer why he would think I did not need him when we, too, had a baby. However, what was apparent to me was the neon sign over this girl's head that read how badly she needed a father for her baby and an income to support them both…for both of these, Dean qualified! The weeks continued. The holidays were drawing near. Our son was almost six months old. For a two-week holiday period, I was encouraged by my husband to go to my father's home, still in another city. This I agreed to do, knowing that those two weeks would enable Dean to pursue his new love interest, without any obstacles or time constraints!

During my holiday stay at my dad's, I innocently became part of a scenario that turned out to be extremely awkward. On that visit, our son, Dean, Jr., and I shared a bed in a bedroom where there was a landline and princess telephone. Our son was still not sleeping well, but both of us had managed to doze off when at full volume the phone rang at approximately 12:00 a.m. Only my stepmother and I were at home because my dad was at the restaurant working late, so the loud ring startled me and brought me back into an abrupt reality.

I quickly grabbed the phone and in a *hushed voice* I replied with, "Hello," trying hard not to wake our baby in the process. Immediately, I heard the female caller say in broken English and with a sarcastic, taunting tone, "I am through with him now. I'm sending him back to you!"

Unquestionably, I did not know how to respond! Nevertheless, with all my social graces intact (my mother would have been proud), I quietly, sincerely, and enthusiastically answered, "Oh! Thank you!" and with that zealous response, there was complete silence on the other end of the line. My caller was speechless, not knowing if I was mocking her or if I had just completely lost my mind!

Of course, this woman thought I was my stepmother, and the apparent ease and confidence with which she performed this cruel telephone call made me aware that she had carried out this malicious deed before. Showing no mercy, this spiteful female felt powerful and mighty at the expense of my father's family.

From that day forward, through different eyes I saw the role of my stepmother; after that call, I better understood her plight. Toward her, I became more compassionate even though I was still aware of the awkward, uncomfortable situation my existence brought not only into their marriage but also to their Catholic religion.

I was that irregular puzzle piece that did not fit in my mother's family, nor did I have a place in my father's. I never shared with my Aunt Mary what had taken place for me that perplexing night. Because of lacking a role in this family, I did not know how to show her my support by lovingly and gently bringing up this difficult subject!

As the caller and I both hung up, I laid there mulling over what had just transpired. The more I mused, the faster my heart throbbed as I sadly connected the dots. I pondered for an unknown amount of time—perhaps fifteen to twenty minutes at the most—until I saw through the bedroom window a car with its beaming headlights driving through the alleyway and entering the garage area of my family's home. Within a couple of minutes, the back door opened and closed, and my father walked through the house, closing the door of his and my stepmother's bedroom.

As I meditated on this subject the rest of that night, and for the balance of my stay, my already broken, burdened heart wept over my father's indiscretion. I struggled with the reality of husbands and fathers not being faithful to their marital promises. I had just left my own husband, threatening to do the very same thing there that my father was capable of doing here where I was visiting!

Was commitment in marriage, and the sanctity thereof, a wasted vow—a promise unable to be successfully accomplished and kept for eternity? Did I not have a hope and a heavenly assurance of having my husband remain faithful? I could find no ready answers to my questions.

When at last my baby and I returned home, my in-laws presented me with twenty-five dollars and requested I go downtown to buy a new outfit. It was now after the holidays, so many sales and clearances were in progress.

To my amazement, I found a pair of off-white *Go-Go* boots, elasticized and scrunched up to the knee; a tartan plaid, short, partially pleated, skirt; and a long-sleeved, red, turtleneck sweater—they totaled twenty-five dollars!

I was a knockout! I had broken out of the box and now was feeling very daring.

As New Year's Eve approached, I learned about a party that was being held to which Dean and his date had been invited. While my in-laws babysat, and with me in my stunning new outfit, I drove myself over to the apartments where the party was in progress.

As I crossed in front of the picture window of that particular apartment, the lights within revealed my husband sitting on a couch with his arm around the young blond I had met and spent time getting to know several weeks before. This was going to be my last ditch effort to save my marriage. But I was not going down without a fight!

I knocked on the door, which really was not necessary—all the partygoers had already seen me. Going on within, there was a lot of whispering and shuffling, and outside, as I questioned my resolve, I was scared to death and about to run. Complete with attitude, Dean came to the door and uncomfortably stepped outside for some privacy. Slowly we walked down the walkway and stopped in front of the first darkened apartment.

There I pleaded, reasoned, and gave up any dignity I had left, but, quite honestly, it was not about what I said nor did nor how I looked, it was all about God seriously intervening in this life-or-death circumstance; and, because of His plan, design, and purpose, Dean immediately left with me that night.

Yes, my dreaded washing of Dean's white work shirts with *her* lipstick on the collars was over—and we moved on.

But Dean's anger did not move on, it continued, as did my bewilderment regarding the sacredness of marriage, and, like our wedding vows had stated, *denying all others*, while keeping oneself alone for your husband or your wife.

"I must have asked for this indiscretion," I quietly informed my heart while assuming all responsibility! "It must be that I'm not worthy of having a faithful husband, but I will do better in the future," I counseled myself. "Sandy, you must do better...you must somehow become everything Dean wants and needs!"

And on that day, I determined to never again face anything like this infidelity. I would make sure of it!

From my past I had learned well how to become whatever was required to blend into my surroundings; now my marital relationship was no exception to this rule. I could do this—I, myself, alone with God's help, would make this union work.

Never again would I come so close to the edge of losing the one I loved. From my upbringing, I knew firsthand how harmful divorce could be, especially for kids; and I also knew the extreme poverty that followed close behind single mothers with children.

My marriage was going to survive, *even if it killed me*!

I had been so scared and forlorn during those months as I helplessly watched our marriage vows slipping through my fingers. Now that we were back on track, I breathed a sigh of relief! I was dedicated for the long haul and I could only believe that Dean was also.

Needless to say, I honestly did not know for sure if Dean was newly committed to our relationship because little was discussed that fateful night following that New Year's party. I was afraid to inquire by asking too many questions and unknowingly creating new problems; plus, Dean wasn't volunteering much personal information. So, the entire matter eased into the past, never to be mentioned again.

And my perplexity and loneliness persisted.

Efforts to Keep Peace

After serving in our country's military and once we returned home, I am sure Dean's parents' heavy involvement in our lives was quite obvious to everyone—family, friends, clients, neighbors, and church members.

Each one of us would see them several times a week. We spoke on the phone every day—at times, several calls a day.

As mentioned before, my mother-in-law would come by, pick up our son and keep him for several hours, if not overnight. In many ways, our whole existence was based on co-dependencies.

For several years, our family and Dean's parents attended the same church. After church, there was always lunch either at my in-laws' house or we would be taken out to a restaurant or cafeteria with his parents picking up the cost.

There were some moments when our time spent together was enjoyable, but other times it was forced and embarrassingly uncomfortable! Heavily present in our midst was a thick, strained atmosphere that had nothing to do with Dean, myself, nor our children. Instead there was a frequent underlying current of unrest and turmoil between Dean's mother and father.

Seldom did my mother-in-law enjoy any part of these occasions that centered around food. Because she did not like to cook either, often she would remark how she wished she could "take a pill and be done with it." Consequently, at these restaurants, instead of eating a whole meal with us, she chose to spend that time parading about, dancing with our young son from table to table and in between chairs! I wanted to disappear into a hole...the ill-at-ease faces of the patrons told me I was correct in my reactions.

On the other hand, my father-in-law loved to eat and to create new recipes! He loved it all; therefore, he was overweight and my mother-in-law was not. It was like the nursery rhyme about Jack Sprat and his wife, but reversed. Therefore, if Dean's dad was eating too much, Dean's mom would kick him aggressively under the table! My father-in-law, through clenched teeth and calling her by name, would snarl back at her, "____, if you kick me one more time, I'll..." As our children grew older, secretly this became a family comedy, and we would hold our stomachs with laughter. (It's always better to laugh than cry, right?)

It did not matter how much we tried to make the best of these weekly events, the dysfunction was far greater than anything we were able to manage or overlook. As a result, after years of our living back home and enduring this taut, hostile atmosphere, for me, these after-church Sundays were wearing thin; I needed a deserved break from the routine.

On one particular Sunday, I had awakened very early. It was my role to prepare and dress for church our three and a half-year-old son and our one-year-old daughter. Of course, some kind of breakfast was also necessary for us to be able to endure until lunch.

I would try to dress our kids in cute clothing so we could be proud of the way they looked, and they would get some use out of their once-a-week Sunday clothes. By having them squeaky clean, combed and powdered, the other church mothers would know without a doubt, I was taking exceptional care of my children.

However, if at any time during this preparation process the kids fussed or cried, Dean would become quite upset with me, and the children would be taken to the waiting car and to church in whatever they were wearing! At our destination I then had to make the best of what wardrobe existed.

To maintain peace and quiet, I almost begged my children to not utter a sound! (If they had been older, I would have bribed them.) On that particular day after church, again we went out to eat with my in-laws. Sharing time with them had been unusually difficult on that Sunday. When Dean and I returned home without the children, we were both immensely strained and overly tired. It had already been a long day for everyone!

Unfortunately, I made mention that I was becoming weary of this weekly scheduling, thinking that Dean would again agree with me as he had other times in the past, and, perhaps, we could start eating at our house with just our small family present. However, on this day, he did not agree with me at all.

Instead, he became angry and in a rage turned on me; I became the person in the wrong for suggesting such a thing, while openly criticizing his parents. However, by this time, I, too, was over the edge and was incensed, as well.

For most of our history, I would choose to back down during our arguments and would not push my opinion or my preferences. Realizing how upset Dean would have become and desiring only peace and a measure of tranquility, the majority of the time, I did not really care about being in the right.

But that day, I made the fatal mistake of not backing down, and I continued to probe, pushing the subject and demanding a change and a decision. Something triggered inside Dean, after he repeatedly cautioned me to stop! "Sandy, not now, just leave it alone!" But I did not—I would not—and within seconds, to my shock and dismay, he had pulled back with his fist and hit me full force, squarely in the middle of my breastbone.

The blow instantly knocked all the wind out of my body and I doubled over unable to breathe; within a couple of slow-motion seconds, I became aware of how much trouble I was in. However, I had no time to analyze my condition further because I was being picked up, carried through the house, and was thrown like a rag doll onto our king-size bed! He was furiously yelling and commanding me to, "Stay there." He then exited and our bedroom door was loudly slammed shut!

As soon as I landed and bounced on that mattress, an excruciating, piercing pain shot through my chest and upper torso. I was in agonizing misery with tears streaming down my face while uttering half-expressed groaning from deep within; groaning like I had never heard before—even during my two labors and childbirths. Neither was I fully comprehending what had just gone wrong. I was stunned, wondering how this injury had come about. I had never been as afraid of Dean as I was at that moment! I knew if he returned to that bedroom, I would probably breathe my last breath. I was terrified and felt much like an injured, cornered animal!

I hurt like I had not hurt in my lifetime! Once again, I found myself in a horrendous, hopeless position of not knowing what to do and how to help myself.

In our house, we had an extra telephone in our master bedroom. Over a period of minutes I maneuvered myself over to the phone on the nightstand. I was sent into gasping, shallow breathing and muted hysterics with every movement, every breath and every sob!

Quickly evaluating my situation, I knew I had no one else to call but my mother-in-law. And, quite frankly, I was not sure if she would come help me. But with the piecing pain, I needed someone right then!

In profound fear, I watched the bedroom door and dialed her number. Thank God, she answered! Through my sobs and whispers, my muffled panting and wheezing for air, she knew I needed her. Something bad had happened, and she assured me with, "I'm on my way; I am on my way!"

In a fetal position, I laid in agony unable to move without screaming into a pillow. Thank goodness, Dean allowed her into the house and escorted her to where I was! What a relief when I saw her standing with Dean behind her in the open doorway.

I do not recollect much after those moments. However, in the days that followed, I remember visiting my in-laws' neighbor, who had a chiropractic clinic in his home. There he took chest x-rays and notified us that my breastbone's cartilage had been torn and a rib broken. He also shared that this type of injury was worse than having several broken ribs, and he advised a rib brace and pain medication.

For ten months, I wore that Velcroed chest brace, twenty-four-seven. I was absolutely unable to lie down without having it on. Helping in my recovery was the day our three and a half-year-old son was potty-trained; however, our year-old daughter was not walking—nor was she even considering potty-training.

In the months that followed, I had such difficulty taking care of our children. Lifting our daughter into her crib was almost impossible for my condition. Getting up and down to change diapers, pick up toys, providing baths and changing linens, washing clothes; all these chores were unbearable with this injury!

This younger child of mine tried walking at thirteen months, but disliked it a great deal, so back to crawling she went until she was eighteen months old! Then, and only then, was she ready to try it again; then bingo! Accomplishment! This was a banner day at our house!

Difficult Beginnings but Eager for Life

When this domestic violence took place, I belonged to a babysitting club in which we exchanged hours while babysitting each other's children. After this injury occurred, I could not take care of my own children, and I certainly could not help anyone else with theirs.

One day, I conveniently *lied* to be taken off the babysitting roster for an indefinite period of time. I lied because I could not confess to them or anyone I knew about my suffering from domestic violence. If I wanted to continue participating in this club, how could I share with its members the conditions under which my children and I lived? The mothers would never again have trusted my home as a safe place for their kids to visit for two or three hours.

Therefore, I told the timekeeper I had fallen in the dark over an ottoman and had damaged my rib cage. Because of this injury, I was unable to care for additional kids for several months. I would let them know when I could start up again.

No one in my immediate family—certainly not my mother—ever knew what happened to me that Sunday afternoon. I kept it a secret because it was a private matter, and I knew it would not make a difference anyway—and partly because I felt responsible for not having backed down. If I had not pushed so hard for a decision *at the wrong time,* I would not have been hit, I reasoned to myself.

I already knew ahead of time that my mother would not have been supportive if I had shared with her any information regarding my medical condition. During those many months, I certainly had ample time to include her in my progress. However, instead, I considered the times in the past when she would throw it in my face, how that I had a husband and she did not...I guess by having a husband *all* my problems were solved and *none* had been created! Fat chance!

As a result of this accident, I began to better understand why abused women stay in their relationships. We, women, attempt to justify the circumstances, assume much if not all the responsibility, and we slowly begin to build a new hope and belief that such a horrible occurrence will not ever take place again. We are wrong—we are so wrong and how sad for us!

As the painful months passed, my rib cage and breastbone continued to heal and I did start to hope again. "Hope floats, doesn't it?" I asked, trying to convince myself regarding the future of my marriage. At last, my fear of Dean eased and our lives carried on.

Yes, I had survived yet another experience. Surely I was getting stronger, wasn't I? Because we were about to find out.

In time Dean did almost complete our treasured college education. He came within seven credits of having a bachelor's degree in business administration, with a minor in economics! That is where his education abruptly stopped…heaven forbid, our G-I Bill had run out; and as a couple, we also were out of stamina, courage and ideas!

During those college years we had given birth to two children, while paying a mortgage and establishing a home. At times Dean had worked three jobs, all while attending school. Most of this time, he worked the midnight shift as a college security guard, but also worked at a small, family-owned Laundromat as an attendant—washing, folding clothes and cleaning up thereafter.

I helped him as best I could with his school work by interpreting his required reading, creating his book reports, taking notes, writing mega papers and then typing all of the above on a difficult manual typewriter.

We were both exhausted and weary of this year-in, year-out regimen, while also attempting to manage our lives in general. Seven more credit hours might as well have been a hundred more hours. We were broke and needed an adequate full-time job quickly.

After several attempts at jobs, Dean decided he would apply with an oil company in a metropolitan area, several hours from where we were living.

Glory be to God! He was hired, making more salary than we had ever seen in our married lives! But we would have to move! However, one of the benefits of this new company was they would move us at their cost! Hey! We could not beat that. It was all so good!

We immediately made plans to leave home and to go where the jobs were, which, at the time, this city had a notorious reputation of being the murder capital of the world! Yes, how inspiring this move was going to be for our young family.

I have to admit an anxious secret: I had an apprehension about leaving our dysfunctional families and moving to a city where we knew no one. In a weird, bizarre way, we had grown comfortable and accustomed to having grandparent built-in babysitters and having extra money available sporadically, for those times when we could not make financial ends meet.

What if we again had domestic violence problems; how would I manage, who would I call? When I began working and the kids became ill, how could I hold a job? What if our car broke down, etc? But we moved anyway, into a townhouse in a strange part of our new city. I enrolled our son in public school kindergarten and left him crying on the first day, totally confused as to what was happening to his life. Against my better judgment, I began working at a daycare center with our two-year-old daughter in tow. It was a large daycare business—a chain—with several locations throughout our metropolitan city.

Each day at my new employment, I had at least ten three-year-olds all to myself! Few of these toddlers were potty-trained...and ..."Why do parents insist on buying clothing with hard to fasten buttons, jeans with belts and tucked-in shirts or pantyhose, one-piece bodysuits and frills?" I shouted from the rooftops!

Crazy, crazy! But I gave it my very best shot and tried really hard to succeed, but did not! I failed on this one. Now the question is, "Why?"

The simple answer is as follows: When I would arrive by eight o'clock in the morning, many in my little group of kids had already been bussed in from another daycare location where they had arrived very early and traveled long in our metropolitan city's bumper to bumper traffic. They had already eaten breakfast where I worked and then I started my day with them.

When I closed my door in the late afternoon, once again many in my little group of tiny, baby-faced kids would stand in single file while holding hands, and would march out of the building, boarding one of our busses to be transported to a twenty-four-hour location to await their parents. These babies were no more than three years old!

I needed a job and we needed the salary, but I could not survive this travesty—the process was breaking my heart in this new, big city of ours! Plus, I had two little ones of my own to take care of once I clocked out and we arrived home. I was exhausted emotionally, mentally, and physically.

I lasted two whole weeks in this daycare business, and that was accomplished by gritting my teeth and stretching my stay by several days!

Soon after my doomed first job, I filled a secretarial position at a prominent church's Christian school—kindergarten through twelfth grades. There, my two children were on property with me and I could check on them throughout the day.

During my first and only year, my two little ones had back-to-back allergy outbreaks, colds, strep throat and chicken pox (both at the same time). I could stay home with them or house them on the floor next to my desk. I did both, because I had to become extremely creative; there were no babysitters in sight!

Our son's kindergarten teacher at seventy two years old came out of retirement and caused a devastating insecurity in our five-year-old due to her impatience, weariness, and thereby harshness. For him, this daily stress developed into an acute case of stuttering; plus, he began sleepwalking, as well.

I also believe that this insecurity was compounded by my husband's overreaction and going overboard in his discipline of our children. There was aggressiveness and a severity that neither child deserved.

Dean and I had good kids—sensitive, warm, loving, gentle, and well-mannered. However, PTSD reigned in our house and Dean was not able to effectively respond to his parental duties without irritation and anger intensifying.

After our Christian school employment, we moved into a new VA house. Dean had changed jobs; we were praying for a miracle for our son and his inability to communicate without great effort; and our daughter started pre-K.

I would work, pick up our kids, do homework, clean, cook, bathe kids, and read bedtime stories.

Every so often, my body would shut down with a migraine that would send me to bed to recoup for a day or two—no lights, no sound, no movement! All because I did not know when to say, *"Stop the train; I need to get off a moment!"* I did not sense I could afford that luxury; I was afraid it would upset Dean.

So, I was Super Woman, the Duracell Bunny. Our suburban household even had hamsters and dogs.

By this time, I was working in the church office and doing all the bookkeeping, *plus* I was accounts receivable, accounts payable, and the insurance desk in my spare time.

I was good at my job. I always had an uplifting attitude, a smile on my face, and this ability to pull out from deep inside ways to accomplish all that was asked of me in any situation.

Yet, when at home, Dean and I were still not doing well in our marriage. I suggested and was prepared to go to Christian marriage counseling, but he would not hear of it. At each mention, he would angrily reply, "No!" and refuse it all.

In a pathetic way, I was relieved when he turned the counseling down. Opening old wounds was not something I was looking forward to either. At those thoughts I cringed realizing I had become like him. I was now like Dean; "secondary" PTSD had come to dwell within me—this is the added benefit of surviving a PTSD household—it requires the infection of the whole family!

Our two older children remember their early years, oftentimes with much disappointment and anger of their own. They reenact the time when their dad became livid in a department store because the two of them were playing in and out of the clothes racks. He demanded them to stop making a scene, but they were having too much fun; they could not stop laughing and their play continued.

After a short while, we were back in the car and pulling out of the parking area when Dean stopped the car and took both of them behind a billboard sign—there, they were excessively spanked. They returned to the backseat sobbing with huge, red eyes and my heart was broken! I had no answers for Dean's behavior. We had grown afraid to trust him. But now, our children could not trust me either because I was not stepping up to protect them against their father.

That was not the only whipping they received. Other times, the spankings would occur quite often at our house. He would take them into the hall bath and whip them good, resulting in whelps on their bottoms and upper legs.

By now, I was out of my league. Growing up, I, too, received whippings with a leather belt decorated with the old, round, raised gemstones of different dark colors. I was a good, awesome kid, also, and yet, I felt I had been punished exceedingly and without mercy.

However, now these spankings were happening to my own children. The pent-up anger and aggression within Dean would be revealed considerably during these times.

Nevertheless, in spite of this, I knew it was essential to our family for Dean to continue to step up and be the one to discipline our kids. I also knew if I began interfering by saying or doing anything, he would either make it worse on the children or he would throw up his hands, leaving me with it all.

I was already doing so much at our home. I felt it was necessary for Dean to at least do this part of parenting. I hoped and prayed that he would become more lenient, which eventually happened about five years later with our third child. By then, he was ever so indulgent—almost to a fault! Our older two children would often resent our younger daughter because she was like a grandchild, with no spankings and she could do no wrong.

Subsequently, for many years since, our adult middle child (older daughter), especially, has many hard feelings regarding her early life at home with its unfair corporal punishment. Just like me, she feels that she, too, was a good kid and did not deserve such harsh treatment.

I completely agree with her. Yes, she was a great kid and has become an even more wonderful adult. As a child, she was an angel and had the sweetest, most amazing temperament. Her angelic face, dry sense of humor, and sneaky fun ways were all so innocent and magical!

Yet, she fell into the PTSD irritability, anger/rage, and emotional numbing reactions of her father—as did our son. Not one of us was immune to his frequent and unpredictable mood swings—times when Dean would suddenly change in his feelings and behavior resulting in his phases of anger, rage and over all unhappiness.

Walking again and again on those *huge* eggshells became normal in our family; it was our standard way of life! The ground was continually shifting and we learned quite well to impulsively shift with it—always waiting to make an adjustment according to the mood/the atmosphere within the house. Not one of us wanted to live one moment with the results of having angered the head of household!

We went to great lengths to keep the peace, but even still our peace and harmony was shattered many times over, leaving us and our lack of safety wondering what had just happened? Waiting for the "other shoe to drop" became normal.

I have spent endless hours and years hashing through how we could have avoided these unnatural consequences. Nevertheless, eventually and out of survival, Dean's extreme, confusing disposition became our norm; this was just how it was, and we adjusted and accepted these occurrences as our routine living environment.

For all of us those were hard, extremely challenging years. Though in public we smiled, laughed, and did the usual light and classic family activities, privately we were baffled and tormented with the undercurrent that ran full course through our home and our kids' maturing spirits.

We were stunted in the development of our hearts and souls. Our life force was not functioning with courage and strength; it had become anemic. In addition, our view of God became limited because of underdevelopment and daily assault.

But, as we all know, life goes on—with us or without us! Thus, our family continued marching in step, putting one weary, heavy foot in front of the other, like scientific robots while hoping that surely our ominous tomorrow would arrive instead as a brighter, sunny day.

I did not tell a soul at my church job nor did our church family know about our dilemma. As many times before, I had looked around extensively and believed there was absolutely no one to tell, to confide in, to sincerely care, and no one available to make a difference! No! There was no friend who could listen or understand any part of what was taking place every day in our house; there was no wise person to offer some helpful advice or to provide a loving hug of support.

If, on a foolish occasion, I would make mention of a circumstance at home or use a hypothetical situation, the person listening would weakly shake her head, give me some feeble advice or excuse, perhaps advising me to kick my husband to the curb because I deserved better than that! I would walk away frustrated and feeling violated for having been so silly as to think anyone would have a clue about the challenges I faced. No one in the whole world was going through misery the way I was.

I would be prayed over during church services. I would cry out to God. My cries would hit the ceiling and fall back, because though I worked for a church, my faith and my trust had been shattered. I could no longer see the sky and I had become weak in my belief; my hope had hit rock bottom! "Sister, it seems you are on your own. Just pull up your big girl panties and find a way to deal with it!" was repeated over and over. For a time I did just that. I stuffed and crammed and buried my wounded feelings and my deep sense of sorrow; my mind pretended that I was fine, at times actually living a life of plenty and living out the American dream!

So did my beloved children. Our fun, loving, harmless, helpless, innocent, dear, and precious children!

(Please refer to the Resource section for information on "The PTSD-Impaired Household" where it speaks about children *not* being resilient. The information tells how our kids are only surviving instead of thriving because of their lack of resiliency. Yes, they can survive life but only because of their in-place survival mechanisms which will then hinder their adult relationships.)

God's Unchanging Presence

O nce again, we moved! However, this time we moved into our two-story gorgeous dream house. It was beautiful and brand new, with four bedrooms, two and a half baths, a den with a separate formal living and dining, a breakfast nook, and a three-car garage on a pie-shaped lot...Yahoo! I thought I had gone to heaven when I awoke our first morning in that wonderfully designed house! I just knew we had been totally honored and adored by our heavenly Father...

One of the unique, impressive features of this particular floor plan was the open Cathedral ceiling showcased in the den with a full two-story fireplace. That was the view our occasional visiting guests first observed as they glimpsed beyond the foyer.

Our older children cherished the two-story concept, *for the first ten days*. After that, no one fancied climbing those dad-gum stairs for the remaining seventeen years!

Therefore, early on, the kids developed a unique system for transferring the dirty clothes housed upstairs. One of them would throw the clothes over the open balcony railing down to the first floor, while the other child would catch them and carry the grubby clothing onto our utility room for washing.

This great system also worked well for toilet paper and other toiletries; essentially it was football indoors! There were mega toys, folded clothes, towels and sheets, always stacked on the stairs' landing, waiting patiently to be placed in personal drawers and closets.

It was a great house, even though there was a lot more walking within those 2,400-plus square feet. The kids also loved the cul-de-sac feature and the thirty trees in the yard—front and back. This connection with nature in such a usable, stunning setting was like nothing they had experienced. Life was going well, except for the ever looming monthly expense. By moving farther into the suburbs, we had more than doubled our budgeted mortgage and our travel costs…

Another great feature the Cathedral ceiling provided was the height necessary for our family to later play volleyball inside! Once the stair railing and upstairs banister supplied Dean with the anchors needed to secure the stakes of an inside tent. Due to the tent rope ties, we often *hung* ourselves; but the enjoyment the children experienced was more than worth it; and the tent stayed up for days and then weeks!

Now on two campuses, I continued with my job at the same large church facility; there I was still the accounts payable and accounts receivable department. I performed my responsibilities well, while reaching out to be a blessing to those around me. Often I could be found shining a little light into the darkened tunnel of others in my attempt at trying to provide a measure of hope for someone else.

Frequently, a smile with compassionate eye contact can go such a long way to those who are forlorn—to those filled to the brim with sadness and longing desperately for a friend.

Isn't encouragement cheap? It requires so little from us to offer compassion to this world to make it a better place, to make a difference in someone's tedious life. Why do we withhold from others a daily lifeline?

There is an anonymous quotation that states, "Encouragement is the oxygen of the soul." It is our life's blood, and we sadly retain from those around us our one free available gift—one that can be used to cheer and save from life's horrors many that are broken, weak, and lifeless!

Ultimately, my family was broken, and I myself could have benefitted from such encouragement.

In those days gone by, we were extremely busy living our lives—so much was taking place in such few packed moments. When we first moved into our dream house, I was five months' pregnant with our younger daughter. The pregnancy was going well. I was actively climbing on chairs, hanging curtains, stocking kitchen cabinets, and decorating our kids' rooms, which now also included a nursery.

On occasion, I would take precious time out to sit alone and bask in the blessings I knew came directly from our Almighty Father. I was awestruck and humbled by these miracles. While relaxing in that positive mind-set, I was hopeful that each and every one of our problems, mistakes, pain from our past, was over, hoping our lives had reached a fresh and new start—a new beginning in a our brand new house.

A funny incident happened close to the timing of this transition; one that I would love to share .

At my job in this large metropolitan church, we posted donation contributions the old-decades way: all by hand on index cards and totaled at the end of the year. However, our senior pastor sought to upgrade our system and asked the two of us involved in this process to attend a seminar in another large city within our state. We were to receive training in the newer computer methods.

Our church receptionist—a delightful, blond, blue-eyed, cute as punch, single woman of twenty-eight years, and I made plans to fly to this computer seminar for a few days.

The day arrived. We flew nonstop, and, upon entering the airport terminal, we began our adventure by first leasing a Volkswagen—a stick shift, red beetle bug. This Volkswagen was to be used throughout the days of our stay.

However, my sweet companion did not know a thing about using a stick-shift; of course, I did, but only because of my mother's old, 1955 Nash Rambler, nicknamed G.G. because she only ran by "God's Grace!"

My friend and I "ditty-bopped" throughout the city, and I might brag and say that we did quite well. For our seminar classes never once were we late, nor did we arrive mutilated.

When the final day came to depart, we were right on time at the airport. We returned our leased vehicle without a scratch or dent and waited to board our plane. I felt exuberant! What a great, fun trip this had been.

At exactly 2:00 p.m., we turned in our boarding passes and began our ascent through the *accordion-thing* that connects the aircraft to the terminal. As we were trudging up the inside ramp while dragging our carryon's behind us, my seminar buddy called back to me jokingly, "Wouldn't it be hilarious if this plane was hijacked to Cuba?" (Hijacking planes to Cuba was becoming quite common in those days.)

Laughing, we both split a rib, vividly envisioning the frightening possibility and reasoning that quite possibly we could extend our "vacation" with this great excuse and cool opportunity!

At the front door of the plane, only a few feet from the cockpit, stood the male steward cheerfully welcoming everyone aboard. Still giggling to myself over what my colleague had just shared, jokingly, I inquired of the gentleman, "This plane isn't going to Cuba, is it?"

The attendant promptly smiled back and was going to go along with my *Ha, Ha,* until the overly serious-minded, professional pilot took offense to my questioning comment. This humbug aircraft leader was standing just outside his cockpit and was very close to where we were still waiting for an acknowledgment.

Without a smile on his face, our illustrious pilot slowly walked the five steps toward both me and my colleague, causing us to backup as he boldly stepped forward, while firmly stating, "Ladies, please step off the plane!"

Please step off the plane? What?

"No, no, you misunderstood. It was only an amusing "question, " not a statement, not an order!" I explained it quite well, I thought (even if I kinda' sadly trailed off at the end). And, honestly, how were we going to hijack a plane without a weapon? Plus, heck fire, I had barely arrived and boarded the plane and, of course, I was not prepared to disembark over of a small misunderstanding.

After all, I was still smiling, and I honestly thought that our renowned pilot must be joking, like I was, and that he would break out into a grin at any moment! Yes, indeed, I was patiently waiting for that nonexistent grin.

The smile and laughter never came! Nevertheless, from across the connection in the floor, separating the *accordion-thing* from the plane's front entrance, someone commanded with threatening authority, "You both stay right there. Security has been called!"

"For what?" I squealed again from deep within, but with less and less confidence!

Oh, yes, I was *still* smiling, but my brain was preparing for an aneurysm! I only wanted to run like crazy. However, I was not able to run. No! For way too soon, it seemed, security arrived with guns drawn. How could this be happening—hijacking and now guns drawn?

"Oh, my dear, precious Jesus, I need you now. Do not even delay, 'cause I'm in a bad way!" Inaudibly, I yelled inside my brain so that Jesus from on His throne a million miles away could hear me clearly.

While trying hard to keep up, we were speedily escorted through the *accordion* and then out through the boarding area in front of hundreds of staring, gaping, fellow passengers who had not yet boarded! I guess they had never before witnessed a pair of mindless, churchy hijackers with no weapons!

It was not but a few seconds and perhaps one hundred steps later, before coming from all directions, were a dozen or more security guards with fully-loaded weapons drawn. I found myself looking around expecting to see *Candid Camera* or a movie crew; however, Mel Gibson was not in the building, and we were not actors performing our high-dollar jobs! I know this is hard to believe, but, yes, I had gone into shock and was having hallucinations.

After our gun-toting escort, we arrived within minutes at the FBI Airport Office where we gave them our personal information. Then, for hours and hours we sat in that glassed-in reception area, knowing full well we were in deep doo-doo but unable to retract or explain away what had been asked at that aircraft's entry. And our airplane for which we had reservations had departed anyway!

In Terminal B, outside the FBI's glass door, several times during our uninvited hours we observed numerous agents in a circle, huddled together, discussing our dim fate.

They frequently looked over their shoulders at us through the glass. ("Oh, heavenly Father, please help us!")

As I continuously paced the floor, I was saying over and over again, "I can't believe this! Never will I be able to believe this. Why did this happen to us? Unbelievable! They've got to be big-time kidding me!"

You know the saying, "Everything happens for a reason;" well, it did not apply to this situation! Did not apply at all!

And my co-hijacker traveling companion would get upset and would remind me to, "Shut up. Hush. Remember we aren't supposed to talk!" So, as I paced and paced, my blonde friend would get all panicky and start shaking as she held her head in her hands! But, how could we not talk? This was a crisis!

Several hours later, we were at last allowed to call home! First we called our senior pastor to notify him of our holy predicament.

He chuckled, all the while trying to remain serious and making a sincere effort to be understanding in between the giggles, but he was sincerely unable to imagine our story!

Bare Bones Reality Struck: Let me get this straight. The FBI arrested us for attempting to hijack a jumbo jet from America, the U.S. of A, while demanding to be taken to Cuba! How insane is that? I have no gun, and I don't know anyone in Cuba! Why would I choose to go there—isn't Paris still available?

Finally, by eight o'clock that night (and no dinner), we were told that now we were being allowed to fly on that airline. We later learned we could have been refused passage that day and air privileges *for the rest of our lives*, and we would have been on someone's *list*! I repeat, how insane is that?

Yes, we were released and allowed to walk to the gate for our trip home. Our families had been called and knew what time to be waiting for us. Afraid to make a wrong move, we deliberately walked stiff-legged to the airplane entrance.

For obvious reasons of course, we had *coach assigned seating!* However, several rows behind us and across the aisle, was a tall, starched and suited, muscular man—whom my hijacker friend and I deducted was an airline security agent, like an air marshal with a hidden gun!

Throughout our flight, we did not look to the right nor to the left—not once did we look anywhere but straight ahead! I think we would have stopped our hearts from beating, if it had been possible.

We were met at the airport by our families, all grinning in a "tongue in cheek" manner! We would have grinned, too, but exhaustion had hit us and we were too tired. It had already been a long week, followed by a mind-boggling day!

Fortunately, this incident never appeared on any federal government computer list of "enemies of the state."

This valid, and official, information was shared with us after we called a friend of ours in our state's FBI Headquarters. We were so relieved and thankful for small favors.

Yes, there were several other religious trips that were made during my tenure at this large church; and during each one I participated in, I managed to create havoc in some form or fashion. How does an innocent, goody-two-shoes accomplish so much mayhem without even trying? I never knew. Quickly, I'll share two-and-one-half instances of this suggested havoc I am talking about:

1. One year our highly talented, hundred-voice church choir was invited to sing at a huge, overseas, world church conference. There were two hundred and fifty of us on that trip. We were like a traveling small city!

When we first arrived, we spent our time sightseeing, and joy riding from subway location to location, as well as, hanging onto fast moving and crazily driven yellow cabs. It was very late and we were weary when we returned to the hotel!

The next morning was the music rehearsal with the performance following soon after, and my roommate—a fellow secretary who played the harp for the choir—left early. I forgot I needed to ask her some questions about the day's schedule, so I madly shot out of bed and bounded into the hotel hallway to hopefully catch her, but she had already disappeared from sight.

However, when I tried to open the vacuum-like hotel door to re-enter our room, to my dismay, it had slammed shut and was now *locked!* The enormous suction from our open window had pulled the door closed, leaving me in the God-forsaken hall—without wearing a housecoat, in my bare feet, and with my hair wild and bursting in all directions! It took a frantic fifteen minutes for me to cautiously knock on multiple doors up and down that sterile hallway, finally finding some of our church people who offered to go down to the lobby to ask for another room key! There were some gigantic holy hee-haws over this one!

2. On that same trip, we included a several-day visit to the country of Israel. While in Israel one evening, ten of us walked the distance from our Arabic hotel on a hill down to the Wailing Wall. At all the entry gates were armed soldiers inspecting purses, etc. "Possibly looking for weapons?" I pondered.

We made our way to the immense central area of the Wailing Wall. There, I naively asked those in our group, the ones who had traveled there many times before, if they thought I could take any pictures. Just to be sure, I asked first, because I did not see anyone else doing so. I was confidently informed with a, "Sure, go right ahead—not a problem," and with that answer, I did—with my flash on—because our already perfect day was quickly moving into early evening.

As soon as my camera flash exploded and registered on everyone present, a colossal, gargantuan, threatening roar went up into the heavens, which said, "Ah!" I have no doubt it was heard for miles! I looked around and quickly looked around again, not knowing what this meant because it came from hundreds, or perhaps, thousands, of young people who were standing in groups throughout the general outdoor area... And then a creepy hush fell over the bystanders.

As one gigantic body, with thousands of agitated eyes upon us, the measureless multitude began advancing from all directions towards the ten of us, while I, without dropping my gaze, swiftly released my camera into my large, dark handbag. One of our ten souls was able to find his voice and thus instructed the rest of us, "Quickly, form a circle, facing outward!" Immediately, we did so, asking no questions, while holding hands. The crowd continued to press in. Surrounding us, they pressed in within three feet!

While I stood there with bowed head and in frozen embarrassment, our now official spokesman started negotiating with their spokesman—the whole issue was over the crowd wanting my camera to destroy the picture taken. In the end we were allowed to leave instantly. The alternative would have been being arrested on the spot by those same gated, armed soldiers and sent to spend time in an Israeli jail!

What had been the problem?

We were at that site, at that moment, during Yom Kippur, the holiest of Jewish holidays! By taking a picture, I had disrespected thousands of Jewish citizens on their holiest of holy days!

Our solemn tiny group almost ran back to the hotel. When we arrived, I was breathless, shaking immensely, and was a social nervous wreck! Later that evening when I had a clear, non-shaking, quiet moment to check my camera, I realized I would never be developing that particular picture because it was nowhere to be found! It was forever gone! Do I think God had anything to do with this final, unexplained result? Oh, yes! I do.

To this day, our small group's spokesman continues to remember that event. He laughingly will not let me forget it! And there were other trips—trips like the one where Dean and I did not have passports like everyone else in our foreign mission's church-rebuilding group. You know, the required passports to return into our country—or passports to pass from one foreign airport to another—or from one South American country into the next. Somehow we had overlooked the necessity of such *terribly important* items—and now we were in great need…again!

And each time my very sizeable, heavily-freckled, pale-skinned, hazel-eyed husband and I (with an olive complexion and dark brown eyes and hair—and very few freckles) stood in line with the rest of our obviously white, twenty-person group, we would all stare innocently at the customs officers; they would stare back, scrutinize, whisper to each other, re-inspect our notarized citizenships (the documents for which we ran crazily through the Miami Airport at midnight to obtain after we became aware we each needed one to board the plane to South America); then these officers, against their better judgment, would reluctantly pass us on.

It was nerve-wracking being so klutzy as a *world-renowned traveler!* It soon became a given that when Sandy was on a trip, in-country or overseas, I was criminal material and no one wanted to travel with me! Go figure!

In addition to numerous gratifying trips, while living in our dream house, our family had many moments of enjoyment. In the seventeen years we dwelled there, numerous enjoyable events took place while all three of our children were growing like weeds.

Some of our pleasurable and humorous events are as follows though it is hard to pick a few because there were many:

There was Little League Baseball for the girls; they were league champions for two of those years and they were correctly named the *Angels*.

There was Boy Scouts for our son, and we were Den Parents. And Girl Scouts was available for our older daughter.

There were illustrated book reports and hard-as-all-git-out science projects of every description (each year I became apprehensive seeing that season approach).

There was summer camp, swimming and life guarding lessons, as well; or how about the chiggers and diesel fuel, Q-Tip remedy, and poison ivy from head to toe.

And, of course, there were school fundraisers for the three kids—*all at the same time.*

There were summer vacations the kids spent alone at home where they would try painfully to kill each other. As parents we were trying to earn a difficult living, which became impossible to do with the continuous complaining phone calls.

With other neighborhood kids, there were secret rafting trips on beach floats down the shallow, rat-infested drainage ditch—better known to our family as "the gully" behind our backyard fence.

Or there were neighborhood roller skating teams out on the cul-de-sac.

Or hours of bike riding on the Green-Belt trails and duck feeding at our community's pond, while running for our lives from many angry geese—there we would also fly kites for hours.

Or the kids would have pet parades and circuses with the resident inside and outside pets, all dressed up in doll costumes.

We would have confetti-filled Easter Egg Hunts with at least a hundred hidden eggs—only for our number-one son to grab the water hose and spray us until we were all soaking wet.

Our Easter Egg "Battle" Extravaganza

Or there would be mud balls thrown at passing cars from the backyard fence of one of the neighbor kids—the same Dennis the Menace who would pull all our flowers off their stems, so that he could make colorful potpourri. And we also had Kool-Aid/ lemonade stands.

Or there was the time when pickle juice was fed to a neighbor kid no one liked. His enraged mother was at our front door claiming he had a huge case of diarrhea as a result of our kids being naughty.

And there were stitches, as well as fractured ankles and casts, cut-open chins, boo-boo's of all shapes and sizes.

And pets and pets—all kinds, except for reptiles (*absolutely not!*)—but there were birds, fish, guinea pigs, rabbits, hamsters, kittens, cats, dogs, and puppies. At one time, we had eight different varieties of pets in and around the house.

Too many times we had countless kittens and puppies, so, on a steamy Saturday (or a cold, rainy one), we would position

174

ourselves outside the H.E.B. or Kroger grocery stores with a "Free" sign, and prayerfully we would kiss good-bye to each one.

Each year we made an event out of the downtown Thanksgiving parade, complete with folding chairs, hot cocoa, donuts, coats, gloves, hats, leg warmers, and blankets; it became an anticipated, yearly family tradition for us and friends.

How about the three Christmas tree, wooden cutout decorations of different sizes (one for each of our three children)— with the littlest wooden Christmas tree outfitted for our youngest with a diaper? That year, our cul-de-sac won the neighborhood's Christmas "Best Block Spirit" Award.

Last, but not least, was the Family Pizza Restaurant gift card all five of us won at a school sponsored talent show while performing, "Ob-La-Di, Ob-La-Da," by *The Beatles* from 1968!

For this talent show, the five of us dressed in large yellow trash bags with cutout holes for heads, arms, and legs—real white feathers glued on the back tail area and more feathers glued around our neck openings. Each of us wore an elasticized rubber chicken's beak, white knee-high socks, and a variety of straw hats!

We entered the contest as *The Fulkerson Flock! And we won hands down!*

"The Fulkerson Flock" in Full Uniform

Dean and I tried extremely hard to make as many good things available as we could in order for our children to experience enjoyable times and live rewarding, normal lives.

As a result, oftentimes our kids would hesitate at length to make their weekend plans with their friends, waiting to see first what the family was planning. For the most part, our good times worked out and life was pleasant.

Until, on other days, the PTSD demon would raise its ugly head and loudly remind us that there was still a dark side, coursing beneath all those good times. There still was a trigger-happy anger and fury dwelling inside my husband. It was like PTSD was on a mission of spreading depression and misery, infecting the five of us!

As a type of Rambo, the military had done too well a job of programming and desensitizing Dean as a warrior, but then failed to consider depressurizing him upon his return into civilian life and readjustment.

Yes, the moods, the pain, continued and plagued our American way of life. Dean's wounded state of mind, this disorder of the brain, heart, and spirit also transferred into his abilities to hold sufficient employment, even though his work ethic was strong.

Usually he was able to obtain the job—after all, he was in sales—but long term, he could not sustain the job, due to lack of sleep, hyper-vigilance, depression, nightmares, subsequent fatigue, all draining his resolve and tenacity.

Yet, through it all, he had a mental, emotional disorder that had not been acknowledged, diagnosed, nor treated. However, this in and out process within the job market was not his fault— this behavior was not my fault, and none of these problems were our children's fault.

Vietnam and Agent Orange had come to abide in our house. War trauma had come to dwell in the Fulkerson household— along with the terror and the images of the many souls lost on both sides of the battle; and, of course, there was always the possibility of the wounded or dead having been left behind in that country.

Dean's soul was injured; his mind was perplexed and his identity was in question. There were disturbances in his emotions and behaviors. After Vietnam at best, Dean's reasoning abilities were often confused and limited.

With great difficulty, jobs came and went and for our finances to remain in the black, a major lifeline was necessary. Our once excellent credit rating became a thing of the past. We were spiraling downward.

Too often, there were those times when we were living from hand to mouth; our utilities having been cut off and very little was visible in the refrigerator. There were numerous nonsufficient checks bouncing at our bank of the suburbs, along with the bank's many extra fees and charges depleting our already bleeding-out finances.

Our teenaged son once asked in almost a whisper, "Mom, are we ever going to have any money?" This question was in response to my once again stating to him that we could not do something he wanted to do because of finances. I gave him a heavy sigh and said promisingly and longingly, but with uncertainty, "I hope so…"

I stretched every dollar, every grocery purchase, and every clothing need. Our in-laws pitched in here and there, and thereby sadly enabled us to continue to survive.

I cooked meals and used questionable leftovers that an average household would have discarded without hesitation. My family today has no idea the over-the-hill ingredients and the expired dates they ingested in those days. I know only God saved us during those many years from the possibility of serious food poisoning.

And in fear and trembling, while living in terror of foreclosure, often I would remain awake at night examining the dark street outside our bedroom bay window. My eyes would play tricks on me because I would imagine seeing multiple cars and men boldly approaching our front door, seeking to move us out and claiming our home for foreclosure and subsequent auction.

For our children, we attempted to fiercely create an atmosphere of lightheartedness, of normalness; however, secretly our children were very much aware of the stress and strain residing in our home. They were attuned to the fact that something was at odds; there was serious unrest in our midst. Because of their discernment, they quietly strived to assist us in developing a normal life rather than the front and center consumption developing daily in our PTSD-impaired household.

But, yet, the bottom line of all these many positive and negative events was the love—the ferocious, tenacious, committed love that held us together—that unstoppable, unbeatable, relentless bond that flowed through our veins, minds, and hearts.

We were survivors—we are survivors—God designed us to do battle for him and for one another. This is what we did extremely well and still do today. We hung strong, in prayer, with intensity and fervor.

A better life was ahead, I just knew it; one of freedom from oppression…and we could hardly wait to witness those miraculous events! We believed without any doubt, our miracles were coming; and from that date, we began looking for them!

Patience—staying power—a little longer.

Perseverance was what was required.

Observation: In my life's later years, I made a discovery regarding God and His proven miracles. First of all, I learned well that without negative occurrences in our lives, there is certainly no purpose, no reason for miracles to take place.

Please allow me to explain: We do not need miracles when everything in our lives is positive and going well. Sadly, too many times we hardly need God or anything He has to offer, period. It is because of our huge needs, the intense darkness, and the hopelessness that the path is paved and the spiritual bread crumbs are dropped, for miracles to be revealed and made known to us within our negative circumstances.

Since this heavenly disclosure, I thank God for all the past negative moments—the many negatives that troubled us, that brought us to our knees; which, by the way, is the perfect position to hear and to communicate with God.

God has a way of turning our life's lack-lustrous events into positive, glorious ones: our negatives always become positives in God's world…this is what makes God good all the time!

For me, my life of many trials and tribulations became the springboard for creating a Sandy that would house the compassion, the empathy, the zeal, the fervor, and urgency for reaching others that are hurting just as she was before God revealed Himself in a new profound way and met her many needs.

I like who I am today, but who I am today is only because of the unpleasantness that plagued me prior through those decades. Yes, those painful experiences created who I am now, and that is all good for me and my loved ones.

Let's learn early not to fight against how God desires to fashion us. He has a plan—a design—and his intentions are always miraculous! Let us search for the bread crumbs on purpose—they will never lead us astray. We must begin looking for our miracles; and, unfortunately, if we are preoccupied and focusing on life's other circumstances, we may miss them and what a senseless, tragic loss that would be!

The Price of a Dollar

There were those many years in which we hopelessly struggled to make mortgage payments, car notes, and utilities; plus, early on, we also had a ski boat payment! As much as I disliked the purchase and cost of that boat, I have to admit our family did receive a lot of pleasure from its purchase.

By having a boat we were able to spend more time together. We camped out a great deal in rented, primitive cabins, or in a tiny, two-person pup tent for all five of us, complete with biting flies and using the only dollar we had to purchase a fly swatter; the cereal-and-chip-eating squirrels; and the multitudes of chiggers, mosquitoes, and fire ants! We entertained ourselves and others with water sports, and in ways we would have never been able to do without this boat.

Of course, I still wrestled with my motion sickness problems, but over a period of time, I discovered how to modify my illness. Mainly, I believed family time in any capacity was urgent because of the heaviness under which we lived with PTSD and all it brought into our home. We had to have fun as a family unit! Therefore, I would find ways to force myself into overcoming my motion sickness handicap. Overall, those were truly fun times and we have precious fond memories.

After four years of ownership, we were compelled to sell the boat. We needed those funds to pay toward our mortgage installment because once again, we were behind on our home's loan payments. It was a weary, defeating day when the boat sold and we watched it being pulled away on its trailer out of our lives. Surprisingly, however, after it was gone awhile, we adjusted and did not miss it that much.

For several years Dean owned a small janitorial business. Everyone in our immediate family learned how to clean commercial buildings, as well as rental car lots around the international airport and elsewhere in the city. We would be found on many holidays cleaning our accounts, in lieu of our handful of employees, who refused to work on those special days. Instead, we as a family would work in their place to maintain these seven-day, twenty-four-hour business accounts.

Therefore, though our kids grew up in the suburbs and were considered privileged, they discovered early the value of a dollar, and how many nauseating urinals it took to earn that dollar!

Our children learned not to shy away from grimy, smelly restrooms, kitchens, or break rooms. When customers or our commercial-account employees looked down their noses at our family doing an honest day's work, we held our heads higher and did an even better job than if they had not considered us beneath them.

You would think that employees would be thankful having a clean environment and that they would assist in moving their chairs or even their feet to make way for our mopping and vacuuming; instead, many of them gained pleasure from making our jobs even more difficult while acting superior.

Those were humbling experiences. At one time, my younger daughter and I cleaned several used car lots two times a week where we dealt with chauvinistic salesmen—alone and unarmed, late at night, our son cleaned rental car lots in frightening areas downtown. In the late night hours, our older daughter earned her small amount of monthly mad money by cleaning a creepy mall of offices.

On the surface, though these janitorial opportunities and encounters may not sound like times of humiliation, we, ourselves, were surprised at how our sensitive egos found it hard to willingly lower ourselves to some of those uncomfortable, sordid levels...

There were stretches of time when Dean would have great difficulty with the negatives of having a day-to-day, week in and week out, all-night janitorial company. This was especially true when he would work in our office for eight daytime hours, and then would have to fill in for a sick employee, or, perhaps, he would personally tend to an account for which he alone was responsible, having to clean it on a regular basis because of cash-flow troubles.

There were those all too frequent weeks when our employees would be paid, as would our office rental and utilities, but we would not receive a paycheck.

Always during nights, Dean would either be cleaning an account, or he would be hyper-vigilant, on military alert, and would be up all that night protecting and securing our home's perimeter. Neither way was he getting enough sleep. Weariness and exhaustion were setting in.

When we added all of this together, plus the PTSD symptoms of poor self-esteem, negative self-image, irritability, and depression—that is when we acknowledged that most things were not going well.

Dean's fatigue was obvious. It revealed itself in lack of patience, high degrees of stress, frustration, poor concentration, moodiness; it became harder and harder for him to function and to keep everything running smoothly or, at times, running at all.

Post-traumatic stress was doing a number on our family, but we did not know what its cause was, much less what to do about it. We had no tools with which to function; certainly we had none to flourish!

At times, Dean would simply shut down. Go to work, come back home, and shut down for the period of time he was off. Go to work, come back home, and so on. For years, we lived under these conditions.

Knowing I could not or should not depend on him, I began taking care of most things at home. There were very few times that

I could question him on what to do about a certain circumstance because either he was not wanting to communicate and problem solve at the time, or he was experiencing apathy and would make unsound judgments and poor financial decisions.

I recall when we were dating how secure I felt when he made simple decisions for me, for us. At the time, I did not perceive that ability and blessing as part of a controlling personality. However, after Vietnam and several years into our marriage, I came to the conclusion that, in reality, I had exchanged my controlling mother for a controlling husband.

However, the controlling part was not the nastiest problem. This particular problem became a crisis for me when Dean grew angry and hostile as though I was the enemy and would withdraw his inclusion and affection, leaving me isolated and emotionally cut-off for days on end!

His reaction was my payback; for what, I was never sure! However, my true trauma was revealed in the not knowing if, this time, Dean would be finished with me and our marriage would be considered a thing of the past.

I am a slow learner; I readily admit that. Thus, it took me several years to face the truth that Dean was controlling me like my mother had done when I did not accomplish things exactly as I was told. She would emotionally abandon and leave me out on a limb, alone, as punishment! When young I was often left with the frightening feeling that my mom found me so repulsive that she could not stand to look at me!

In our marriage, this continued behavior and lack of a dependable, affectionate, secure relationship would drive me into absolute devastation; it would knock out the legs from under me, and I would become hopelessly suicidal! At best, my emotional foundation was distorted and illogical, but, nevertheless, it was what it was, and that was all I had.

To most, I know none of this makes sense, but I did not and could not repair something that was so deep and consuming—so very deep within. In all honesty, when I married, had I jumped from the pan into the fire? Perhaps now, with this massive quantity of PTSD in our lives, I truly had!

Oh, my, I look back at those early years in my mother's house and gasp at how vulnerable I was. I was in such emotional poverty; so hungry for attention for all the right reasons; so thirsty for affection—sincere, unconditional affection—true love from a parent, either parent; love for who I was, or, even more so, love for whom I should have become!

It takes my breath away when I am truthful with myself. I candidly believe if I had not fallen in love with God, my constant companion, and all his blessings during my mid-teenage years, I suspect, without a doubt, I would have pursued darkened paths. I believe when a child has been sexually abused—not assaulted, but abused nonetheless—taking that sinister road into threatening directions seems a fair and easy transition. For me, because of the lack of genuine love and outward affection being withheld by my parents, as an early teenager, I reasoned that negative attention would have been far better than no attention at all.

Thank you, God, for drawing me by your Spirit into an improved life and, in particular, for protecting me from my own mother and her inadequacies!

While in my late forties, I confronted my mother and emotionally fell apart. She looked at my younger sister who was present and asked, "What is wrong with Sandy? What is she talking about? I don't understand!" And as she sat there later, all her body language became a giant question mark! I was the one tormented, while she sat there experiencing neither pain nor remorse. No "I'm sorry's" were ever spoken to any of her children.

When someone has wronged us and does not take at least a portion of responsibility for those wrongs, the door slams shut and is sealed on those damaged, bloody emotions and soul injuries.

For all four of us children, this lack of apology and acknowledgment was the end of the story. We had no recourse, no remedy, and no chance to heal—and according to my mother, we were dreadfully mistaken about our wounds under her rule!

For many of us as young adults, we often seek our parents' blessing—a recognition as in Bible days of old of how proud they are of who we have become. A seal of approval—just a few words to let us know we have honored them by walking uprightly according to God's Word, while holding jobs, paying taxes, being faithful in our marriages, and raising respectful, awesome children and grandchildren.

When we fail to hear that approval, fail to hear those longed-for words, and never receive that sought-after blessing, we grieve the loss of that support and that endorsement! No one else in this world can replace our parents in this way. That intense hunger and yearning to witness their pride in us remains forever lost, and we weep and mourn within ourselves.

However, on a lighter note, a series of funny events happened early one year as our children continued growing like weeds. Briefly, I would like to tell about those events. Now in looking back, I think everyone will agree how truly amusing they are—one of those "wow" Sandy moments!

In those years, somehow we always had a menagerie of pets, strays and otherwise. For several years, we had a tortoise-colored cat that frequently had litters of kittens. Most of the time we were short on money, so this poor creature never made it to the veterinarian to be spayed.

Our house was designed with the three-car garage connected to the home by way of a breezeway. Literally, anything was able to crawl from the garage through the breezeway and into the two-story housing area between the lower ceiling and the upper floor.

Once again, Crissy, our tortoise cat, had given birth to several kittens in that narrow area above our home's downstairs ceilings. In truth, all that activity was unknown to us until the kittens' eyes opened and Crissy's little ones started to navigate. Above the kitchen, breakfast room, and den, we could hear them meowing at all hours of two very long days and nights.

But that was not the awful part. The really terrible part came when they started falling between the walls of the den, utility room, and kitchen! At one point, the meowing was right over the sink, and then we were sure it transferred to behind the dishwasher, and then the sound was in the den walls, etc. These helpless sounds were driving us crazy with worry!

We recognized that these little ones would die in those spaces if they could not get back to where Crissy was, or if Crissy could not rescue them. So unless we helped , dying was a sure thing— and then our house would have an unbearable odor—*for a very, very long time*!

Dean volunteered and took on the mission—I was extremely thankful! First, he tried to get to the kitten over the sink— that was one hole. Then he tried to get to the one behind the dishwasher—to no avail. He even attempted to get to the back of the dishwasher by way of the accompanying wall of the utility room's broom closet; there was then a sizeable hole there, too.

After that he tried to get to a kitten meowing in the den's wall behind the intercom unit, but when removing the unit, at first all he saw was a long, thin, emaciated, white tail hanging in what used to be a vacant opening. *He freaked out, thinking it was a rat's tail*! After some effort, out came the kitten. Oh, yeah, we were well on our way to a successful mission now!

With the other kittens, Dean was not going to be defeated. When he could not get to the kitten behind the dishwasher from the inside, he went outside and proceeded to remove several bricks from the kitchen's exterior wall.

All of this effort did have a happy ending, however, except for the holes and bricks not being repaired or replaced any time soon. As a result of these peculiar events, what happened next was really bizarre!

After the kitten episode, it was but a short time before I heard some commotion in the utility room's broom closet—the one with the larger hole in the wall still present. I gingerly opened the door, ingenuously thinking the noise was being made by one of our pets finding itself locked within. Boy, was I in for a shock.

As I stood there frozen in place and staring into the small area for possibly two or three seconds, glaring back at me with beady slanted eyes was this large, pointed, brownish face of a rat! Thank God I was able to slam the door shut before the very substantial rat ran out into the house!

I danced around in place for several seconds not knowing which direction to run, terrified that the animal within would eat its way through the door and I would be next on the menu! Finally I breathed and what came rushing out was, "Oh, Oh, OH, OOOOH NOOOO, DEAN!" I shrieked, paralyzed with fear!

Thank goodness Dean was home that late afternoon. We determined that the creature had entered the house by way of the breezeway, went down the inside wall, through the unrepaired hole, and into the broom closet. And now, he was *ours...to keep.* This was more than just awful—what were we going to do?

Still not fully believing my colorful description regarding the size of this living thing, our home's fearless leader nonchalantly delegated the duty and sent me to our upper-class, suburban hardware store, while he free of embarrassment relaxed at home. Upon arrival there I knew I must downplay my situation and not mention why I needed a mousetrap the size of Texas!

Therefore, I gave the generic man behind the counter a weak smile and calmly inquired as to where the mousetraps were displayed. As he escorted me, picking up one about the size of a postage stamp; I focused on the business at hand. As I looked further I located a very large trap. Then I softly commented, "No, I think this one is more the size I need..."

Of course, being a male and a well-informed hardware man in mousetrap sizes, he shook his head and lightly chuckled at my selection; after all, we lived in a ritzy, rat-less part of the county!

But then when I reached down to collect all <u>three</u> of the large traps, he lost it! I continued with a cool and composed facial expression, but the whole time I was croaking within. Promptly I paid and left him grinning from ear to ear!

In the meantime, the beast at home was still banging around in the closet. After I returned, things quieted down; we hoped he had found his way back out perhaps by way of the missing bricks outside the house! By this time, Dean had been made a believer regarding the possible size of this four-legged animal. He methodically baited one of the traps, tied a thick twine to its mechanism with which to pull the rat out, and placed the trap strategically on the closet floor among all the other stuff the rat had knocked around while performing unspeakable acts!

We sat and waited; the kids were ordered upstairs. Then, yahoo! The trap went off, and "Katy, bar the door"; the thing in the closet began to bash into the door and three walls! Nothing was sacred in this arena; as though that was not enough, it was making squealing, curdle-your-blood offensive sounds like nothing we had heard before! The ogre was in pain to be sure and enraged at its circumstance.

We determined from the sounds and noise factor that even this trap was not big enough. As Dean slowly opened the door, he saw where the apparatus had come down on the rat's neck all right—but the rat was walking around on all fours with the trap attached! Oh, my goodness!

I literally had my fist in my mouth to keep from screaming when Dean pulled that trapped rat out of our closet. With the rat's tail dragging on the ground, they went out the door and behind the garage! In just a few moments, Dean returned to our kitchen, selected a very large, sharp butcher knife and quickly went back out. I thought I was going to keel over!

Yes, my brave husband had to slit that rat's throat! It was well over a foot long without including the foot-long tail! Because of "the gully" behind our property being a shelter for critters of this caliber, for quite a while all three of those traps served us well, as

Dean set them over and over again, all with ropes attached, and proceeded to line up the dead bodies behind our three-car garage.

At times, as a family, our economic despair caused us to earn our finances in other ways depending upon the year, and Dean's mental and physical health.

We had to set our preferences aside, as well as our pride, desires, and dreams; all were placed in check as we attempted to hold onto our homestead, after many years of great sacrifice. Many months it became impossible for us to make those large mortgage payments. For two years, I worked two and a half jobs—the combined hours amounted to approximately sixty-seven hours a week!

For six years I worked for a Christian school where our children attended. I was the receptionist, accounts receivable, accounts payable, payroll, and the school nurse. Yes, I was experienced in all of those areas, except for the school nurse!

I could handle everything sent my way, apart from the nursing duties. On those many special occasions, I would call the students by name and then emphatically say to the little kids, "All I ask is that you please do not bleed, and don't throw up—and if you should find it necessary, also, please don't wet or pooh-pooh in your pants." They thought I was either kidding or crazy! I was neither; I was just smart!

One of my other jobs was, of course, the janitorial one that I performed with my younger daughter; however, for over two years, I also worked at a department store at our area's mall. In this retail store's office area we posted charge account payments, employee records, counted money, made deposits, and were forced to perform those dreaded gift wrapping duties.

One of our most attention-grabbing financial ventures was when in a weekly neighborhood newspaper, I found a summer, seasonal job selling fireworks for the Fourth of July. The possibility of earning two thousand dollars over a ten-day period was too enticing!

Surprisingly, Dean went along with the idea, but, hello, we were desperate and were facing yet another financial crisis!

So, Dean and I went for the interview, looked around at the others there in the waiting room, and for a moment, wondered if we had walked through the wrong door. But we quickly got a grip, smiled at the right times, and were hired to man a fireworks stand at a location within the suburbs.

We were told what a great business could be done on our particular corner and how it had actually earned the last year's recruits two thousand dollars. That was all it took; in a moment we signed the contract and became professional fireworks dealers! I was excited. What a project; what a blessing! We were exactly two thousand dollars behind on our mortgage; we could do this for ten days—it was possible, wasn't it? Sure it was.

And so we began—twenty-four-seven. It was a large stand and had two storage areas, one on either end. One of the ends we used for inventory, and the other we used as our sleeping and/or resting zone. We made it as comfortable and homey as a makeshift fireworks stand can possibly be.

A valid question from someone might be something like, "Did we know anything about fireworks—you know, the product we were going to earn money selling?" Well, I could blow smoke and lie, lie, lie; instead I will say, of course not. We did not know a thing—not one single thing! We knew how to light the sparklers—that was it!

For the first two days we had been selling little bits here and there, learning and sharing with each other any selling tips. Then quite suddenly by accident we discovered our ace in the hole!

Early each morning, some of the nine to twelve-year-old groups of boys would come by and purchase several of the unknowns on our shelves. As we were interacting with them and bagging what they had chosen to buy, we started asking questions as to what this firework or that firework would do—exactly how did it explode, were there different colors, did it go straight up with repetition or did it zigzag, was it popular, and so on?

By the end of five days of concentrating on a variety of questions posed to "safe" customers, we had become educated and fluent in the world of fireworks! We were selling everything in sight; we could hardly keep the shelves stocked. Each day we received a large shipment of almost the whole lot!

Doing this was almost fun—except for the forever and ever hours, the heat, the bugs, the lack of a refrigerator, and no commode! Some other lucky vendors had travel trailers pulled onto their properties for comfort; we were not one of those.

Our contract required us to have a staff of at least six able-bodied people available all day on the Fourth of July. From stories we were told beforehand, we knew it would be busy, but six whole people? *Really?*

Nevertheless, we called in the troops, including our son and daughters; we were there in full force. It was not any time at all before everyone started arriving and fighting over parking spaces. Midday we had six lines, ten people deep, and while we chuckled and laughed out loud with comforting relief, we processed orders at lightning speed!

By eight o'clock the night of the Fourth, we had little inventory left. By midnight, the bewitching hour when we were required to stop selling, I counted five small "chasers" still on the shelf. Besides those, everything else had been sold!

My goodness and thanks be to Jesus! Because of him and our willingness to put ourselves out there—plus, with a wee bit of creativity—we had made our necessary two thousand dollars, and our home was safe and still ours for a while longer. *More bread crumbs on purpose—thank you, God!*

For five years our only son played sports for the two upper-grade schools he attended. He was talented at men's volleyball, soccer, flag-football, and basketball.

Dean III before Open-Heart Surgery

During practices as a high school freshman, he began having difficulty breathing while running. As he ran with his team conditioning laps around the gym, often he would turn an appalling grayish, purplish color and would sweat profusely—more than what was considered normal. Nevertheless, our son would push himself until the end because he never wanted to be treated differently and did not want to draw negative attention.

However, the most troublesome problem was the *extreme,* fast, heavy pounding of his heart. After taking him to doctors who ran EKGs, echograms, treadmill stress tests and provided twenty-four-hour halter monitors, for the next two years, none of that testing revealed anything abnormal.

Another heart specialist placed him on a beta blocker, which nearly killed him. We tried many things and many prescriptions, until within Houston, Texas, we at last came under the care of the Baylor College of Medicine.

There in their reputable hospital, his heart was mapped, and it was determined that for his heart to function in a healthy manner, there were two-and-a-half too many electrical circuits. I took off work to perform daily and overnight stays with our son for a week while the doctors were mapping and testing various heart drugs. His excellent heart specialist wanted to prevent him from undergoing invasive open-heart surgery. The doctors concluded our son could more than likely tolerate one of those tested heart medications.

Within two weeks of taking this drug, Dean III had become a *Dr. Jeckel and Mr. Hyde.* The transformation was alarming, and his actions were nothing less than weird. He himself determined he required surgery and made the final life-changing decision!

Within four weeks, during the month of June, we returned to the same hospital, same team of doctors, and our son of seventeen years prepared himself mentally and physically to undergo this large-scale surgery!

That frightful day as he was being prepped in the hospital room, I knew I had to remain strong and brave for both our sakes. But as the nurses and interns wheeled him down the hall toward the operating rooms beyond, leaving me behind after telling him I was praying and how much I loved him, I completely broke down.

Through my tears, one last time I purposely glanced at his chest peeping out from under his gown while fading into the distance. I took a mental picture knowing full well the next time I would see him, his young man's chest would have an incision from his collarbone all the way down to his waist, with his sawed-in-two breastbone held together with numerous metal staples.

Heart complications had become the final straw on our camel's back—this was more invading than we could emotionally and physically handle. The enemy of our souls had generously injured Dean and me, but now rising up in our hearts and spirits, he was forbidden in God's mighty name to come near our kids; our soul's enemy was not allowed to harm our children!

With us our pastor spent hours and hours in the surgical cardiac waiting room. Feeling terribly responsible for taking up his whole day, we genuinely thanked him and tried to encourage him to go on with his busy schedule, but he would not hear of it. He did not leave primarily because he knew what to expect after this type of surgery—and we did not.

Our pastor stayed until after we witnessed the aftermath of open-heart surgery back in the days before lasers!

Words cannot describe the alarming sight! In the recovery room Dean and I stood in place astounded and speechless as we watched our son, now all bandaged up (but still revealing a large amount of blood,) gagging and retching up all this thick white mess from deep inside his impaired body. I was too stunned to cry—and he was too sick and overwhelmed to know we were there!

It took the rest of that summer and into the beginning of his high school senior year before our son was stronger and feeling fully recovered.

By February of the following year, he was once again able to play basketball for his school without experiencing his heart racing and fluttering at over three hundred beats a minute!

Yes, my employment's insurance paid for this high-priced surgical procedure in its entirety. Our family had witnessed and participated in yet another miracle. The showing up and showing off of our God was not taken lightly.

All three of our children played sports and contributed to the patriotic team spirit of their schools. Our youngest was also a cheerleader two of those years. Oftentimes it was quite difficult to support and schedule all of these practices and competitions, but rarely did we miss one. Our kids did not always want to play sports for their school, but as a parent looking back, I believe overall it was beneficial and gave them purpose and a feel for team unity.

During all her high school years our older daughter played girls' volleyball; one of those years she was a part of a gifted team that won State among private schools!

This was a huge accomplishment for such a small Christian school; thankfully, Dean and I were present at that monumental event, and we were still there when the fantastic trophy was brought home to the school's trophy case!

The Ultimate Final Straw

O ur son graduated high school and was functioning well with a normal heart. After a couple of years, he had chosen to attend a well-known aeronautics school in another state. His leaving for tech school left us at home with two children—one in high school and one in middle school.

After our son's departure our younger daughter during the month of January began to suffer from panic attacks. Because we did not know what the nature of these episodes was, we automatically began worrying that she must have the same ailment and heart configuration as our son had had previously.

We began taking her to doctors; like our son, she also wore a halter monitor during her school days and while sitting-out during basketball practices or actual games. Nothing was revealed to us as being out of order, but then we recalled that our son's early testing disclosed nothing as well. Therefore, we kept trying to discover what could be lurking and causing her so much discomfort and fear.

Dean and I highly suspected that perhaps these could be birth defects in our children due to Vietnam and the Agent Orange chemical contamination. We requested church prayer and continued seeking answers because we realized that she, too, was the same age as our son was when he first began showing such off-the-chart symptoms.

We had become so weary, so jaded, of this regimen. We had been fighting this battle for many years. The word "stress" did not come close to the agony we were going through! All we could imagine was that, yes—Agent Orange, the herbicide widely used to eradicate the thick jungle foliage in Vietnam, must be the culprit causing these uncommon deformities in our children.

Our anger and bitterness climbed to record highs, while our despair and frustration reached record lows, over financial limitations due to mounting doctor bills, testing fees, and medication costs. All these issues were occurring with no employment insurance coverage, unlike the full insurance we had the previous years for our son's doctors' care and major surgery. We were living by faith regarding all our family's medical emergencies.

Our hearts were in our throats, and we held our breath as we pursued different avenues attempting to find help for our second child experiencing new heart issues and health concerns.

It was not until March, the spring of that year, when one grave Saturday afternoon my young daughter came into our bedroom and told me tearfully that she had been raped at the end of December during her Christmas holidays. Immediately I sunk into a hole of despondency, helplessness, a wasted state! I could not wrap my weary mind and raw emotions around such information. This was an off-the-chart tragedy! Where could I turn for bracing, assistance, advice?

Our thirteen-year-old, our beautiful, innocent, baby daughter had been raped by an eighteen-year-old, a friend of her friend's brother. She had gone over to her Christian school girlfriend's house to spend the night during the Christmas/New Year's holidays, only to return home the following day violated, traumatized, and anguishing over an assault! A trap had been set by her girlfriend, who was like a sister to this man of eighteen and an older male friend of his. As if injury was not enough, these people heaped insult upon her as well, when our daughter was asked by her attacker if she knew what had just happened. Speaking through the alcohol they had provided earlier, which along with them she had warily consumed, she replied that she didn't. He then proceeded to nonchalantly inform her that he had just taken her virginity. Because he was her first experience, he bragged that she would never forget him and consequently, she now *belonged* to him and was to do what he said. After that vicious experience, they were still not through with her—for months there was continued talk and plans regarding a life of prostitution and escort services.

In her innocence our child calculated that as a result of this sexual act, she was then probably pregnant. Her fear and dread reached enormous heights, thus the additional panic attacks. To bring about a desired and welcomed miscarriage, with her fists she would pound her stomach without mercy, causing severe bruising and injury.

All these many lonely weeks our daughter had lived in silence with the memory of that assault and these "friends" continued harassment; lived with it for almost three months without adequate support, comfort, or medical attention! No, her panic attacks were not due to a heart condition at all; they occurred from a violent attack resulting in rape and the continuing confusion and shame brought about by the attacker and his accomplices.

Though much of these details were withheld initially and only recently have been revealed to us, now evaluating those weeks and months in both our lives, I must secretly admit I feel incredibly guilty over not adequately, emotionally connecting with her! I did not have an excuse *then*—and certainly, I am not saying I have an excuse *now*.

At that time I could only cry out to the hills, to the stars, to God in heaven, and plead, "Why? Why? Why?" Truly our hearts were breaking! This was yet another brutal wounding I was incapable of handling properly and sensitively. Even with our limited shared information, I was shattered with what was happening all at once—and all that had been happening within our family for years!

Nevertheless, now I want to publicly apologize and express to this daughter, whom I love with all my heart and soul, how sorry I am for not having been the mother I should have been and for whom I believe I would have been if life had not already beaten me up from all directions, leaving me bloody and shattered!

199

As her mother, I take full responsibility for not being there for my daughter the way I would have wanted and needed someone to be there for me if I had been in such a private, relentless nightmare as she was—the tortured state into which she innocently found herself!

Now I question if my mother felt as helpless and hopeless in her own private torment, unable to do anything more or go any further than what she had already accomplished. What about the caring emotions she failed to show us children over those many years—unable to go there because life was also beating her up from all directions, leaving her bloody and shattered as well?

Now standing and viewing from a mountaintop—*hindsight,* they call it—yes, my then immature vantage point could eagerly criticize my mother for not feeling, loving, understanding, or doing enough—but what if that was all she could do and what if she was already doing more than she had ever thought possible considering her temperament, her physical strength; and what if she was throwing all she had at not committing suicide instead?

God help me for not being more appreciative and empathetic. I now comprehend, as humanity and as parents; we can only use the best we have at the time, in that moment, in those hours, in those circumstances. And oftentimes, even though we may and do frequently come up lacking, God knows our hearts and sees our souls and judges us with a different scale than the one we use for each other. Thank you, Lord, for being lenient and merciful to me! (Thank you for my mother!)

I can only hope that my (baby) daughter can forgive me and will see my heart and understand that, yes, I was there, but I was *buried alive* in difficulties and trauma. Nevertheless, my love then was alive and well and promised to positively rise again to do everything in my power to make a difference for her in this world!

About two weeks later after extensive searching and after a consultation about our daughter's attack, we made an appointment with a female doctor, rationally thinking a woman physician would have more compassion and show more sensitivity than a male doctor. I took off work again. This absence from work just had to be; my job would need to wait, and it was okay for my desk to stack to the ceiling.

But wouldn't you know, this female doctor's bedside manner was immensely lacking and without any sensitivity. Nevertheless, although she was without mercy and kindness and caused excessive pain for our *baby girl*, who had tears rolling down her face as I tried to comfort her, the doctor did do a thorough exam, confirming the act of violence.

Our young daughter was tested thoroughly for HIV and numerous sexual diseases, which all returned negative... Thank you, thank you, thank you, God!

I cannot begin to explain how catastrophically our house was functioning. Additionally, we were upset and angry over our youngest not wanting to press charges against this man of legal age who had gloated, intimidated, and had taken great pride in having stolen her virginity! She was yet another notch in his belt.

I do not know how my Vietnam-era, sizeable husband, complete with PTSD "up the kazoo" kept, not only his sanity, but his *kill-at-will* war mentality in check! Although I know that during those years he was extremely overworked, overly burdened, and had sleep deprivation to huge degrees.

So though we thought we knew the reprobate's correct name, we did not pursue getting his address to pay him and his family a visit. He has no idea how close he came (except for God) to being confronted by the Fulkerson clan. It would not have been a pretty picture!

Therefore, the lowlife got away with it all and left our family in a heap on the floor, licking our wounds while desperately praying to quickly find the path to the recovery process not only for Dean and Vietnam but now for our younger daughter—for both of their PTSD woundings!

Soon after through a series of contacts, we were put in touch with a Christian female psychologist who had written a book about her own recovery from a rape experience.

We made an appointment and once there filled out the necessary papers to see about qualifying for a reduced counseling rate. Thankfully, the request was approved, and the rate was reduced somewhat; it came to almost $100.00 a session, all of this out-of-pocket. Of course, the sessions were being scheduled very close together—finances once again were more than impossible to budget. God knew we had no finances and therefore no budget.

We kept maybe four appointments until our child reached a plateau from which she was choosing not to advance. Because she could not reveal any more—the counselor had accomplished all she could until our daughter was ready to pursue a deeper recovery through future visits. Thereafter, not once did our daughter choose to return, and our counseling visits were laid to rest.

What did happen next was a referral to a psychiatrist for a prescription antidepressant. This our youngest did do, and we began taking meds each day; very slowly she appeared to get better and better.

Nevertheless, in her subsequent future teenage years, she had her many, many instances of rebellion! As a helpless mother, there was a heartbreaking moment in which she confided, "Mom, what have I got to lose? My virginity is gone. There's nothing left. Nothing will bring it back! What more can possibly happen to me?" I was broken again and again, facing yet other devastations I could not repair nor make better!

From day to day my husband was living crushed in spirit, and now this daughter was also on the verge of self-destruction.

My goodness! Our family was still not out of the woods; there were future chapters of promiscuous behavior, nights and nights of staying up 'til the early morning hours waiting for our younger daughter's arrival, only to appear at work the next day on time, fresh, and choosing not to mention the late and early hours I was keeping and why.

Many nights, I anxiously thought and prayed, "I'm going out of my mind with worry. I must have some peace—some relief. Lord, bring me some solace and reassurance that you hear and know my heart's cry and that you will save our daughter from devastation."

And God would hear and seemingly our lives would settle down for a while. God's bread crumbs were present and soothingly alive and well.

By no means in those early days in the suburbs was I super woman, a marital saint! I had my moments when I would reach my mortal limit, when I would have enough of my husband and what he was dishing out, and I would pack and leave our home, sometimes in a car and other times without one.

Some nights I would walk out and sleep in our secondhand van in the garage, where it was hot in the summer and cold in the winter—and where no matter what the season, there were always hungry mosquitoes!

But even though I was miserable outside in the elements, for the time being, it was worth it. Then in the early morning I would return to our bedroom with a new ability to continue.

While using my mother's old car, I spent nights on a Kroger grocery store parking lot under the bright lights for security. The noise factor made sleeping there almost impossible. But, regardless, I would persist in spite of the mental and physical pain; and the next morning I would drive home, go inside early before the children had arisen, and would prepare for work as though nothing had transpired. Indeed, on those mornings I not only looked bad but I felt worse!

As a result of one of those occasional confrontations Dean and I had, once I did pack and asked my mother-in-law, who then lived across the gully, to take me to my aunt's house inside an older, ethnic section of the city.

My mother-in-law was frequently Johnny-on-the-Spot, more than willing to take my place within our family. In no time she was eagerly waiting in the driveway! However, briefly before her arrival, I had sat in our calming, finely decorated formal living room, looking around the room and the foyer at mementos and pictures that I was leaving behind, sadly not knowing if I would ever see them again.

The sick feelings were overwhelming, and the forlorn emptiness I felt within was killing me. But soon my mother-in-law was honking for me. I picked up my suitcase, informed the children that I was going to visit relatives for a while, told them good-bye and that I loved them, and reluctantly closed the front door of our special house behind me.

Before I am unfairly judged, please allow me to better explain my then situation: Grieving as unto death I had to leave my children behind—without transportation, I did not know how long it would be before I could find a job. I did not know how I was going to eat and take care of myself, let alone take care of them. With them in school and their needing to be provided for, I was well aware it was not rational to cart them from pillar to post. I had to be realistic, *but I loved them so!* However, the worst part of all and the one I felt most guilty over, was the reality of leaving them to the mercy and control of my unpleasant and ruthless mother-in-law and a father who was too ill to alone adequately provide for them!

I walked to my mother-in-law's car like I was participating in a death march, and longingly gazed, purposely memorizing the front of our house as we drove away. She did some talking along the route. I was too morbidly sick to hold a conversation. Because of circumstances I had played right into my mother-in-law's eagerly awaiting hands, and I recognized it. But for my trip to my aunt's house, I needed her to take me because in advance I had decided to leave my marriage without any portion of the small amount of money in our bank account and without either car. I would begin life anew and make it on my own, starting from scratch.

I walked up to my aunt's house—a tiny house in a fifty-year-old, low-income neighborhood. I pressed the worn doorbell; her car was gone, and no one answered. Now what?

Not knowing how long she would be gone, we drove back to my in-laws' house. Confused and crying, I took a nap in the spare bedroom. When I awoke at 5:30 p.m., I called to see if my aunt was home. Sure enough, she had arrived and I was free to return.

Again we made the trip to my aunt's house. As I walked into the small living room with my single suitcase, my dear aunt had a bewildered look on her face. At that instant I had a clue, a red flag; for me there was no future in that house. I was in for a disappointing ride!

She escorted me into her master bedroom where I was to spend the night while she had made arrangements to sleep in the second bedroom.

What a mess! I was tired, I had not eaten all day, I was lonely, and now I was not welcome. At best being there with her was awkward. I could tell she did not know what to do with me!

We both sat at the kitchen table, after she had looked into the empty refrigerator, only to further inform me that there was nothing at all to eat. The only item housed in that old 1950s refrigerator was a six-ounce can of grapefruit juice! I knew I could not put grapefruit juice into my already acidic stomach; therefore, I declined the offer and chose water instead.

In spite of my fatigue and sorrow, I tried to explain my life's difficulties to her, but with her not knowing anything about PTSD and "the elephant in the room" and my not knowing how to effectively describe the symptoms of PTSD, all my marital troubles sounded lame and whiney! How could I do a fair job of describing my problems to anyone when I myself did not have any explanations? Nothing I mentioned that night was a reason to leave my husband and not go back. By the end of our time together, she gently asked me, "Is Dean really *that* bad?"

As I heard those words repeatedly ringing in my ears ever so softly, but ever so final, I knew this door had just been closed shut; my initial intuition had been correct, and my future stay in this house had come to a close.

On an empty stomach, I took one of my mother-in-law's antidepressants and fell asleep crying, feeling at the end of my rope. Now I literally had no place to go—no place to start over! Once again in life, I did not belong.

The next morning I considered throwing up but knew I was completely empty. I felt bad, felt foolish for being at my aunt's, was nauseous, and had a mega headache. By ten that morning, Dean had called and asked if he could pick me up. I felt compelled to say, "Yes, of course." As Dean picked up my unopened suitcase and we both stepped out the door, my aunt was all smiles. Her load had been lifted, but mine had returned!

Dean and I quietly drove home; our lives continued nonstop after this brief hump in the road!

In our home my walk-in closet was my refuge; it was my "safe place"—the only place that belonged completely to me. I could hang there with no expectations, no demands, and no rules. I did not have to dress a certain way; I did not have to wear makeup; I did not have to be on time or act this way or that... I could just sit or lie there and chill. This was my sanctuary, my hole in the mountain where I was protected and could be myself, whoever that was.

On this day, I was particularly saddened. Dean was home but was not available; he was in that detached stage. I and the kids did not often fit into his thoughts and plans. He frequently, on an emotional level, would live his life and work out his feelings on an independent, disengaged, and separate track.

Individually and collectively from time to time, we, the family, would try as best we could to squeeze ourselves into his life, his space. But usually, we would be deeply disappointed and left to question ourselves as to what we could do better or what we should not have done in the first place!

Yes, we as a family were Dean's PTSD's *collateral damage*! All four of us were laid out in shambles behind him—not believing we had any capacities, any abilities for pleasing him and of generating a deeper and more rewarding relationship.

This particular morning as I lay in the closet, I was becoming more and more despondent as the moments passed; finally with my tears flowing, I knew I had reached my *final breaking point*! I had tried pretty much everything, and I could not continue rising to the occasion as though nothing was wrong with my world.

There was a lot wrong in my world; I did not know why or what, but I was convinced it was in chaos! I must have thought it was hopeless that day because the aloneness, the seclusion, was suffocating me. By degrees I was fading mentally, emotionally, and spiritually! I needed out. I cried for a change in my life! It had become a slow death, but it was a death nonetheless!

And I made a decision...

In Dean's closet on the top shelf, we had stored a gun and bullets. It was a small automatic that we had purchased for my protection while Dean was stationed at the El Toro Air Station and working late-night hours. I stretched on my tippy-toes to reach it in its case and brought it down.

As I removed it, I checked the clip to see how many bullets, if any, were still in it. There were none. I loaded it with five or six bullets. I do not remember how many.

Without saying a word, I quickly walked by Dean who was sitting on the couch with his back to me while watching television; he did not speak either. We were not speaking that day; it was yet another day of not speaking! I continued through the breakfast room, utility room, and out into the backyard.

Yes, I was fearful; I was extremely nervous and was on the brink of terror. I questioned myself as to the sanity of doing such a thing, but inside my house, I knew, because of the millions and millions of other times, there was no emotional response present there for me. There was no true relationship to be had with my husband who was indifferently watching something unimportant on TV while his wife of twenty-plus years was taking her life… *committing suicide* in their backyard!

From that point on, my compassion grew, and I better understood the many desperate women in this world! When we are trapped with our backs to the wall, like imprisoned spirits, while frantically searching for someone, anyone, to stand with us in our darkened corner, to give us hope and encouragement that things will work out, but we hear and see no one! Without a doubt, for us there is no one there.

As we witness this authenticity, "There is no hope!" is driven home. What are we to do with this truthful realization as we attempt to stand on our own two feet without adequate tools? No, there is nothing we can do because it has already killed us— inside and out!

I aimed, closed my eyes, and pulled the trigger. *Nothing happened…*

I opened my eyes and looked at the gun and fumbled with the clip holding the bullets while trying to remove it. As I held it in my shaking hand, I stared at the bullets still there, realizing the first bullet had jammed and the remaining bullets in the magazine were out of alignment!

"What has just happened?" I asked out loud. In that instant, I experienced a queasiness, and I was still shaking badly. All I could think to do was to go back into the house and ask for help.

Dean had not moved off the couch. I handed him the gun as I complained, "It jammed. Don't ask any questions! Just unjam the gun!" While he held the gun, he gave me this unbelieving, pitiful look and said in a faint, feeble, accusing voice, "Sandy, what are you doing?"

For a brief moment, I regained my composure and halfway shouted, "Please, can you fix the gun? I just…need for you…to fix the gun. That's all!" But he quickly replied, "No." He would not do it. Immediately, I felt even more dumb and ridiculous—and certainly not visibly loved and cherished!

Probably because she was called, my mother-in-law appeared shortly thereafter. She was there to take the gun home with her, but she could not miss the opportunity of literally smiling at my ignorance!

I am sure on that day I felt like my mother had on the day when she had spoken of suicide, and our pastor had laughed at her inability to handle life. Now on my day I felt her pain and her confusion. She was desperate, her back was to the wall, and she was weary of life and its troubles. Now I understood so much more. I almost understood it all!

Our older daughter overheard the three of us shouting and me crying. She came into the master bathroom with a shocked expression and tears streaming down her angelic face, begging me not to do anything "like that"! And my heart broke as I witnessed my older child's tears and heard her sobs, saw her visible exterior, and felt her internal pain. How could I hurt her that way?

Those many years ago, I had been my older daughter. I had been the one terrified that my mother would indeed kill herself, and now here I was replaying that scenario, and my own daughter was hurting and pleading for me not to do anything *like that!* How awful—how heartbreaking! I was so sorry for showing that weakness in my makeup and causing such anguish in the heart of my child whom I cherish with a love that remains unmeasured!

Within I was shouting and crying for help. I just needed someone's love! That was all—not too much to ask. I did not know any longer how to breathe, how to live, how to grow and succeed in my life.

I literally had nowhere to turn, nowhere to run! I desperately needed support and a shoulder to lean on, someone who understood me and would cry with me, if nothing else! However, there was no one at all.

"Jesus, I need a sympathetic ear, a compassionate friend who, too, knows the pain and anguish I have stockpiled, the torment I have stuffed into my heart and soul!" I cried into the universe! Life had become too difficult, too unrewarding, too unyielding, and too loveless…"

It was all draining me, leaving me empty. Little by little, I fearfully was losing my grip on my faith and my trust in God, the very one who had been there and had supported and ushered me through my whole life.

I held my heart as I wept, "Somebody, please see and care enough for me to come to my aid. This unnamed monster of isolation, depression, hostility, distancing, emotional numbing, anger, and rage is sending me over the edge to the brink of devastation!" Like David in the Bible I groaned and travailed while seeking God.

The friendship(s) I was desperate for did not come for a while longer; those friends came much later, and, therefore, my life continued to mold me into the person I was to become: the person who would reach out to those who needed hope, that someone who would declare that just with a little light, a little faith, a few dreams, the someone who would do whatever was necessary to aid a fellow wife or female veteran crying her last breath and unable to face another tomorrow!

Yes, I was being birthed and designed for the days, the work, when I would stand erect, with my head held high and no longer a victim, no longer just surviving, but instead striving, thriving, and succeeding in inspiring others not to lose their hope in this life.

Nevertheless, during those days after my attempted suicide, I backed down, just like I had always done before, revealing the lack-of-courage soul and peace lover I was. At that time I remained defeated and felt pathetic once more.

That afternoon I looked at my strange, distraught reflection in the mirror, knowing with certainty I did not have a "snowball's chance in hell" of ever becoming a lifeline for someone else when I could not provide encouragement and success for myself.

However, my Lord and Savior was preparing my future's bread crumbs. No, I had nothing to fear; all was in control!

The Joy of Parents

It was the early 1990s and our son, a Christian high-school graduate, had fallen in love with a very pretty senior from the same Christian school where his two sisters were still attending, where I was also working, and where Dean had worked for a year as a coach and civics teacher. As we all know, when we are deeply in love, we are in a big hurry to get married and to begin life. He and his girlfriend were in just that kind of hurry. Our son was still an aeronautics student in another state; therefore, their plans were to marry at home, and then they both would set up housekeeping where he was attending school.

We carried out his wedding according to plan. But needless to say, we again had numerous embarrassing moments due to our nonexistent finances. As parents of the groom, there were obligations, and it became necessary for us to bring out our "Monopoly" money for certain aspects of this epic wedding.

Therefore, we braced ourselves for more of life's awkward, uncomfortable opportunities or trials and tribulations! Surprisingly though, we pulled it off, but with much less than the skin of our teeth.

For instance, we began the rehearsal dinner preparation by using an inexpensive smoked brisket that Dean had barbequed and then taken to a butcher shop to have chopped for use in barbeque sandwiches. At a discount, I found loads of red potatoes for potato salad, and there were chips, pickles, onions, and desserts—all arranged according to the usual rehearsal dinner specifications. We managed to prepare "oodles and gobs" of everything!

However, there arose one big problem. The great smelling, inexpensive brisket we had so proudly prepared when left in a warm oven started to release way too much grease, and it was literally floating in the pan.

Therefore, in a strange church's kitchen when I first became aware of our brisket's condition, I broke into a cold sweat! I knew it was not proper for me to serve our meal floating in grease, so I hurriedly found a large spoon, and I clandestinely drained off the fat as quickly and as covertly as I could. What I did with that grease is "top secret"!

The low-grade meat quality probably would not have mattered to anyone attending the rehearsal—however, I was carrying my children's first wedding expectations on my sleeve and just knew the "egg on my face" was not only showing but glowing!

For weddings usually only the bride wears something borrowed—but not for this wedding! Fortunately, I had been offered a dress that would blend well with the wedding colors; I happily and thankfully accepted it and gratefully felt that this gift had been presented to me by an angel! God bless her; she had no idea how frantic I had become. My father and his two sisters flew into town for the purpose of attending the wedding. Of course, all three of them made plans to stay in our home!

My relatives planned visit made me officially a hostess, which, combined with our family's other daily drama, my situation was quickly becoming a crisis. This production was creating serious consequences in our house!

Not only did I need a clean house for my once-in-a-lifetime family guests, but I also needed matching sheets and pillowcases, enough pillows, sparkling bathrooms, newish towels, and complete menus. Gee whiz! Where was the money, the time, and the energy coming from? However, somehow miraculously it all came together. God was so kind to us! The entire rehearsal dinner went off without a hitch. And because we had over-prepared-to-a-fault, we had enough food left over for use in feeding all of us the following evening and more additional servings into even the second day. When we arrived at the church bright and early the morning of the wedding, we ladies were handed corsages and the men had pinned boutonnieres on their suits. We were then ushered into the church library to be photographed by the already stressed-out wedding photographer.

For pictures, in my borrowed dress, I looked pretty first rate, and Dean in a much used but spiffed-out, navy blue suit was not looking badly either. Our daughters as bridesmaids were in their special rented dresses and dyed-to-match shoes. Without having been on the inside track, no one could have guessed the difficulty involved in how we financially accomplished this feat!

As different ones were busy with pictures and others of us were on the outskirts waiting to be posed, I looked over at my stately, suited marine husband who was standing strangely inside a cornered area with his back to the wall and both hands neatly folded. For me, his stern and wrinkled forehead gave him away. I was apprehensively curious but instantly became distracted.

Before the picture-taking phase was over, I sided up to Dean and hung my head low while inquiring under my breath using my plastic smile, "Are you okay? Why are you standing away from the others?" To my astonishment and dismay, his whispered answer was frustrated, angry, and troubled, "I split my trousers all the way up the back, and I'm trying to hide the tear!" Indeed, the material of that worn navy suit had rotted away and could not hold together under this day's stress.

Boy howdy! I knew exactly how those pants felt! There was absolutely nothing we could do about Dean's current humiliation-filled moment. We had a long day ahead of us, including the wedding's *front-row* seating and the immediate reception's greeting line thereafter!

Whoa! It was a long, tedious day indeed! My husband spent most of it leaning against a variety of walls, sometimes tugging at his jacket or sitting down away from the crowd—except for the moments spent standing in the front of the church for the wedding itself and then performing the congenialities of the ceremonial reception line.

During the ceremony for the benefit of covering "the accident" from being seen by anyone standing behind him, Dean did his best to camouflage the giant, at-an-angle split boldly displaying his blue and white boxer shorts. What a trooper, my marine!

We presented our son with a hundred dollars to be spent on his one-night honeymoon before our newlywed couple would leave for their out-of-state school responsibilities. We were embarrassed and very reluctant to offer him so little in monetary funds, but in his kind, gentle way, he was exceptionally grateful and humbly thanked us. Our son is truly a priceless gem, a one-of-a-kind pearl of great price, and, even today, he honors and supports us in every way possible!

After a little over a year, Dean III and his bride returned to Texas, choosing to live with us. They were expecting their first baby so they stayed with us for eight months; that is, until my mother also moved into our house!

During the summer months prior, I had received a person-to-person long distance call from Adult Protective Services about my mom's appalling, unspeakable living conditions. It was not like I did not know how atrocious those conditions were; after all, I grew up in them. But none of us kids had been able to talk my mother into budging off her insane decision to not move for any reason—except when we happened to mention "the man that lived under the house!" During those discussions, she was more open to making a change.

"The man who lived under her floor," as the story went, would come into my mom's house at night and steal her food from inside her refrigerator. We knew this was not true, but she was convinced and would go on at great length as to how he would rattle the pipes and make other noises throughout the day and night! Nevertheless, he must have liked it there because he stayed for many years!

Thank goodness she had been invited to move into her brother's and sister-in-law's spare bedroom back in our original hometown. Her brother had suffered several mini strokes, and his wife thought my mother would be a big help and a good companion. Dean, I, and our two daughters made the trip down the coast to where we had originally met and married. During a phone call in a rational moment my mother had eagerly agreed for us to pack some of her things and to physically move her three hours away. But when we arrived, ready to start and very much on a timeline, she was having serious second thoughts. We talked and talked, packed as we talked, and tried to ignore the anxiety she was expressing and obviously feeling!

Again, it was another humid, sultry Texas August on the coast; inhumane and brutal was the heat in this un-air-conditioned, unventilated, and cram-packed house with only a narrow walkway down the middle of each room! My mom would not allow us to open any windows. But we were carefully choosing our battles with her, so we kept quiet and endured the sweltering heat and unusual pesky bugs.

Dripping with sweat and giving us ready-to-kill looks, our daughters busily wrapped china and packed boxes while I stuffed my mom's hatchback Chevette with dozens of black trash bags full of dirty clothes. I believe the clothes had been in those bags for many years because the smell outside the trash bags was pungent! *But she had made it clear*: she would not travel anywhere unless those clothes and her car went with us! Sadly, I knew she meant it.

Dean and one of my brothers loaded the U-haul with some of the main pieces of furniture. Then came time to load the refrigerator! However, before Dean moved it even slightly, he first unloaded four giant trash bags of Styrofoam containers and other storage boxes from Meals on Wheels! We were all wowed!

The man under the house had not done his covert job well; the refrigerator was still filled to capacity.

As this appliance was rolled out of the filthy, stacked kitchen through the tiny hallway, into the living room, and out the front door, there was a continuing wide trail of murky, dark-brown liquid readily draining with gusto. I thought our daughters would not survive the revolting smell of months and months of spoiled, rotten food billowing from what had emptied out onto the floors! Outside Dean courageously hosed down the refrigerator and loaded it onto the U-haul.

By the time we finished all we could physically handle, it was almost sundown, and we still had another three hours of driving. All of us that were making the trip, except for my brother, climbed into the vehicles, my mother included.

However, before doing so, for a long while my mom hesitated leaving. I felt compelled *to lie* to my mother by gently agreeing with her, "Yes, Mom, of course, we'll be back really soon to get the rest of your things. Everything here has been secured and won't be stolen." (Liar, liar, pants on fire!) I had no idea that this was a prophecy in the making.

Without my bold-faced lie, my mother would not have relocated. Realistically, while working nonstop, it would have taken us at least two weeks to load the rest of what she had in that house into at least four U-hauls! We did not have the bodies and manpower for that or the money required. Doing the move this way was the best we could pull off. After hours of driving and arriving in town at ten o'clock that night, we drove my mom to my aunt and uncle's house where we left her with some clean clothes and her secured Chevette automobile outside at the curb. Now my mother would be safe and well cared for and the Adult Protective Service office was satisfied! The next day after unloading the U-haul truck at a storage unit, we started back home because we were scheduled for work first thing Monday morning!

Within less than four weeks, my aunt was frantically calling, "Please, come get her," she pleaded apologetically. "I'm sorry, I can't do this! Please come soon—real, real soon!" Then she proceeded to fill us in on the chaos my mother was causing within their home. "Oh, God, what are we going to do?" Where was my mother going to go?

We stretched out my aunt's frantic calls into an extra life-saving two weeks, at which time we drove back down to The Valley, and after driving seven hours, we loaded my mother and some of her belongings. The two of them, my aunt and my mom, had a parting of the ways and now could hardly tolerate one another.

My mother, of course, in her mentally confused state was accusing everyone present at my aunt's house of stealing her possessions! Out of survival we left her stowed items in storage, unable to face the work and required stamina involved so soon after the first move!

When we returned home with my mom in tow, it was just two weeks before Halloween, and then, of course, the major holidays were soon to follow. Our shoulder-breaking load had just become heavier; we now had a full house of seven and a half people, most of who had little to no money to assist us in providing for utilities and groceries. What little currency we did have we owed to our many unpaid bills!

I was quite worried. I did not see how we could afford our new tenants; however, I knew from lots of previous experience, I could always stretch the grocery dollar, and I could create from leftovers appealing and filling *gourmet* meals! Thankfully, we did well on the subject of food; we just did not manage skillfully in other areas!

Never in our wildest dreams had we anticipated my mother moving in with us; and because of not anticipating, we were also not on any senior-citizen housing list, which would have enabled my mom to very soon have her own place.

Upon checking into those accommodations, we discovered they had waiting lists of dozens of names waiting their turn for senior housing. There might as well have been hundreds of thousands! Nevertheless, with a hope and a promise, my mother's name was added to the bottom of the long list! Therefore with no other choice, we were forced to coexist with my mom who could be rather cruel, even on a good day. This my happy-go-lucky daughter-in-law soon discovered.

For our pregnant daughter-in-law to survive during the day while we were all gone to work and school, she would lock herself in our master bedroom where there was a bathroom for her use. Good naturedly she would rest and watch TV all day, and, from time to time, she would sprint to the kitchen for some food. This lasted for about seven weeks until one day our son rushed her to the hospital. After a long and hard labor, our first grandson was born—the prettiest baby ever. Our son and his family chose not to return to our house; instead they moved in with our daughter-in-law's parents who lived in another city.

This left our two daughters at home, alone, during the Christmas holidays. However, it was not long before they, too, packed their bags and chose instead to stay at my in-laws' house. Before exiting our house and leaving their maternal grandmother in their dust, there was something shared with us about my mom placing curses on them! Without much effort she had managed to run them off also!

Nearing the end of December and the New Year, I was beside myself. I did not know who to call and how to improve this awful, declining arrangement! During this particular time in our dismal family life, our home phone had been disconnected due to lack of payment; therefore, for over a year and even with teenagers in the house, we had managed to exist with no phone.

In desperation and with total abandon, I found myself at a grocery store using an available payphone beside the cosmetics department. There I tearfully called my older brother *collect* and begged him to take our mother for at least a two-week period, just long enough to give us a breather. He informed me that all his family had been suffering with the flu; plus, he had no room in which to house her—only his living room couch! Frantically and hysterically, I sobbed that these temporary accommodations would be just fine and that his couch was "perfect" for her—just a few days—please!

I beseeched, I implored, and I even dumped guilt on him. My brother and his wife refused to allow our mother to enter their house due to a previous experience with her. They already knew firsthand how grueling and damaging her presence could become.

In addition, my mom was having health issues. With great difficulty, I would take her along with her Medicaid information to a clinic or to a private doctor, but before she would get into the car to go to any appointment, I was required to move out of our house all her stuff—everything she owned in its entirety. Her every hairpin was packed into her Chevette vehicle and locked; she carried the keys!

When we returned two or three hours later, a move-back-in session would ensue. Reluctantly and with a deep sigh and dread, I would place all of her possessions back into her room, which had become a modified, bedroom version of our formal living room.

Not only was this weekly moving of her belongings becoming a huge dilemma, but with each medical visit, she would consistently accuse the sensitive family doctor of attempting to seduce and violate her while I stood there as a witness, unable to speak out of sheer embarrassment!

After several times of going through these paces, my mother was bringing out the *beast* in me; I just knew I was going insane! I am ashamed to admit this, but in my weaker moments, I would scream at my mom to please not ask what she was requiring of me! However, her mind was not there, and I knew this all too well. But even so, she would still dig her heels into the dirt and would not budge from her point of view or way of handling and exacting certain things.

There was no changing my mother's mind, no reasoning with her; no amount of begging or pleading would make a difference. It was going to be her way; it had always been her way, and now was no different.

It did not matter who was being hurt, who was being imposed upon, who was having to spend money they did not have, or who was losing their mind; my mother basically did not care.

Near the first of the New Year, at last, we received a call from a senior-citizen complex about thirty minutes away in a neighboring small town. They had an opening in a duplex combination just right for my mom. She qualified, and we prepared to move her in.

But first, Dean and I had to go back down to where my mother's brother and sister-in-law lived to get her furniture and other items out of storage. We traveled down seven hours, loaded a U-haul, immediately turned around, and traveled back seven hours! We were wasted; we had become way too old to be doing such backbreaking, heavy lifting, and back-to-back traveling by ourselves!

Once we were back, once again, our heavenly daughters came to our rescue and assisted us in moving this now exceptionally strange woman into her new dwelling! We helped set up my mother's bank account, her phone, transferred her Social Security check to the new bank, and stocked her cabinets and refrigerator. Dishes, pots, and pans were ready for use; her television was set up, as was her bed with clean sheets on it.

We gave her a good-bye kiss; quickly said some encouraging, highly spiritual and lofty words; and rode off feeling good about ourselves! Things would be different now—and we breathed a deep sigh of relief. After their exile, our two daughters moved back into our house. Our son and family would now come by to visit, and our PTSD lives returned to "normal"! Glory be to God!

Isn't it amazing how at times we think our lives are the worst they can get and will ever be, that our lives have reached an all-time level of despair and dreadfulness. Until something new occurs, like my mother moving in, and all of a sudden we see how really great we had it before and did not recognize and appreciate it. But when the new thing, the new predicament arrives at our front door, all of a sudden we know without question we have been driven to the brink of insanity!

After my mother's accomplished move, we were rocking along for two weeks; then it was time for me to physically check in on Mom. Dean went with me this first time; he entertained her while I cleaned her apartment. Bless him.

Just for the record: I would always take my own cleaning products and my equipment with which to complete this cleaning task every single time I went to visit my mother.

At each cleaning occasion, the stack of dishes and other *indescribable items* found in the sink would send out aromas unknown to mankind! Absolutely nothing—not one item—had been washed since my last visit of two or three weeks prior. I would gag, I would heave, literally holding my nose and closing my eyes while I rinsed the nastiness down the drain!

We already know about my mom and refrigerators, so, of course, her then current refrigerator with its looming science projects safe within was no different than the sink!

For several months she would go with us to the grocery store to buy her monthly groceries. It would take us several hours. She was like a child in a candy store! My mom would stop to speak to many customers or staff members or children. We were made well aware that every single aisle held treasures calling to be uncovered and investigated!

When we would finally arrive back at her place, if Dean was not with me, which became less and less often, I would be the one to unload, unpack, and put away the groceries! Exhausted from the trip, she would leisurely remain in her chair, watching television.

I would then proceed to clean her apartment, followed by my traveling thirty minutes home to all my remaining duties there.

As bad a toll as all of this was taking on my mind and my spirit, I pressed onward for over one and a half years. Physically it was hard for me and my family, but emotionally, it was far worse.

What really would hurt and anger me beyond imagination was when she would be insulting by eagerly showing me the previous grocery bill from our last visit with several items circled, accusing me of stealing from her and taking the circled items home. Not once did I even consider doing such a thing, and, of course, she was not taking into account all the supplies and equipment I gladly provided. When my mother would tell me how she had not been able to find this or that grocery item, I would go to the cabinet and show her where those items were; she would then comment, "Well, that takes care of that one. Where are the rest of these things?" And my anger would climb to record highs, as did my blood pressure. All I could do was boil and then cry out internally in exasperation!

After all those many months and months of caring for her by myself, at around ten o'clock one muggy Sunday night, I was returning home alone with the windows open. After church early that afternoon I had arrived at my mom's and had spent many exhausting, grueling hours. But that night I was sobbing and with my open bare hands I was madly banging the steering wheel while discharging all the pent-up anger and frustration that had built into exasperating mountains of stress!

I pulled over to the side of the dark backwoods farm road and allowed myself to empty out all the pain, hurt, and anguish that I had stuffed in order to continue in my support of my mother's life. But I was so weary! My true limitations emotionally, physically, even spiritually, had been reached.

I was spent. I was wasted. I was void of any more willingness to sacrifice myself and my family any longer. I wanted out of this sole responsibility role of mine. I unloaded it all onto God. "You know, God, how tired, how "done" I am! I need help! I need relief! I must have some help here! Listen to me! Please listen to me," I whispered between my vast groans. "Please find a way to help me. I must have some respite, because as you already know–honestly, I cannot carry this load anymore!" And I wept and wailed the remaining way home!

Amazingly, by Thursday of that same week, three o'clock in the afternoon, at work I received a call from my older brother (the one whose home was not available for our mother to visit in the years prior). My mom's housing office had tried calling me at home with no success—they also sent a constable to notify us. As he approached our front door only to find no one home, our dog bit him instead; therefore, they called my brother to tell us our mother had passed away that day. That morning when someone had checked on her, she was found resting in her favorite chair!

In his way God had answered my prayers! At eighty-two years old, our mother was at that moment where she had always wanted to be—next to Jesus; and I could now completely devote myself once again to my unwell husband and to our struggling family structure—our family and our daughter, who was also experiencing and suffering from primary and secondary post-traumatic stress disorder .

However, the real heavy-duty miracle of this occurrence will "knock your socks off!"

In her later years, my mom believed beyond a shadow of a doubt, with no exception to the rule, she would not die like all, average, mortal humans do. She would live to see her Savior return to earth and forever set up his kingdom of which she would be a large part.

Because of her mind-set and these staunch beliefs, she had no need for life insurance, a will, no extra names were necessary on her bank card, there were no unimportant do-not-resuscitate signed forms, no burial insurance or pre-burial plans, and definitely, no need to grant anyone on this planet her power-of-attorney! This worked really well for her because she had huge suspicions and mistrusts of us kids and typically was wary and doubted everyone. She was still doing life her way.

Here comes the miracle part: At the time of her death, I had already been working at a funeral home for ten months. Only because of my employee status, was our family able to bury our mother in a plot of our choice at the funeral home's perpetual-care cemetery, complete with casket, graveside service, flowers, and piped-in music; all for three thousand dollars!

Plus, the company was willing to wait for payment until we probated her estate! Yes, lots of miracles were still happening for us.

Additionally, after I returned to work following the burial, within four weeks, I had a falling out with my superior to whom I gave my two-weeks notice; I was no longer working in a funeral-home capacity within six weeks after her death!

Coincidence? I do not think so! A truly, unquestionable bread crumbs on purpose blessed moment!

God had provided for us and had settled all the agonizing fears and anxiety I had harbored for many decades about what this time in my mom's life would mean to us as a family. Those many questions about how we were going to afford to take care of her in her final years and then those last few days?

Yes, God provided for her and for us; she never spent one day in a nursing home—there was never a need for hospice; and to our astonishment, when her estate was probated, her bank account totaled over $7,000! By accessing her account, she paid for her own funeral and more!

"Thank you, God! We praise you for your care and heavenly provision in all our behalves. Thank you for listening and for showing compassion for my many limitations. Thank you for your heavenly Bread Crumbs on Purpose!"

God Listens and Answers

Our older daughter graduated from the same private Christian school from which her brother graduated. She had done well, she had friends, and she had developed into her own exceptionally, distinctive person. Seemingly her feet were planted solidly on the ground; she knew what she wanted, was willing to pay the price, and chose to attend a university in our city.

We were proud and sought only good things for her, but also we only wanted what she would choose for herself. In our early years, Dean and I both had lived under unhealthy expectations from our parents; we had lived under those expectations, but we had not thrived!

Therefore, we chose not to place those lofty burdens and goals on our children. We may not have communicated those thoughts properly, but God knows our hearts were in the right place.

A four-year college was not a requirement for each of our children. We tried to encourage them toward those goals, but we were just as proud and content when two of the three decided to go to a vocational school.

All we asked of them was to love God, with their children to attend church as often as they could, to become good citizens and to stand by their families.

When this daughter was a baby, she and I became very close buddies. What a joy she was! I learned so much by observing her and her sweet disposition. She was my little anchor, and I enjoyed caring for her. Much of the time she made my lonely days bearable. We were friends!

She was the child that on a particular Christmas, when she was eight years old, she wanted so badly to give her dad and me a Christmas gift but did not have the money. She became creative and uniquely gift wrapped what she found.

That Christmas Eve, her exceptional gift was given to me for opening; as I unwrapped it all I could do was smile and then chuckle over and over again! I was flabbergasted!

Our precious, generous daughter had collected our mail for numerous days and prepared it as a gift! In the Christmas spirit, on the outside she decorated the package with peppermint candies! Pretty ingenious and clever! What a treasure she was that Christmas Eve as she still is today. It was the best gift I had ever received! Daily I was amazed by her.

When this daughter of ours graduated from high school she dedicated her ceremony to her grandfather, Dean's dad, who had passed away three weeks prior. She and her grandfather were close, and she would choke up, with a trembling lip, when she spoke of his death. We know he would have been full of pride and delight attending her notable graduation service.

De'Anna at Graduation

He, no doubt, was the one who rescued her from her grandmother and would show her a measure of kindness because our son was the one who held my mother-in-law's heart and full attention. Even as a four-year-old little girl, she noticed the preferred treatment her brother would receive. Her grandmother would usually leave her for last, as an afterthought.

This bothered my daughter enough to mention the preferential treatment. Many times this behavior I had already observed also. But how does one coerce a person like my brash mother-in-law to choose to do what's right when their heart is directing them to not care as much for one grandchild but to care for the other in huge concentrated servings of fondness and affection?

Therefore, this child and her grandmother were never close, and over the years, their relationship became more strained. Our daughter was obedient, respectful, and compliant, but she was also highly observant, discerning, and very little got past her. Dean's mother only thought she was getting away with her shenanigans!

Ironically, this teenaged-crown-prince son of ours also observed his grandmother and determined at an early age that he would not be leaving his future wife nor his future children alone with her. Fifteen years before my mother-in-law died, our first born had already broken off his relationship with his paternal grandmother due to her prejudiced and cruel ways of reasoning and living!

I have a strong feeling my father-in-law died unnecessarily. I believe he gave up hope for a better life. He desired to travel, but my mother-in-law was not about to take him anywhere, except for perhaps an overnight visit to her family.

He wanted to go places and do as many activities as his physical limitations would allow; but she was intent on saving their money for a rainy day. Instead she chose not release a cent for adding some fun and excitement to their mundane lives. Near the end his expectations withered, and he started not to eat. By not eating and with him being the cook in the family, my mother-in-law was forced to prepare meals for both of them. Without the task being heartfelt, she presented the food in a hateful, unloving manner followed by unkind, spiteful words.

Those many years when we would all have meals together, my mother-in-law would be watchful of everyone else at the table. She would scrutinize how much each person swallowed and would find a way to mention the quantity and calories they had consumed and what that meal would mean to their already expanding waistline.

As my father-in-law limited his food intake, he became weaker. Toward the end, we think he was having second thoughts about what he had purposed to do, but it was too late. He was sixty-nine years old when he died. I believe that even with his many ailments, he could have lived longer if he would have had a partner as eager to live life as he was.

As I stood by his casket in Central Texas, I wept and thought, *What a waste!* The ones that should stay in this world do not, and the ones that should not stay, do. Such an injustice!

I looked at him and whispered, "You really did do it. You accomplished what you needed to do, and now you are with our Savior having the time of your life. Do some 'traveling,' Jack. Bravo for you!"

Dean's sorrow over his father's death did not help his daily life. He grew even more distant and less responsive than he had been before. Our family and his job-maintaining abilities were suffering more each month.

It was not long after Dean's dad had died when his mother began absorbing and requiring more time with him, leaving our family with less. We were also becoming more conscious of the unknown, hidden role his father had played in my in-laws' relationship. Apparently he had been my mother-in-law's faithful sounding board. He had been her daily encourager and would soothe her fears and doubts and build up her self-esteem. Now that he was gone, Dean was his replacement.

There was not enough of my dear husband to go around. It was obvious to me that the little I had of him was quickly dwindling.

Dean's mom was like my mother in the fact that it was of no concern to her how little was left for our family of my husband and our children's father. Without guilt or remorse these two women were selfish enough to send home to us the remaining bits and pieces of a man we so desperately wanted to be whole and ours alone.

It seemed I had become the mistress in Dean's and my relationship, and my mother-in-law had become the most important woman! She managed to persuade Dean to do things around her house that for years he had not had sufficient time and stamina to do at ours; her control was relentless, and I knew I had no chance when it came to competing with her. Sadly enough, Dean had a deep-seated anger quandary when it came to his mom—all too often, it was a love-hate bonding. Because she had not been the mother he so desperately needed; his mother's mother was the one he loved with all his heart and soul. His maternal grandmother had cared for him; she had sacrificed and shown him what a genuine, unconditional love looked like! Dean honored her and still speaks of her today with immense admiration and wonder! His most cherished childhood memories revolve around his times with his grandparents, especially his highly regarded, greatly missed grandmother.

This anger issue towards Dean's mother only became worse after his father died, and she started monopolizing so much of his spirit and strength. It was not until much later before his temper and wrath, fueled by his PTSD, really got the best of him. Unfortunately during the lifetime of his mom, she would never discern the reality of his pain and heartache!

Once in the course of one of our frequent hurricane seasons on the Gulf of Mexico and immediately following the historical Katrina hurricane that came ashore that year at New Orleans, a huge percentage of our metropolitan city evacuated when the area was threatened by yet another impending storm. On national news for weeks we had witnessed the catastrophic devastation in Louisiana; as a sobering result, our hurricane threats had now taken on new meaning and more significance.

Nevertheless, in spite of these forewarnings, Dean and I had decided to stay at our house within the city; soon our son and his family joined us after they were left with no utilities. We later learned that Dean's mother had traveled a hundred miles up the Texas/Louisiana border with a well-meaning friend and his family, taking refuge at another residence they owned.

Apparently to gain this family's undivided attention and undying assistance, my mother-in-law must have played on their emotions by sharing with them how we (Dean) were not caring adequately for her. She was in need—in danger—and Dean was coldly uncooperative through his lack of concern. Her Oscar performance must have been exceptionally effective because soon thereafter we received a fiery call at dinnertime. Our son was on the road doing his job and not present, but his family was. Dean took the call. On the other end of the line was the son, now in his twenties, of his mother's friends who was now demanding that Dean rise to the occasion in the care of his mother or he would teach Dean an unforgettable lesson!

Yes, Mr. PTSD was very much present that day and lodged right under Dean's friendly demeanor. Instantly, Dean was yelling back into the phone with an anger I had not witnessed in awhile. He advised the young man to meet him at his mother's house within thirty minutes so that both of them could "work something out" and this youthful crusader could follow through on his threat of setting Dean straight! We were in for it now!

In a rage, Dean threw back the chair, left his dinner, and, grabbing his keys, he was storming out the front door. I yelled if I could go with him. Fortunately, he bellowed back with the answer, "Yes!" With that we peeled out of our driveway and left rubber at every corner, stop sign, and stop light for the next twenty-five miles.

Nearing his mother's area, there was road construction at one of the exits. Dean turned the car into the road blocks and hefty mounds of dirt after he had taken us down the freeway at ninety miles an hour! I was holding on with both hands and praying under my breath. From years of negative experience, I wisely knew this was not the time to speak or even to pray out loud… (Timing is everything with PTSD!)

We arrived and with tires screeching drove up onto my mother-in-law's front lawn where in the dark she was seen waving us down and smiling with a huge grin on her face and later a chuckle in her voice! We were both baffled by her insolence, but I was not surprised at her smile. That victorious grin I had seen many times before.

With enormous hostility, Dean threw open the car door. I solemnly exited the other side. On her remote, Dean's mom clicked open her electric garage door (now recall, she supposedly still had no utilities), retrieved her purse from her car, and then proceeded to climb into the backseat of our vehicle, ready for us to take her to our house for "party time." From Dean's position outside our car, my husband screamed at her that she was not going to our home, and with that said he walked out onto the black-topped road awaiting his appointment with his mother's champion!

We looked toward the corner of the street, and there slowly coming around the turn was a large truck with its headlights beaming. Dean stood in the middle of the road with a wide John-Wayne-cowboy swagger. The truck pulled alongside with the passenger-side window open, and the young man asked Dean if they "could talk." Heck no! And PTSD hit the fan!

Swiftly Dean climbed onto the running-board and threw half of himself into the truck's cab while attempting to grab with both hands the steering wheel and the driver. To get away from this out-of-control situation, his mother's young advocate gunned his truck. As it lunged forward, and without Dean's hands strongly attached to anything, my husband fell backward out the window and onto the street.

Frantically I reached out, trying to save my warrior from more injury, fearing that he had injured his neck or broken his back, but Dean would not acknowledge my help. While holding onto his left arm, he rose in a stagger and then continued unsure step after unsure step advancing toward the truck that had reached the street's dead-end and had reversed to pass by us one more time.

In the bright headlights, I yelled to him, "Dean, please, stop! You're hurt! We can go—please!"

"No!" he countered. "I still have one good arm. I can kill him with one good arm!" Now like a madman and with his broken arm hanging limply by his side, he continued pressing forward.

In my horror I realized my husband was back in the country of Vietnam. My Rambo had returned there and was fighting for our cause. Under my breath, I whispered, "God, where are you in this?" I knew if God did not intervene we were about to witness a murder!

In a flash, the truck had again reached us, brushing closely by Dean, who stepped slightly backward, but at that instant the young man wisely decided to drive along the edge of a deep drainage ditch to avoid another confrontation. Directly he gained some speed, drove onto the road, and left the ugly scene behind him.

In anguishing pain and with great difficulty, my husband stumbled to our car entering the passenger's side; there he leaned his head against the headrest and breathlessly begged me to take him to the VA hospital for treatment. In my mother-in-law's dark yard, we left her standing, still holding her purse—but no longer grinning—as we turned around and rapidly maneuvered the many miles into downtown.

On the way to the hospital, our younger daughter met us and with us arrived at the ER. Our frantic daughter-in-law had called her when much earlier we had left our house to meet our mother-in-law's mighty defender.

Nine days later, Dean was in surgery for a shattered elbow and a broken upper forearm. He now lives with nine screws and a metal plate in his left arm. The only positive to this story is that not only does Dean's asthma detect impending wet or cold weather, but now his arm is also an indicator as well! In retrospect, Dean regrets this life story occurrence and fully recognizes how his mother manipulated this circumstance and many others to everyone's detriment. In this incident and in the months that followed, we all paid a huge price, but Dean obviously paid a higher cost for the most damages and for agonizing pain and suffering. Post-traumatic stress had dealt him still another blow.

At Dean's mother's funeral in North Central Texas, none of our children chose to attend. In fact, the only ones in attendance at her burial were Dean, myself, and a cousin of Dean's who drove in from West Texas. Her life had touched many people, but on that final day, no one was affected or indebted enough to pay their respects.

I was angry at her large extended family. She had attended in full regalia and had contributed high finances for the funerals of many of their loved ones; she had put many of them through tech schools, had purchased needed clothing, etc., and, yes, she did much of this assistance only for glory and recognition; however, whatever the reason for her support, they owed her a final farewell of appreciation!

I was sad for her. I am sure it was heartbreaking for Dean, but he has never spoken of the hurt and disappointment. How awful those days were for us! I strongly believe every person's life should be celebrated, and they should be honored for having lived and, hopefully, contributed to society's positive advancements.

Nevertheless, what Dean has done because of the many family members who did not attend my mother-in-law's funeral; he has turned it around, and since his mother's death, he has made huge efforts and spent much money to attend each one of the family's burials. (Hopefully, someone is keeping score and has noticed.)

On that cool morning under a metal shelter in the middle of the dried-up, non-perpetual cemetery, the three of us present gathered around her casket along with a funeral director or two. Dean offered a well-meaning prayer, revering his mom's life, and spoke only of the positives and what she had meant to us. Lingering, we said good-bye to her and walked away. Unlike his father's passing, few tears were shed that day.

I fully understood and recognized our children not being able to pay the "price of attendance." In their short lives, they had already paid the price hundreds of times over, but what about Dean's mother's remaining sisters, brothers, nieces, and nephews? Really? Only God knows. Perhaps they, too, had already paid an unknown price.

Within the next few years of my father-in-law and my mother's passing, my aunt died as well. This was the aunt I went to stay with overnight so long ago. She had died suddenly, and the whole family was reeling due to the unexpected loss.

When the extended family flew in to take care of her funeral arrangements, we all congregated at her little house. There was a dozen of us going through her important papers and pictures and dividing up her belongings. My father was pacing from room to room in a daze while wearing my aunt's blonde wig and drinking beer after beer to ease his emotional pain. Of any of the siblings he had been the closest.

Her official will and testament presented me with a couple of her things—priceless items! Her home was part of her estate; therefore, we encouraged our son and his new family to buy the home as a starter house instead of continuing to rent.

He turned it down, saying it was in a bad neighborhood and school district. By the time he made the decision to not buy it, we had already realized we should move into it ourselves.

It is a good thing we did because we were within three weeks of being evicted and having to move due to foreclosure proceedings. No longer did Dean and I have the creativity or the energy and stamina to try to save our homestead. Neither of us had the heart to continue to fight any longer! We gave our dream house up, walked away, and chose not to look back after seventeen years of blood, sweat, tears, and never-ending struggle!

On my aunt's house, we had made an offer to the rest of the family; it was gladly accepted, and we began moving in. It took us awhile to determine what we were choosing to take with us, being that we were coming from a house with over 2,400 square feet into a house of only 850! Yes, it was going to be a smaller-space shock, a culture shock, and a location shock! But we had been blessed and in no way were we going to complain about this "gift horse."

After a foreclosure status on our credit report, we concluded we would never again be able to purchase a house. So when we made the decision to move into my deceased aunt's house, we were appreciative. It was our miracle—our last chance to own property!

To facilitate the move, quite a few things were stored in my in-laws double-car garage, other things were stored in our new home's single-car garage, and many things were just discarded or given away. By the Christmas holidays of that same month, we had pictures on the walls, a decorated kitchen and bath, and our Christmas tree was waiting for Santa.

Simply because we did not have the funds, without adding on or remodeling, we lived in this tiny house for three and a half years. But we did manage to pay it off, and we continued the insurance coverage that my deceased aunt had in force while she was alive.

Dean, in particular, loved this little house; he would brag and say, "I can reach everything in this house by sitting in one spot, and I don't have to move an inch!" It was good enough for him and me.

At this time in our history, I was still working and Dean was working off and on. Our marriage continued to rise and fall—moment by moment, month by month. The misunderstandings and misconceptions ran rampant through the rooms of our miniature house. We were not happy—as happiness goes—but we were committed; each one of us still secluded and bewildered.

Wanting to earn spending money, our daughters began working at an area amusement park on a part-time basis. It was there our younger daughter met her future husband, a fellow employee, and fell in love. In what seemed like no time, she was pregnant and expecting a baby by the springtime season of the following year.

Dawn at Graduation

For over a year this daughter had been in tech school training, taking classes for X-Ray and Lab. Now she had to place her schooling on hold because of the radiation danger associated with x-rays and the possibility of harming the wee child growing within her.

At the beginning when she first learned of the pregnancy, she was having great difficulty making a positive decision regarding keeping and giving birth to this baby. Instead, rather than waiting any longer, within two days she had made an appointment for an abortion. She was not choosing to carry the child full term, nor did she want to go through labor to deliver it.

Today it is her well-known, publicized Christian testimony that the main issue in this pregnancy was that our daughter did not know for sure which of the men she had been with was the father of her five-week-old unborn child.

Needless to say, our daughter did not keep that abortion appointment due to a conversation she and I had concerning this new phase of her life. I vaguely remember some of the aspects myself. Truly I must have been both emotionally and mentally challenged.

Nevertheless, she relates the story in detail and how it impacted her decision; she says that during our talk while sitting at the kitchen table, I had wrapped a small prescription bottle in a dish towel like a baby is wrapped in a blanket, and as I rocked it, I spoke of it as a life, as a part of her, and offered to care for the child until she was ready to accept responsibility, and until she was ready to love it as we knew she would.

We held our breath, and she went through with her pregnancy with both her father and me encouraging her. At the delivery, both her baby's father (and future husband) and I were present and witnessed the miraculous birth of their beautiful, healthy son!

What a glorious day that was. He had not been aborted; he was now occupying a special place in our family! Four grandsons as Fulkerson descendants—what a blessing. Praise be to God!

It had held true: no one in our family was going to be thrown away! As long as we were alive, Dean and I would hold to those principles no matter what the circumstances.

Prior to the birth of our younger daughter's little one, a difficult event occurred that I must include in this story, hopefully to aid for a better understanding of our lives and how God has intervened. This occurrence came about during the summer of 1998, when our daughter was only two and a half months pregnant.

My cousin and I had put together a family reunion for my father's side of the family. It was our first reunion ever, and we were excited about all the possibilities.

Close to a well-known beach resort, we rented a building equipped with a kitchen and plenty of tables and chairs. After the food was purchased, we began our plans for laying out the food and decorating the facility. About fifty or sixty family members attended; it was very much a sensation, and some in attendance were already counting on another reunion.

On a Saturday, about two weeks after our family's return from that success, in the middle of yet another stifling August afternoon, something was said that triggered a negative reaction in my marine husband. He declares that our pregnant daughter and I were laughing at him and making fun at his expense.

He responded with great hostility and his perpetual anger and rage; the more I tried to reason with him to find out what had been said or what we could do to repair the damage already caused, I quickly grasped there was absolutely no room for logic. It was over and done; there was no going back and apologizing. He wanted us out of his face and out the door!

His fury physically sent me out the front door and onto our small front yard alongside the oak tree growing on the left hand side. When I hit the ground, it promptly knocked the wind out of me; once I gained my breath back, I discovered I was sobbing with my face down in the lawn, all the while inhaling dirt. Upon opening my eyes, I remember I could see all kinds of bugs traveling through the root systems and onto the blades of grass.

I slowly started moving my legs and arms and pushed myself up. My head was spinning, but once again as many years before, I did not have adequate time to further evaluate my condition because I could hear my pregnant daughter inside crying and screaming. I knew I must go back in quickly; she needed me.

I managed to stand up, and then I pushed my way back inside the house. Through the living room I ran and into the short, narrow hallway. However, already coming down the hall was my husband pulling my daughter by the hair. He pushed me aside, moved quickly through the living area, and then physically threw her out the front door onto the grass, exactly as he had done with me.

What I had missed witnessing was my daughter holding a large kitchen knife against her father's hostility! With a kitchen towel he had overpowered her grip on the knife, chased her down, and proceeded to drag her in the direction of the yard.

I tried hard to be effective in protecting her, but my husband was massive; I did not have a prayer against his size. For the second time, I again was thrown, this time landing next to my recovering daughter!

I was astounded and speechless after witnessing our two-and-a-half-month pregnant child bouncing across the ground! We managed to get up slowly, both of us weeping and making our way to the front door. Cautiously I turned the knob. It was locked!

In wild-eyed terror, we hesitantly knocked on the door. He gruffly answered and I nervously appealed, "We need our purses and keys to a car." In short order, he produced the purses and keys, and we left with nothing more in our hands. Both of us had been thrown out onto the street!

My two visits onto the yard had bruised my ribcage. I was not sure if it was only bruising, but I was quite sure of the pain. Nearby we had a small hospital emergency room; in response to the standard questions, I said I had been hurt accidentally. The triage nurse called the police to investigate possible domestic violence!

After the policeman spoke to our daughter, he tried to convince me to make a statement with regards to the accident; I ruled against it. No such statement was ever made, leaving my husband's record clear.

The x-rays taken revealed no breaks and my daughter's pregnancy was unharmed as well. We left the hospital and began traveling to find an inexpensive motel room. After stopping several times before finding one available, right away we went to sleep, only to awaken the next day, on a Sunday morning, in the pit of hell!

Knowing full well I had to be at work that Monday morning meant we must go back to our house to get our clothes. It was noon, almost one o'clock, when I stopped at a payphone and quickly called our son to tell him what had happened and where we were headed. I made him aware just in case something else should go wrong at the house; he would then know where to check for us.

On the way there, I was very nervous, very frightened, not knowing what to expect from Dean. However, when he promptly answered the door, he was okay and was agreeable to letting us remove the clothes we needed. We loaded our little car and headed over to our son's home, knowing how disgraceful this all was and how pathetic it must sound and look to someone outside the perimeter.

The next morning I left for work, leaving my daughter in bed for the day while staying with my daughter-in-law and her two children. This arrangement continued for two days until we realized we must make other arrangements for everyone's benefit.

At the motel where we had spent that first night, I had seen a sign suggesting that there were kitchenettes available for a weekly rate. As I inquired I learned that there was one left; we put down our deposit and moved in on a week-by-week basis. I was using my paycheck for this purpose and not paying bills.

By making a trip to a dollar store, I was able to purchase kitchen supplies, including pots and a frying pan, cups, glasses, utensils, etc. Then it was time to go to a grocery store and stock up on some essentials. Something that soon became a major priority was bug spray from Home Depot for the fleas in the carpet and the mass production and miscellaneous trails of roaches in the kitchen!

Many years ago I came across a saying that read, "Until You Spread Your Wings, You Will Have No Idea How Far You Can Fly." At that time, this quote resonated in my world in more ways than one.

We spent three weeks in that below-par motel. I will never forget the experience! I was amazed that I had been able to stand on my own two feet during that time. I had proved to myself I was a survivor. I learned I could provide for myself and my daughter while utilizing my own God-given ingenuity and resourcefulness. Never in my life had I been as alone and scared—however, with God's presence, I was capable of managing my own life and the life of my pregnant child!

On occasion, I would hear from Dean—we would talk while I was at work. After two weeks, he started asking me when I was going to return home. I was flabbergasted! I told him I had no intentions of *ever* returning home!

At the time I had no ingenuous plan, but I was again totally suspicious of his harmful capabilities! I knew in my lifetime I could not—I would not—end up ever again on the front lawn, bouncing upon the ground, inhaling dirt! I like to think he was surprised and regretful. I am not sure if he was! We have never discussed it.

However, during those phone conversations I did not share how afraid I was to live with him again. I did not believe it would make a difference, so I would just keep quiet on the phone and let him talk. Finally, one day he volunteered to move to his mother's home so that the two of us could return and live in our house once more. The door had been opened so to speak, and I took advantage of the invitation.

Knowing how troubled and terribly frightened I was, the decision was made to change the outside locks of our house! Once again I went to Home Depot and purchased two sets of locks. I believe it was our son who installed them; that alone brought much security and peace to my mind and soul.

This was how it remained for another three weeks; my daughter and I were doing well. I was extremely sad and emotionally spent, but I was determined to live on my own for an indefinite amount of time. I now had no choice!

I do not know how long I would have been alone; God would have to have done something different in our lives.

Sure enough, God did have his own immediate plan—and it was nothing that either Dean or I would have dreamed of in a million years!

Be prepared to be amazed!

Dean had been calling and asking if we could at least date every so often. Here I was scared to death of his ongoing explosive temperament and he was suggesting dating! Finally, one day, after his voice and presence seemed quite settled, I said "Yes," and we made plans to go to a movie on a Friday night, the eighteenth of September, 1998. Wow! What a night that would prove to be!

But dating was all it was going to be. We were not going to get back together, not for a very long time, if ever! This post-traumatic stress disorder thing of which we still knew nothing about had done a number on me and our family. I needed a whole lot of time away to regroup and heal from many, many injuries and scars. I felt like a walking infirmary.

In years gone by, I had gone back to Dean numerous times, but landing in the front yard had been my wakeup call! That violence caused me to feel more stupid and ridiculous for living with him than any of the other injuries. I did not want to feel brainless and pathetic anymore. I needed a change, a new view; I needed a brand new Sandy in my life!

And our young daughter needed the assurance that her father's love included restraining himself from acting out in anger and threatening the life of his unborn grandson! Mothers can absorb many things within the marriage, but when violence is shown toward our children—that is, when we become warriors! No one messes with our kids! No one!

Dean and I went to a movie—and as we were walking back to our car, Dean's pager began sounding off. Several times on our way back to the house, it continued to signal an incoming call.

At last, I asked Dean to pull into a gas station where I decided to return the number listed on the pager. When I placed the call, our next-door neighbor gently informed me that our house had caught on fire and that six fire trucks had just left our neighborhood! Denial set in; I could not grasp the picture; I was speechless!

For the next fifteen minutes, we drove in a panic until we arrived at our street! There we found our daughter, her husband-to-be, and our next-door neighbors, each wanting to tell us the story and to show us by flashlight the shell that was left of our house.

The story was that our daughter and her boyfriend had decided to give our Maltese dog, Tucker, a bath. The dog was in the warm tub, lathered down, when they heard an explosion coming from the other side of the house. The boyfriend being a curious person decided to go see what had happened, but our pregnant daughter begged him not to leave her because our dog never liked baths and was relentlessly clawing to escape the tub!

After reassuring her, our future son-in-law left the bathroom, quickly checked outside, and discovered billows upon billows of smoke exiting our small one-car garage.

Immediately he yelled for our daughter to call 9-1-1 while he turned on the garden hose and courageously attempted to put out the flames that were well on their way to rising even higher than the tallest fifty-foot neighborhood trees.

Because of the closeness of the small houses in our chosen neighborhood, there were six fire trucks called, and everyone living within blocks was all standing on the streets watching this enormous residential fire. Yes, our house was on fire and going up in smoke!

By the time we arrived, there were no longer any fire trucks, no nearby neighbors, all utilities had been disconnected, water was dripping from the gaping holes in the ceilings and the walls; what was left of our house was in shambles. Our homelessness was now official; my daughter and I had nowhere to live!

My husband invited us to go to his mother's home—we had no money to do anything else—and we were sincerely appreciative that we had any option at all available to us. So off to grandmother's house we went.

The next day was a Saturday. We called the insurance company, and I called and broke the news to my coworker who was in charge of my employer's office. We then waited at our burned-out house for the insurance adjuster who by appointment was to meet us there.

Our son came to offer any assistance, and our kind next-door neighbor ran an extension cord from her house, providing us with a fan to help with the still existent summer heat and humidity.

The adjuster agreed with the fire department's assessment and documented that the fire had started in the garage with a faulty gas water heater; that was the loud explosion our daughter and future son-in-law had originally heard. From the garage, it spread through the attic to the entire remaining house—850 square feet did not offer much resistance.

The adjuster left forms for listing all our furniture, clothing, and household items, encouraging us to list everything down to the dog's bowls and chew toys, and gave us tips as to how to calculate the cost and replacement values.

He informed us regarding the process he would follow in filing our claim. He alerted us as to how much money we could expect for living and out-of-pocket expenses, and then how much we could expect for rebuilding, if that was what we chose to do.

This man was amazing; surely he was an angel in disguise. Without his coaching us, we would not have received the amount of money we did—and God knows we needed all of it.

After spending most of the day at our destroyed house and keeping our insurance appointment, we realized we needed clothing if we were going to church the next morning. We wanted to thank God for the total tragedy which he had spared us from experiencing. Our daughter and son-in-law-to-be could have been killed, as would our unborn grandbaby. The house was too small to not have been engulfed in flames in seconds. Instead, our daughter called 911 and for a couple of minutes stayed on the bedroom phone as requested by the operator until she was forced to evacuate through the smoke-filled rooms.

Promptly we visited a twenty-four-hour K-Mart to buy clothes and shoes for our daughter and myself for Sunday morning's service. That morning, as always, I sang in the choir and lit up when our son and his family entered the sanctuary. In support our family filled one and a half church rows, because that weekend a measly residential fire had not defeated us!

As the praise and worship service started, I was flying high that morning! My God was the "bestest" God ever! As we sang a particular song again and again, I literally flew down the stairs of the platform; grabbed my husband, my son; and started leading a march around the perimeter of the church sanctuary!

As the music played, more of our circumstance-knowing members joined in our "Jericho March" until we had encircled the interior of the church two or three times. We had been spared! We had been blessed! *Our testimony was that God was good, all the time!*

On that same Sunday and in the weeks to follow, we were given donations upon donations from many individuals, from my employment, from the church, and last of all, a church shower was held for us to replace needed sheets, towels, and miscellaneous household items!

Nevertheless, much of our life was lost in that fire. Besides losing furniture, lamps, area rugs, linens, etc., we lost keepsakes, the children's handmade Christmas decorations, and many pictures, and even the priceless letters written to one another during our Vietnam War era!

Within the next two weeks we had a "fire sale" and sold much of our remaining fire-smoke-and-water damaged possessions, including our mattresses. In so many ways, it was a nightmare! In *the natural*, we had been stripped yet again!

What we did not lose by moving into a tiny dwarf-like house from a very large one, we lost in this all-consuming fire. Much of our life as we had known it was gone; we were starting over. Our marriage was starting over as well. Now, without a doubt, we were back together as a family, ready to face the unknown future.

Much of the above documentation makes it sound like we were feeling no pain in this transition. Quite the contrary! We were hurting, we were grieving, we were sobbing, our losses were gigantic, but we were alive and together!

In these tragic times, we swiftly realize that life can always be so much worse than what has just happened to us! Yes, things were awful, but we could have been planning funerals for our loved ones instead of worrying over lost furniture and sheets!

Our unity was strong once again; after all, *we were the "Fulkerson Flock" and flocks wing it together!*

Miracle upon Miracle

After the Friday night fire, by Sunday afternoon, the three of us agreed with unified certainty we must find a better place to stay than my mother-in-law's home. She needed us out of there even though she had two extra bedrooms, and we needed out also to maintain our sanity. Another large reason we needed to relocate was to keep Dean's mother from knowing our daughter's quickly-becoming-obvious pregnancy secret.

Our daughter-in-law had generously taken on the task of finding a suitable apartment for us to lease. We gave her an approximate location within the city, and she stayed online and on the phone until she found a couple of complexes that she felt would work well for us.

While I was working, my husband, my daughter, and my daughter-in-law visited several of these apartments, finally deciding on one in particular. Afterward, I joined them at the apartment office, looked at the downstairs, two-bedroom, two baths, patio unit, signed the papers, and walked out without writing a check for the customary, *always required*, two months of advance apartment rent!

This metropolitan city apartment complex already knew our family's unusual circumstances; therefore, they took us under their wing and allowed us to move in without a dime being exchanged! They took us at our word and believed us when we said we would be receiving some insurance money within the next two weeks. Another miracle!

The available apartment was ready for inhabitants. The utilities had not been disconnected; therefore, for the next two weeks our utilities were furnished free of charge.

We loaded what little we had left and said our thanks, waving good-bye to my seemingly stressed-out mother-in-law. By the Tuesday after the fire, we were moving into our new apartment. The floor plan was more than adequate for the three of us. Our daughter was now four and a half months pregnant and doing much better than she thought she was.

During the year and a half that we lived in this apartment complex, we had an occasion that became yet another embarrassing instance in the lives of the Fulkersons. Because we had had old, broken-down cars for many years, we believed we needed to upgrade and trade in our dull, ancient-gold-metallic van for something more reliable.

After looking in the newspaper for several days, I called a dealership and was put through to a salesman who in the end became a "member of the family." We arranged a time to meet and chose a great-looking car—perfect for me. The understanding was for us to bring in our trade-in the following Saturday. Our salesman was graciously calling our trade-in van *his* car. (Aww... bless him!)

The day came for us to take in our van. One of the requirements was that it had to be able to *roll* into the dealership. This we were confident it would do, so we hopped in and began our journey to pick up our new car.

A few months earlier, our van had been vandalized while innocently sitting on the apartment complex parking lot. As a result, we already had plywood over one of the broken, elongated rear windows. Hey, it did not good, but it kept the rain out and the most-of-the-time, but not always, air-conditioning in.

One of the other things our van was missing was its rearview mirror. That item was nicely resting on the floor between the two front seats. I knew it was important for the van to have a mirror for safety and cosmetic reasons, so I tried *gluing* it back on! As I applied additional glue, it continued to slide down the windshield leaving a trail of white Elmer's Glue behind. No amount of time of holding it in place made a difference; its weight was working against me. Finally I gave up, leaving the infamous mirror on the floor; however, on the windshield remained a huge big glob and smear of Elmer's—it was obvious to the world the vehicle desecration that had transpired!

As we arrived at the gate to exit our apartments and begin our journey, for this task we already had a documented system in place. The shotgun passenger, me, would run around the short nosed front of the van; I would swiftly punch in our code and then run like the dickens back around again, flying into the van before the gate closed! This was all necessary because Dean's driver's side window would not go down and amazingly nor would his door open from the inside.

When we pulled into the dealership, our salesman was already outside, waving recognition. We stopped; he yelled, "Is this 'my car?'" And we hollered back, "Oh, yeah, it certainly is!" Knowing in advance that Dean was going to need to exit the vehicle through the double-doors on the van's side, we parked indiscreetly on the car lot where no one would see us. Clandestinely, my extra-tall husband folded himself in half and stepped out through the side doors. We completed remaining paperwork; they gave us a generous trade-in allowance only because our van "rolled in," and then our salesman nonchalantly asked us to bring our rundown van around to the front of the showroom. His manager needed to drive it! Dean and I hopelessly looked at one another. With an assured smile for our new family member, we plodded back to the van and brought it around; hoping a gigantic parking-lot hole would soon open up—burying us with our humiliation!

Oh, yes, the manager was able to enter the van through the driver's door—after that we looked away because we knew he would not be able to exit. He looked at the mirror and windshield, looked at the broken-out window, looked at what used-to-be gold carpet and beautiful leather seats, and then dripping with sweat, he jumped out through the double-doors on the side; we were mortified!

Everyone smiled. We were given the brand new keys, and even though we now had a fancy rearview mirror mounted with great glue on our spanking-new windshield, we never looked back!

As soon as we settled into our new living quarters, we began searching for a reasonable contractor with equipment to bulldoze our worthless, burned-out house, purposely leaving us a cleared lot on which to rebuild. Of course, for rebuilding, we needed a homebuilder as well. Fortunately, I had a job that allowed me to spend quality time on the phone making calls, checking prices, and scheduling appointments.

Finding a homebuilder that would modify an established, existing blueprint was a trick. Until on a weekend, we walked into a builder's office where a single employee was working on that Sunday. Just the day before this lady employee had modified an existing blueprint for another client. We discussed what we needed due to the measurements and configuration of our property and, thus, how we needed it built and what we would like to have included; right there she created our house! That was the last time we saw her—we know God had her there just for us.

Blueprints were drawn, money was funded by a credit union and we began choosing our brick, roof shingles, paint, hardware, lighting, carpet, etc. Within six months, it was finished, and we moved in! During our one and a half years in our miracle apartment, we had again become grandparents, this time to an awesome little kid with big brown eyes; dark, thick curly hair; beautiful, long eyelashes; and a charming personality! Our daughter's Medicaid pregnancy, long labor and difficult delivery had produced a bundle of joy. Our son-in-law-to-be was still a part of our family and completed the fatherhood necessary for this delightful baby boy!

Within six months of moving into our brand new miracle house, we had a remarkable wedding and a cherished baby dedication for our younger daughter and our spanking new son-in-law. They paid for much of the wedding and reception, for which we were grateful. Our guest list included our friends and theirs, working colleagues, and church members, all rejoicing with us over this positive ending. For their honeymoon, the new bride and groom went to San Antonio; we gladly kept the baby while they were gone. They lived with us until our daughter began working in her field of radiology and lab, at which time they moved into their own apartment. However, for the next several years, regardless of where they lived, their marriage was in turmoil. I am not quite sure why, perhaps due to a lack of maturity on both their parts. We helped in funding their expenses; we counseled and encouraged them until we could counsel, advise, and encourage no longer. We posted an arrest bond, we helped pack to move them again and again, and we ran interference all hours of the day and night.

At long last, they were both working and earning adequate money when they decided to buy a small brick house in a subdivision about fifteen miles away from us. After a while, church attendance became a thing of the past. Usually on Saturdays we babysat their two children with additional hopes that the parents would be refreshed on Sunday morning and able to attend church themselves. Instead, they took these opportunities to drink, to do drugs, and to stay out with friends until the wee hours of Sunday morning. There was definitely no church for them the next day.

For numerous years, we took our daughter's children with us to Sunday school and to Wednesday night service. These two children became active in the church's girls' and boys' programs, and for several years, our tiny granddaughter became an accomplished ballet dancer as a result of the dance classes into which we enrolled her.

I am so appreciative that our daughter and son-in-law allowed us to do these things for their children. We enjoyed picking them up from elementary school; taking them to What-a-Burger for hamburgers, milkshakes, and chicken fingers; and then caring for them until either their father picked them up or we would take them home later in the afternoons.

For two consecutive years we were Santa Claus and Mrs. Santa Claus for the children's elementary school. It took many hours for hundreds of children to file through for the purpose of being posed with huge smiles on Santa's weary, numb knee, as their pictures were taken. Most of the fourth graders—some taller than I—chose to sit on Santa's worn-out knee; and Dean, by now sweating profusely, but loving every moment, would gladly accommodate each and every one!

An exhausted Dean was absolutely thrilled to do this for his grandkids! And our grandchildren never told any of their friends that Santa was truly their grandfather.

Sadly, things were not going well in our younger daughter's and son-in-law's lives; these kids were struggling to pay bills. However, their limited money was being used in other directions, such as, their times out with friends after work or on the weekends, the three or four packs of cigarettes a day that our daughter was smoking, etc. Many of these darkened roads were leading them into a downward spiral, one that swiftly led to debilitating pain, poverty, and destruction. There were certainly no *bread crumbs on purpose* on those lost pathways.

Then in just a matter of months, God answered our prayers, and swiftly it all began coming together. First of all, our daughter began inquiring and making plans to attend a Bible school in our great state of Texas! Promptly she was accepted, and the packing and scheduling activated, as did the leasing of their three-year-old house. Even their pet dog, Pepper, was given away to a new home.

I was so relieved, but I could hardly believe it. The godly change had been so drastic and so complete! Having run out of ideas, Dean and I had stepped back, removing our hands from what was taking place in our daughter's and son's lives. It seems that only then was God able to come to their rescue, having spoken marvelous words to their hearts and souls and through the Christian actions of others.

Because of God's intervention, our daughter, husband, and family have completed their third year at a Bible college. They are licensed, have a bachelor's in leadership and pastoral ministry, and soon will also be ordained as ministers. Now there is also talk of a master's degree and points beyond.

At the end of this year, we will be involved in moving them once again, but this time it will be to Phoenix, Arizona, where their godly calling will begin, and there others in need will also be blessed by what God has created anew within their lives. Isn't it *crazy awesome* what only God can do?

After speaking on numerous occasions to her college's student body assemblies, early this year our daughter wrote her testimony for publication in the institute's monthly, worldwide magazine. Her testimony has been circulated around the world regarding the hand of God on her young son's life and how God's spirit intervened in preventing her older child's abortion.

Our daughter currently has several speaking engagements scheduled, and many others she already has to her credit. Her miraculous personal testimony is still in progress, in addition to their ministry's vision of providing a center for those many teenage women and young adults choosing instead to walk away from abortion clinics. Our children are in hopes that this center will be in place in the very near future. Other aspects of their ministry will be crisis pregnancy centers, teenage purity emphasis outreaches, as well as offering a hand to homeless teenagers. And there are extended plans to open additional centers in Florida and Pennsylvania.

Dean and I are humbled by what God has miraculously brought into our lives!

A couple of months before our younger daughter moved with her family, our son had already moved with his family to the northeastern portion of our state. After being laid off from his job as a long-haul, eighteen-wheel truck driver, our son and family experienced a drastic, sobering year of questioning God's direction and provision. Amazingly, prior to that year of retrospection, he and his two sons had been involved in the moving of our daughter and family into their nice three-bedroom, two-bath apartment in one of their Bible college's family apartment complexes. One year later we were also moving our son and his family into their nice three-bedroom, two-bath apartment within the same building as the one our daughter's family was still occupying! Within the next two years, our son and his wife will also be ordained as ministers and will be graduating with a bachelor's degree in leadership and pastoral ministry with a focus on missions!

Our oldest grandson is currently participating in online ministry training and is part of a team assisting in the crusades of a national and international youth evangelist. God is good—*all* the time!

The above two moves away from our area left me, Dean, and our longtime friend, Mr. PTSD, alone in our house! No more overnights, no more Sunday dinners, babysitting, dollar movies, spur-of-the-moment trips to Galveston with the grandkids, eating out as a family, no more attending church together, etc. The silence, the strain, the awkwardness, and the aloneness was deafening and would bounce from wall to wall, room to room, while the *three* of us endeavored to find a place of our own and a way to live abundantly and successfully while doing so.

For several years, my job had been my salvation. I had a place to be each day and a schedule to keep. Our newer second car had been repossessed. Life was still hard.

In the end, I had fun employment as a fine arts secretary for a high school. There I worked hand in hand with choir and band directors or drama and drill team instructors. I scheduled fundraisers to raise money to fund students' competition trips for band, choir, drama, drill team, and speech. I also made reservations with hotels for end-of-the-year awards ceremonies complete with all the trimmings.

However, the best part of all was actually traveling with these awesome kids (many from low-income families) on these trips and being present while they performed, winning against strong and advantaged competing schools, and proudly bringing home multiple, hard-earned awards and trophies!

On certain days of the week, Dean would take me to work and pick me up in the late afternoons. Yes, I would worry about him during the day—home alone—but emotionally I was not prepared to quit working and to live twenty-four-seven with Dean Fulkerson and his post-traumatic stress all day.

Then one afternoon I had a rude awakening when Dean started telling me about how he had spent his day. I had already brought him up to speed on mine, and I then inquired about his.

He described the morning and then began explaining how he had pulled a lawn chair onto the middle of the driveway facing our backyard. There he sat in the middle of the day, in the sun, by himself, for an undetermined amount of time—yelling to no one present. Out of loneliness, he was yelling, "Hey!" And louder, he yelled, "Hey!" And even louder, he screamed, "Hey!" Our eccentric next-door neighbor looked through her blinds to see what could be wrong but decided to do nothing. There was no one around to talk to, no one to answer him.

On other days, close church friends would call, checking on Dean and graciously praying over the phone.

Because of Dean's personal experience and restoration process, we have since learned the hard way that each vet suffering from war trauma must be held in loving hands in order that he or she might be able to deal with their current life—in preparation for the healing and recovery of trauma that will soon begin. We must be prepared for re-experiencing trauma during counseling, which has the potential of causing lives to become temporarily worse before they get better.

In Dean's last days of trying more employment and attempting to make his life work, he was not sleeping but three hours a night and then working nonstop all day. By June of 2003, Dean was finished; he had no more tolerance for life. After admitting to himself he could no longer rise to the required levels of employment, he confided to me that he fell apart realizing he could no longer handle what he had experienced in war.

Dean knew his life was about to change drastically, but he was not sure what form the unknown was about to take. When he first started his weekly counseling sessions at The Vet Center, occasionally his counselor there would call him to check in. She was concerned that Dean would end his life any one of those days; she was shockingly perceptive.

For this book, Dean's story has been modified, portions left out, because he has been asked by counselors not to share his complete story. They have heard in detail his wartime experiences and feel that much description, places, and names will affect other veterans in their disability applications. Each application must be verified for its validity and held in confidence until the process is a proven accounting.

I have honored my husband in his confidentiality request. No published book, no awards, will entice me to risk his life and privacy by retelling his story in its entirety. Dean's personal story and his mental health are worth more than reaching out to the lives of others, even though that is "our heart and soul's mission."

Just recently has Dean begun to heal; his five senses are beginning to be restored, as are the little things that act as triggers to his memories of those events gone by. They, too, are experiencing a healing and a true recovery.

However, just three nights ago at 3:00 a.m., his nightmares were so powerful that from a dead sleep his kicking in bed landed him in a sitting-up position, breathing hard, his heart pounding in terror, and sweating freely. As Dean puts it, "Our sheets looked as though *the circus had just left town*," due to the aggravated wrestling that ensued during those most recent night-time experiences.

I knew what my decision to retire was going to mean in my life. I knew this decision had the potential of being one of the loneliest choices I would ever make.

I recognized all too well what I was jumping into. PTSD was *not* my friend, and I was aware of the impending isolation for both of us—one from the other.

Nevertheless, I also knew I had no choice. If something had run awry and Dean had an accident or if he lost his senses with no one there to be aware and to assist, I could not have lived with myself! The guilt would have ruined my remaining life; recovering from this self-centered act of working and ignoring his cry for help would have taken its toll on the rest of my days.

Therefore, I did the deed—I retired! I informed our high school principal of my decision, and though we professionally did not enjoy each other's company, he was gracious in telling me I could return to his employment if I ever changed my mind.

Dean, I, and Mr. PTSD began our daily existence together.

At this launching of our retirement, I stayed busy. There was a lot to do, a lot to catch up and organize, a lot to clean, a lot to paint.

Until one day, it was all done. I looked at myself and wondered, "What now?" I also asked myself, "How am I going to live like this? Oh, God, where do I go from here?" I am a person of purpose. I must have purpose for my life to be worth living!

PTSD was in the house—huge post-traumatic stress was still in the house! The only way for me to stay in the house was to stay busy. But I had run out of things to work on, and PTSD was gaining on me. Now I could not stay ahead of it because by this time, Heaven forbid, I had become idle.

Yes, the day had come when Dean could no longer punch an employment clock; he knew and I knew it was over. He had reached his limit. The mountain of negatives had stacked; he had pushed himself until there was nothing left. Everything was gone except for a thin shred of dignity.

This huge man had been reduced to a vacant shell of his former self as a young man. His spectacular sparkle was gone, the driving force and the twinkle were gone along with the belly laughs and the energy and ambition—gone like sand in a storm. Against our wills, our dreams had leached out and died.

Then one day I asked him again, as I had fifteen years before, "Can the VA (Veterans Administration) help us in any way? Surely there's something they can do now!"

With that inquiring question in his arsenal, he sucked up his small amount of pride and tried the VA one more time. By walking through those challenging doors, we knew he was running the risk of further humiliation and being bluntly told for the third time that there was nothing for him there except pain management and water therapy! However, as if mandated, he found his way to what was called the Peas Clinic. It was there he learned about PTSD and was skillfully directed toward counseling at one of The Vet Centers within our metropolitan area.

Miraculously, his counselor at The Vet Center became a close friend. He proudly says of her: "Jesus saved my soul, but '——' saved my life!" She counseled him once or twice a week as needed for a year or more until the day when he was ready to enter group therapy.

In group therapy when he started there was a total of twelve veterans in Dean's group. These twelve guys bonded like Gorilla Glue! They began going on fishing trips; they would go to breakfast or lunch at every opportunity. They would giggle and heehaw on the telephone like teenagers! Truthfully, I was turning "green" with jealousy.

Already Dean had received not only a VA disability but a Social Security disability as well. As a result of these rulings, he had advantages like The Vet Center connections, the VA psychiatrist,

VA medications, and the government dentists, dermatologists, eye doctors—yes, the government recognized the veteran and was there for his lifetime.

However, on the sidelines stood Sandy, hoping to be acknowledged at some point in her married life. She needed a turn also. I had paid a price as well—a huge price. Why wasn't someone on hand to help me?

The Vet Center counseling was a service that was offered to me because of Dean's client connection; however, after mentally walking through the paces of such an initial visit, I decided that my seeking such therapy would have taken away from Dean's recovery. I will never know if this decision was a correct one, but this valuable and available counseling was declined.

Then one day we learned that there was going to be a class for the wives of the vets in Dean's weekly therapy, as well as other in-session Vet Center groups. We as spouses and other family members were all invited to attend. How exciting was this—I could hardly wait! At last I was being acknowledged, and it felt so good. This class had been formed just for me as a wife of a combat trauma veteran!

On a late Monday afternoon Dean and I arrived at the location. The facility was a renovated downtown motel that was then currently housing homeless veterans. Our group leader was a lady whose job was to work with the homeless veteran population.

At that first meeting, several of us walked into a very small motel room into which we heard the air-conditioner humming and saw a table tightly surrounded by a dozen chairs. For several weeks, we were to gather there while our husbands continued building friendships downstairs in what had been the main lobby of the old motel.

The first day of this class, binders were handed out. The title on the binder in black and white was something like, "How to Love Your Combat Veteran," and decoratively on the side was a picture of a red rose. Each week I was dutifully present and accounted for, until the third meeting. Midway through that historical last visit, I came unglued! As our group leader began presenting the chapter for that week, I felt this churning inside my gut and as it kept rising, it was becoming stronger and larger. I knew at the rate it was building, I was about to be in trouble and out of control.

Not wanting to create a scene, with great determination, I cautioned myself, "Sandy, get hold of these emotions *now*. What is going on with you?" Unbelievably, in the middle of everything, without warning I pushed my chair back against the motel wall and stood up, while breaking into sobs, I excused myself by loudly gasping and stating, "I cannot do this. I'm sorry, but I cannot do this!" With that, I left my opened binder on the table, grabbed my purse, ran out of the room, slamming the door behind me. No one followed.

The doors of these second-floor motel apartments opened outside onto a modified, roof-like, walk-around area. Leaning against the wall of one of the other rooms, I cried and wept uncontrollably, not knowing why I was suffering so and not knowing how I was going to get out of there with some decorum still intact.

Somehow I did see my way clear and stumbled onto the makeshift elevator and down to the first floor. As I rounded the corner to the main lobby, I was then more of a basket case than when I first started. Everyone present was deeply concerned, but I gave no explanations; immediately Dean helped me to the car, and we left.

I did not return to our group's meeting the following week; I had no intention of going back. I was through! But I still did not know why I had reacted in such an intense and profound way. I analyzed and scrutinized over that week and the next. Why did I react in that manner? I had to know.

Then one day my puzzling answer was unearthed, and at last it was clear as day! For the first thing, I objected to the title of the course on the binder; but most of all, I objected to the focus of the group on the veteran and how we as wives were requested to further understand the trauma (PTSD) in our spouses. To our soldiers we were to give additionally of ourselves…to dig deep, as in endlessly loving them through their post-traumatic stress disorder.

Yes, I fully understood all this. I got it, honestly I did!

However, by that instance in our marriage, we had been married thirty-nine years as had others within this special group. I had been through a great deal of trauma and violence. I had weathered many storms and was for all practical purposes still in one piece! However, now I was being schooled in 1) loving my combat vet, 2) further understanding his trauma, and then I was being asked to 3) give even more of myself—more than I had already given to this thirty-nine-year marriage! What? Really?

Believe me, I had nothing (*absolutely nothing*) left to give. I was used up and dry. I was so dry I was curling like dried mud! Numerous times I had bled out, and no one had seen my pain or my impending death! "When?" I screamed. When *was* it going to be my chance to receive what I needed—before I became more like the walking dead? Please tell me, where was the class being held for me—to piece me back together as the caregiver? I roared and agonized for a lifeline, a transfusion of life and hope!

For several weeks, I held my ground; I deliberately refused to return to the classes still being held. Dean was kindly supportive of my decision.

But before it was completed, back to that class I returned because I am not a quitter, and I had to prove to myself that I could stick it out. With clenched teeth, that is just what I did!

It was shortly thereafter when I called Dean's counselor at The Vet Center and asked what she thought about an idea of mine. Was there some way I could acquire the phone numbers of the wives of the veterans that were in Dean's therapy group? Some phone numbers Dean already had, but not all.

The big day came when I was ready to phone these wives, of whom I knew nothing. I took many deep breaths, and with a lot of hope, I left messages, spoke to some of them, inviting them over to have dinner and to see where our acquaintances would take us.

This was the beginning of our organization entitled WINGS. I could not believe it; five or six of these wives actually came over! We ate and laughed, and often through tears we told each other our stories. We learned by the end of the evening that we were all married to the same man; we were married to the PTSD iron man!

Post-traumatic stress disorder was alive and well in all our households; because of this disorder, all our veteran spouses acted and reacted in much the same way.

Each month we met—and slowly our grass-roots group grew to include others. I had absolutely no training or experience in leading groups, especially stress groups. Therefore, in the beginning I used 3x5 index cards to write down a word that I thought was of importance for us to know, using Webster's definition and a scripture focusing on the same word. As I became more familiar with leadership, I graduated into 4x6 index cards. Over a year later at one of our monthly meetings, I was feeling like I could fly; feeling like I could soar into the heavens! With Dean and his life, I had been *in the trench* for so long, but now with new found friends who understood my daily challenges and concerns, my hurts and suffering, I was rising *above the trench* of limitations and darkness. Yes, I was soaring above, looking down, and I dearly loved the view and the lofty sensation!

Thus, I described my feelings to my new battle buddies and asked them to consider naming our group WINGS, instead of what we had been called up until that time; we had been known only as "The Vet Wives." "However," I confided to my friends,

"I don't know what WINGS will stand for." We needed an acronym. In no time at all, one of our more enlightened members volunteered, "Women Inspiring Noble Gracious Spirits"; we all stared, with our mouths wide open. None of us had in mind anything more glorious than that! So it was, on that day, WINGS became "W*I*N*G*S"!

Soon after the christening of our support group, late one night I was on the computer looking for possible clip art that would be of value to us as a logo. I typed in *wings*, and Bingo! There on the computer was a pair of pure white, crystallized, feathery wings with a perfect, bright red heart in the middle. It became exactly what I desired to say to the world about this fantastic support group. Yes, we have W*I*N*G*S to rise above the trench of PTSD. Yes, we can soar to special places where we can live and love, where we can grow, but we will always have a love and a heart for our combat soldier. We will remain devoted to them and our relationships; we will have their back—we will have their six—because we love them unconditionally, no matter what the trauma, no matter what their disabilities involve and bring into our lives!

It was not long before we became more acquainted with the organization entitled the Disabled American Veterans or the DAV for short. After Dean became a member and started attending regularly, with him I attended a Midwinter Conference in Washington, DC. From that point on, I, too, was hooked!

Once I heard about the House bills affecting veterans' benefits, once I hiked up to The Hill and walked the long, daunting, marble halls of the offices of our House of Representatives and Senators, met with their office representatives, pleaded the cases and crisis of disabled veterans and their families, toured the cafeterias and ate lunch among government dignitaries, the "movers and shakers" of America, and visited the basement gift shops and post offices complete with the official White House stamp, I returned home with a new zest, a new energy and initiative. I was officially and passionately on board!

All too soon we became officers in our DAV Chapter and Auxiliary Unit. What an honor and privilege that has been! Of course, our organization is not perfect—there are politics and large egos involved. But there is also a passion, an urgency, for keeping veteran affairs before Congress, and God knows this government of ours needs reminding every moment of every day what the cost of freedom is—yes, the home-front debilitating cost of liberty and independence!

Our government must be reminded every minute about the price that is being paid by our youth and their parents, our soldiers and their spouses, our warriors and each one of their children, and it continues on to encompass the generations of their grandchildren and great-grandchildren.

Heaven help a country that forgets its soldiers that have defended that country's flag and have bled and died or have returned to their homeland as a double or a triple amp, blind, disfigured, bed-bound, and a PTSD and TBI sufferer.

Oh, yes, there's tragedy and loss, which are the aftermath of wars, and there is struggle and trauma and pain, and most of us will rise up quickly and say it is worth all of it and we would gladly do it over again! However, it is only worth it all when our country and our government recognizes and sincerely honors the sacrifices and the afflictions brought about by that dedication and allegiance. All too often, we must sound the trumpets to be heard above the din and clamor of our government's elections and re-elections.

Brave on, Disabled American Veterans, Veterans of Foreign Wars, The American Legion, Vietnam Veterans of American, Texas Vets, etc. Sound the alarm, blast away; make whatever noise necessary to wake up this dear land of ours, until our country's defense and those who defend it are more important than budgets, political agendas, or military careers!

"Dear Father, hold close to your heart these your children, and minister new life into their beings, into their souls and spirits. Direct them in your ways, move them into your paths of *Bread Crumbs on Purpose* that will guide them into good decisions, into straight and narrow godly directions. Securely hold their hands for the essential reassurance of your presence and comfort.

"You know their pain; you know the destruction that PTSD has left in its wake. Soothe and heal their wounds, calm their fears, and hold them "in the palm of your hand" that they may receive and bask in the peace and serenity that only you can provide and so willingly bestow.

"Father God, go before them, walk beside them, carry them when necessary—but always be present in their lives. Thank you for your patience and grace and mercy, for they will follow us all the days of our lives that we may dwell in the house of Our Lord forever and ever. Amen."

What I Know Now

Throughout my life, I have looked to God and trusted him to bear me up when my body and soul was stuck in the mud and the morass, in the sludge of life and its challenges and limitations. God has carried me when there was no light and no way out of dire circumstances. Because of his presence I have never been forsaken; goodness and mercy have surrounded me everywhere that I have journeyed.

There is a wonderful, meaningful story behind the gorgeous lotus flower. Its story is an awesome one because this plant grows in mud and yet rises above the surface of the swampy water in which it was created to bloom with remarkable beauty. It is often confused and mistaken for the lily pad, but the difference between the two is extraordinary. Needless to say, the lotus flower is exquisite and much more beautiful!

From the very beginning, the roots of the lotus are buried beneath the mud in murky waters on the bottom of a pond or river. In time, it pushes itself out above the cloudy water reaching for the dazzling sun where it then blooms in radiant glory.

This plant with incredible strength grows in spite of its life in the muddy swamp—the quagmire of marsh, mud, and compost.

Many of us also began our lives in shadowy and gloomy waters with limited available resources and limited futures. On the surface we did not have a chance because our roots began at the bottom of society's ladder. As children we were below the bottom of the river; for many of us we did not have "a hope or a promise!"

Nevertheless, with unbelievable strength we grew in spite of our humble beginnings; we grew toward the sun (Son), and only because of God have we developed into something amazing; we have bloomed and brought beauty and positive living to this world. Above all and more surprising, the lotus flower is untouched by the impurity around it. This flower symbolizes the purity of heart and mind. It represents beauty and success and not just survival.

Yes, we can all become more than what we were born into—more than the seemingly out-of-control tragedies that occurred as we were growing up.

The story of the lotus is my hope for us all. I have a desire for us to rise above the trauma and difficulties of life. Yes, we should still remain who we are, who God made us, but from there we can continue to grow, becoming much stronger in our spirits, our resolve, and our emotions.

Trauma silences our voice. It steals our stamina and creativity. Our talents wither or remain dormant when we are pressed to our limits and can no longer rise to what life requires. Post-traumatic stress smothers what God has created in us, who he designed us to be. Through our giftings our Lord has endowed a piece of infinity. We are unique and given abilities no one else has; to do the work that no one else can do. God has plans to grant us abundance in life; let us look to wellness and wholeness. Let us be inspired!

The following scriptures have been blessings to me; my hope is that you, too, will find comfort and peace from reading them:

There is a scripture in Psalms 57:1–2 (NIRV) that reads:

> I will find safety in the shadow of your wings. There I will stay until the danger is gone…I cry out to God, and he carries out his plan for me. He answers from heaven and saves me. He puts to shame those who chase me. He shows me his love and his truth.

Or in Psalms 91:4-7, 9-12, 14-16 (NIRV):

He will cover you with his wings. Under the feathers of his wings you will find safety. He is faithful. He will keep you safe like a shield or a tower. You won't have to be afraid of the terrors that come during the night. You won't have to fear the arrows that come at you during the day. You won't have to be afraid of the sickness that attacks in the darkness. You won't have to fear the plague that destroys at noon.

A thousand may fall dead at your side. Ten thousand may fall near your right hand, but no harm will come to you. The Lord is the one who keeps you safe. So let the most high God be like a home to you. Then no harm will come to you. No terrible plague will come near your tent. The Lord will command his angels to take good care of you. They will lift you up in their hands. Then you won't trip over a stone.

The Lord says, "I will save the one who loves me. I will keep him safe, because he trusts in me. He will call out to me, and I will answer him. I will be with him in times of trouble. I will save him and honor him. I will give him a long and full life. I will save him."

In Isaiah 40:29-31, we read,

He gives strength to those who are tired. He gives power to those who are weak. Even young people become worn out and get tired. Even the best of them trip and fall. But those who trust in The Lord will receive new strength. They will fly as high as eagles. They will run and not get tired. They will walk and not grow weak.

Many of us find ourselves weary and fearful, lacking in trust and faith, alone in many areas, with no one available to share in life's load and responsibilities.

We discover ourselves outdistanced by PTSD and the negatives it brings. During those times hold to the above scriptures, practice living in the midst of them, wrap your heart and mind around them, and look to God—look to salvation.

As often as I can, I walk the beach. Having grown up on the coast, I love the ocean, the sand, and the wind. It is at the beach that I find God in huge doses. I find God in every unique, one-of-a-kind wave along with each seagull and each sea breeze. It is there that I am free of cares and difficulties. My mind becomes clear, the menacing cobwebs are destroyed, and I can soar into heavenly places.

There is an encouraging saying that reads: "Happiness is a summer ocean breeze, sand between your toes and your best friend by your side." For me, nothing in this world can beat that!

Discover *your* place of restoration. Where is it that you can be rejuvenated? Uncover your renewal spot and allow God to bathe your spirit and soul into recovery. Just ask your God, and you will receive!

There is a Cherokee legend that describes the rite of passage for the Cherokee Indian youths—the passage from childhood into manhood. And it goes something like this:

The Indian youth is taken by his father into the forest in the evening, where he is blindfolded and left alone. The youth is required to sit on a tree stump the whole night and not to remove the blindfold until the rays of the morning sun shine through it.

He cannot cry out for help to anyone. Once he survives the night, he is a man.

He is required to not tell the other boys of this experience because each lad must come into manhood on his own.

The boy is naturally terrified. He can hear all kinds of noises. Wild breasts must surely be all around him. Maybe even some human might do him harm.

As the wind blows the grass and earth and shakes his stump, he is required to sit stoically, never removing the blindfold. It will be the only way for him to become a man!

Finally, after a horrific night of terror, the sun appears, and he removes his blindfold. It is then that he discovers his father sitting on the stump next to him…

His father has been watchful the entire night protecting his son from harm!

We, too, are protected by God throughout our dark nights and are never alone regardless of our circumstances. Yes, God is watching over us—while sitting on *the tree stump* beside us.

Moral of the story: just because we cannot see God does not mean he is not there.

Before the going gets tough, take God's promises to your emotional bank and there build a spiritual reserve.

It was not by accident that our WINGS support groups or our post-traumatic stress disorder seminar outreaches are entitled W*I*N*G*S. This designation was authorized by a heavenly mandate. There was a future plan for the restoration of these groups and for the godly involvement in bringing it to pass.

This year we have begun our eighth year of WINGS within the metropolitan Texas city of Houston. These women have assisted in my wellness, in my renewal and recovery. They are the ones for whom I was crying out to God so many decades ago, but then was not the designated time. I was not ready; I had not yet arrived at my *healthy* destination where I could fully connect with others who are destitute while living in fear and despair.

At this moment in time, I can only hope that I have learned and experienced what is required to reach out to someone so deep in the chaos of PTSD—and hopefully I have enough of the compassion, the empathy, and the concern to make a difference, to make *the* difference for someone else who is as lost in the PTSD realm as I was just a few years ago.

We are currently holding seminars for active-duty servicemen and their families as well as retired military and veterans from all branches, all conflicts, and of all ages.

We have also been blessed with a Christian couples' ability at website design. After much time and patience W*I*N*G*S is on the Internet and will become available to many who seek further awareness and support. (www.wingsptsdsupport.org and www. winsptsdgroups.com)

Post-traumatic stress disorder knows no boundaries—it is no respecter of persons; every one of us qualifies. The phenomenon of PTSD will lead anyone's life into the grasp of suicide and will wreak havoc in a marriage and family by way of domestic violence and abuse of various descriptions. It will addict each one of us to alcohol, illegal drugs, or prescription drugs. If nothing is done to avert it, in a heartbeat it will ruin our lives, those of our caregivers, and destroy our future generations.

Many of us have carried a foundation from childhood on which post-traumatic stress disorder due to combat war trauma or other of life's traumas could build. We already have been traumatized and distressed over childhood circumstances and incidents. PTSD events in our adult lives can then adhere themselves to that already laid foundation and can, therefore, become more intense, more powerful, and longer lasting.

It is to our advantage to seek professional help when we discover that we are unable to help ourselves effectively and that, possibly, we are heavily relying on self-medications to move forward through life.

You may ask, "Are yours and Dean's PTSD concerns over? Are they gone forever?" No, they are not. They still plague Dean, me, and our marriage harmony. A main reason this is true is this PTSD mental/emotional disorder became deeply embedded over many years of receiving no intervention from recognized VA medical facilities.

Early intervention is the secret. It is the key to restoring normalcy to a combat warrior's mind and spirit. It is for this reality that Dean and I have reached out with an urgency that surpasses all else in our lives. We want no other soul to experience the anguish and hopelessness into which we lived for decades.

It is not necessary to undergo such trauma when with some knowledge, some support, friends who fully understand our difficulties, and through prayer and trust, a new and thriving vitality can take over where there has been little to none before.

The *enemy of our soul* would like nothing better than for each of us to continue in our anemic comfort zones, our self-induced isolations and tight-fisted seclusions. The less we talk about the PTSD demons, the less light we shine on this trauma, and the more secretive our wounding remains in the closets of our souls, then the longer we will be tormented by a disorder that knows no ending. As the years pass, the syndrome will continue gaining strength, size and momentum as it lies festering within our hearts, minds, and souls.

Dean and I are more than willing—we are *driven*—to make ourselves available at any hour of the day or night in order to rescue just one life, one marriage, or another relationship between parent and child.

Dean and Sandy at a Houston Astros Game -
Throwing the "1st Pitch" Honoring the Military!

There is an old quotation that goes, "If you're okay, then I'm okay, *but if you're not okay, then none of us is okay!*" Many of us already know that within a PTSD-impaired household, we are all attached at the hip. If our warrior is okay that day, if he or she has survived that moment, then our household has the potential of running smoothly; if not, we will all be challenged.

Sadly, our children can recognize a traumatic crisis before we do, and they suffer in unspeakable ways when this stress is raging uncontrolled as a roaring lion within their home. They have a small, all too often silent voice—unable to speak, to protect themselves, or to change for the better their daunting surroundings. Instead they hide under beds and in closets, covering their little ears and eyes in hopes that everyone will be spared, just one more time— one more day!

When there is a PTSD elephant in our homes—in basically every room—and children are present—because children are *not* resilient, it is imperative for their well-being and healthy development to remove this syndrome when possible or to at least begin the restoration process.

What exactly does the term "well-being" mean? I looked it up the other day; in his dictionary, Webster states the meaning as follows: "When something is in good or satisfactory condition— or comfortable." (Perhaps comfortable in their own skin— perhaps at peace?)

Our dependent children must live with the decisions we make in life, whether these judgments are well made or not. With their futures in mind, let us search our hearts and resources to bring about a healthy life for this generation and the ones to follow.

To this day our own two older children have *well being* issues due to our past PTSD elephant. This elephant is real—*very real!* It is a fact that it has dealt misery and self-esteem issues to both of our older children and will to yours also if it is ignored.

However, one may think that his or her children are different. That they are tough because, perhaps, they are military kids! But are these endowed children tough enough to stand against an angry, PTSD irritated, provoked parent? A parent who is not in control of his or her own body and raging vocabulary?!

Really? Can our children honestly withstand our decision-making *collateral damage?* Or are they the helpless recipients of our untimely selections in life—perhaps good or perhaps bad?

Therefore, we must consider and reflect deeply about what we are and are not doing. We must provide a "safe place" for our children and even our grandchildren. We must seek help for our post-traumatic stress disorder disabilities—our children's lives depend on which options, which directions, we choose.

I would like to encourage each of us to choose to wake up on the other side of tragedy. By doing so, we can all be used of God in unbelievable ways. Needless to say, it is obvious that our spiritual enemy does not want us being used for God's purposes and plans.

However, when we are no longer a crushed victim of circumstances, then we can rise to the occasion with our heads held high—held high into the heavens. Beyond a doubt, we know where to go for the rescue of others. Because we have lived it and succeeded in it—we have thrived. We are then victors and no longer victims because now we are well. Praise be to God!

Let us together become a success story—not a survivor's narrative!

When I pray now, I come boldly into the throne room of God, making my requests known, knowing well that the answer for our darkness and our fear is there and also knowing God is always available and *he is good and on time all the time.*

Eight years ago when I was a mess, I was terribly sad, had no self-esteem; even as a Christian *my back was to the wall.* There were no answers for me as I cowered in a corner while waiting with expectation for the next blow!

Today you, too, may discover that your back is to the wall and that you have no hope and nowhere to turn because things are so messed up and dirty; even though you know without a doubt that the arms of your Father encircle you and that you are never alone. Perhaps it's because you have been the *point man* at the front of the battle; perhaps you have been tragically and dreadfully wounded.

Are you living in fear and trembling? Are you afraid of "bleeding out" because no one has noticed how hurt and broken you are; please communicate with me via our website and email. There we also have a phone number for your convenience. I will do all in my power to make a difference for you; you already have my heart, my devotion, and my focus!

Together we can become friends. Without a doubt, I know if I had had someone in my past to have called upon, what a huge advantage that would have been in my life. I can become that person for you. I think you will be both encouraged and inspired!

There is a song we sing during our church's praise and worship time about being a *friend* of God's. Some of the words are as follows:

"Who am I that you are mindful of me—that you hear me when I call?

Is it true that you are thinking of me? How you love me; it's amazing!"

He does care; we can all trust in Him! We are "friends" with the Creator of the Universe! His love is the banner that always leads us "home."

In Psalms 69: 1-3, 13-17, David the psalmist was truly going through it; he was having a tough time! Some even say that David was battle scarred and had been dealing with combat trauma, post-traumatic stress, himself! While reading the following verses, please also remember the beauty and the strength of the lotus flower and its fragile petals.

> Deliver me from the mire and do not let me sink; may I be delivered from my foes and from the deep waters. May the

flood of water not overflow me, nor the deep swallow me up, nor the pit shut its mouth on me...turn to me, and do not hide your face from your servant, for I am in distress; answer me quickly!

But Lord, I pray to you, may this be the time you show me your favor, God answer me because you love me so much. Save me, as you always do. Save me from the trouble I'm in. It's like slippery mud; don't let me sink in it. Save me from those who hate me. Save me from the deep water I'm in.

I would like to include a poem about how well our Lord is capable of taking care of us:

On Eagle's Wings

You who dwell in the shelter of the Lord,
Who abide in His shadow for life?
Say to The Lord, "My refuge,
My rock in whom I trust."

And He will raise you up on eagle's wings,
Bear you on the breath of dawn,
Make you to shine like the sun,
And hold you in the palm of His hand.

The snare of the fowler will never capture you,
And famine will bring you no fear,
Under His wings your refuge,
His faithfulness your shield.

And He will raise you up on eagle's wings,
Bear you on the breath of dawn,
Make you to shine like the sun,
And hold you in the palm of His hand!

The Marine Corps of which Dean proudly belonged is quick to declare that "Once a marine, always a marine," and I like to add to the quote, "Once a marine's wife, always a marine's wife." I say all this because we are so "gung-ho."

When our spouses are committed to the military forces of these United States, whether they are in an enlisted role or perhaps they have a commission, regardless of which branch, the whole family has been recruited as well. It is unrealistic to think that one part of the family unit can be dedicated to the preservation of our country while the other component serving at home is not affected.

Recently we attended the memorial service of a dear, close friend; a military man. He began his career at sixteen years of age when he was allowed to join the Merchant Marines. Later he continued his profession by joining the army for a total of twenty-seven years before ultimately retiring. He proudly served in World War II, Korea, and Vietnam!

However, his wife and daughter served also. They kept those home fires burning and provided the necessary balance that soldier required to facilitate his MOS (the soldier's military occupation status) and lifestyle while in the military.

Below is what was included in our friend's funeral program of November, 2011. We enclose it as a remembrance and an honoring of this dear dedicated serviceman:

What Is a Soldier?

By PFC. Fuller

It is not the drill, nor uniform, badges
Or weapons that make the soldier,
But that spirit of self-sacrifice for a cause
Which he instinctively feels he must follow,

Which urges him on toward a goal he may never attain,
Or, reaching it, may receive no further award
Than the knowledge that through efforts
Known only to himself,
He has added to the greatness of his country
And to the security of his race.

"Where the civilian pays in gold, the soldier buys in blood.
Where the former seeks material gain –
The good things of this earth –
The latter seeks an ideal which frequently
Can endow him with no immediate benefit.
It is for this reason—
The staking of his life for an ideal –
That right through history,
Which is itself but a relation of wars,
The soldier stands forth preeminent
Among the crowd of lesser men."

The following is enough to say for both our departed comrade and his family: "It was well worth it all. We accomplished the mission—oftentimes, the impossible mission. Nevertheless, our country remains free, and we as a family unit, afforded through much blood, sweat, and tears, the means by which *Lady Liberty* shines brightly and reigns supreme."

In a previous segment, I mentioned my desire to share information from the U.S. Marine Corps. I would like to honor that statement at this time. My husband is proud of having chosen the U.S. Marines; we feel the ethics of this organization are worth supporting in this way.

The Marine Corps' Principles and Values:
Honor, Courage and Commitment are the values that guide us—Semper Fidelis is the motto that bonds us. To guard our nation is to guard its principles, becoming not only an elite warrior, but also a noble one.
Core Values:
Honor = A Code of Personal Integrity
Courage = When other Principles are tested, it's Courage that prevents them from crumbling. It isn't ignoring fear, but being stronger than fear.
Commitment = Commitment is the Spirit of Determination found in every marine. It is what compels marines to serve our nation and the Corps.
Semper Fidelis: Distinguishes the Marine Corps bond from any other. It goes beyond teamwork—it is a brotherhood that can always be counted on. Latin "Always Faithful," Semper Fidelis became the Marine Corps motto in 1883. It guides marines to remain faithful to the mission at hand, to each other, to the country, no matter what. Becoming a marine is a transformation that cannot be undone, and Semper Fidelis is a permanent reminder of that. Once made, a marine will forever live by the ethics and values of the Corps.
Our Purpose is Our Promise: We make marines. We win our nation's battles. We develop quality citizens. These are the promises the Marine Corps makes to our nation and to our marines. They are the reason for our demanding recruit training process. They form our reputation as America's force in readiness and are honored through the reciprocal commitment, between the marine and Marine Corps, expressed in our motto: "Semper Fidelis."
In the last analysis, what the Marine Corps becomes is what we make of it during our respective watches. And that watch of each marine is not confined to the time he spends on active duty. It lasts as long as he is "proud to bear the title of US Marine." General Louis H. Wilson, 26th CMC, 22 August, 1975

Within the pages of two manuals we are privileged to use often in our faith-based seminars and support groups, we find a quotation by Dr. Jonas Salk, the developer of the polio vaccine. It is as follows: "I have had dreams and I have had nightmares, but I have conquered my nightmares because of my dreams."

Valued hope and dreams are the precious serum containing antibodies to be used against PTSD. As we manage to keep these alive, we are well on the road to recovery. Our quality of life becomes strong and healthy. Then as we include a little love and devotion, our warrior and his family grows invincible!

Another anonymous quote about hope is: "Hope *sees* the invisible, *feels* the intangible and *achieves* the impossible." What an inspiration to us all.

Our fantastic military ministry manuals ("The Combat Trauma Healing Manual" and "When War Comes Home") are published by Military Ministry Press in Newport News, Virginia, 2007 and 2008.

On Page 214 in "When War Comes Home," the military spouse and family manual written by Rev. Chris and Rahnella Adsit and Marshele Carter Waddell, there is an educational story about artisans in Italy entitled *"The Beauty of Brokenness"*—please read with me as I close:

> "You are probably well aware of the fact that your journey to new normal will not be easy. As you and your husband work to salvage usable things from the rubble that the war left behind, it is important to be realistic in your expectations. But it's also important to see the process through the eternity-filled eyes of God. It can be a painful, sometimes shattering process, but the end result is *absolutely beautiful!*

"In a certain region of northern Italy, artisans in many of the villages produce beautiful vases, each piece fetching a very good price due to the skill that has been passed down from generation to generation.

"But there is one particular village that produces vases that command ten times the price of any of their neighbor's goods. The vases are so valuable because of the crafting technique the artisans of this village use. They make the vases just as all the other villages in the region do, *but then they smash them, shattering them into dozens of pieces.*

"Then, with the greatest care and skill, the artisans laboriously reassemble the vase, using glue that has been mixed with gold. When finished, every golden vein contributes a magnificent element to the vase, adding immensely to its beauty and value.

"This process is very similar to what you are experiencing currently. Your husband's combat trauma has shattered your life in many ways, but the eternal artisan (Christ) is in the process of rebuilding both him and you. And every re-glued crack, every scarred-over wound will contribute to your beauty and value in ways you cannot yet fathom.

"This is probably why the resurrected Christ retained His scars, even in His glorified body. For all of eternity, they symbolize something beautiful to each of us who were saved by them, to all the angels who observed his ultimate sacrifice of love and to the Father who observed the obedience of His only Son.

"So will your scars—seen and unseen—be gloriously beautiful?

"You and your husband have been in some dark places since his traumatic experiences downrange. You are both probably still fighting your way out of that darkness toward your new normal. God's desire is to help you. The sentiment of what God said to his servant Cyrus can be a promise to you as well:

I will go before you and will level the mountains;
I will break down gates of bronze and cut through bars of
    iron.
I will give you the treasures of darkness, riches stored in
    secret places,
So that you may know that I am The Lord,
The God of Israel, who summons you by name.

Isaiah 45:2, 3 (NIV)

"He knows your name. He knows your husband's name. God has called both of you. He'll see to it that neither mountains, gates of bronze, bars of iron or the blackest darkness will keep you from where He wants you to go. And there are treasures hidden in that darkness He wants to give you. As you receive them, you'll know for sure The God of Israel is the one who has been with you in that dark cave of trauma. *Those who have never entered the darkness will never touch those treasures.* But He's holding them out to you.

"May God give you the sight to see the treasures meant for you; accept them and use them for your healing and for the glory of the kingdom of God.

"And may the golden veins of your restored soul be evident to everyone for all eternity."

Sometime things fall apart so that other things can fall together.

—Unknown

In conclusion, a special prayer:

At times I see glimpses of the man I married, the one with whom I saw a bright future before the war came home with him. The occasional pleasant conversation or the gentle touch of his hand or even that infrequent shared laugh fuels my faith and keeps me believing that you (God) still raise the dead. Father, I ask that you will allow me to see more of my husband—the one my heart misses and loves—from time to time in the months and years of healing still on our horizon. These reminders of what remains enable me to do the work of reconstruction (recovery) and of finding our "new normal."

In Jesus' name. Amen.

Epilogue

Dean Fulkerson
Sergeant, E-5
US Marine Corps: 1965-1969
MAG 11—DaNang Air Station
Vietnam War: 1966 through1967
Communications/Teletype and Radio

Dear Friend:

Unfortunately, I will have this one shot at providing my insight. I imagine I'll rewrite this conclusion several times a day for the rest of my life.

Originally, Sandy and I dated, fell in love, and thought of a scheme to honorably get her out of the circumstances under which she lived. However, while standing in the yellow footprints in San Diego, California, at the Marine Corps Recruiting Depot (MCRD), I thought, *"Boy, Dean, you've really done it now!"*

Just a while ago I was asked what I wanted to be remembered for; after some soul-searching, I think my answer would be, I would like to be remembered as a mentor. In today's soldiers' experiences of having large numbers of daily suicides, my heart is literally worn on my sleeve. There is a sense of urgency under which I live, wanting to reach out and to make a difference to just one more; to help prevent another unnecessary suicide, to waylay another senseless domestic violence episode. So I ask you, "Are you my one?"

Sandy and I desire that the young soldiers of today not wait so many years to get the help they need. Sandy's father was in the army, and my dad was in the navy, both during WWII. My experience in the Corps and my dad's in the navy had its caustic moments. Then our having to wait so many years without help definitely marked all of our lives.

The alarming rates of losing veterans from WWII, Korea, 'Nam, and now Iraq and Afghanistan to suicide are very serious. I feel the politically correct stance that our US Government has taken is tragic and disastrous.

In addition, I believe with all my heart that we *are* a Christian nation—in these last days, I believe we should be an ally and support system to Israel.

However, in all of this, I also feel there is a frustration and stress of living in these very same last days. I often wake up in the middle of the night preaching to hundreds of thousands of people about what we need to do to prepare for the difficulties threatening our country. (If this offends you, I do apologize.)

The message I would love to communicate to our warriors, ladies and gentlemen, is to talk about your PTSD with a professional or with someone who has been through similar traumatic, wartime encounters.

I think Sandy has written this book is such a way as to not be so serious minded that it will turn you away from our idea of this becoming a useful tool for the beginning of your recovery.

I look forward to the future with great optimism—a future where you will receive the assistance you deserve. Please become more motivated to learn about your PTSD. On this subject, vast reams of knowledge are coming forward every day. I encourage you to join a service organization that helps veterans. Their publications will assist you in finding the latest information pertaining to past conflicts, or current medical discoveries, and sometimes stories about people who would love to communicate with past military friends.

I recently had two of my children speak at one of our seminars as to their growing-up experiences in living with my PTSD—

they were to speak with no holds barred. Wow! I am very ashamed of myself! I had no idea the harm that was caused—talk about a reality check of myself, of my life. But, ultimately, this was good for me because I needed to hear the truth from their perspective!

I have had to stop talking and have started listening, and my wife of almost forty-seven years would probably agree with this fact. I can truly say that teaching an old marine new tricks rings true and is benefitting my life.

In looking back throughout all that we have put ourselves through, I often wonder if every portion was necessary for us to conclude where we are today. However, in looking back to thirty-five years ago, I do not see how we could have crammed anything more into our lives.

While watching the movie, *Forrest Gump* and his remarkable story, I look at my life and ask "Why?" Perhaps the question "why" was for me to mentor other folks forward with, "'Do as I say and not as I have lived.'"

Yes, we have been "through the mill," but through it all, we have tried to stay in church while keeping our focus on God. As a testimony as to what God can accomplish: By this year's closing, Sandy and I will be licensed ministers through The Fellowship of Ministers and Churches, a division of Christ for the Nations Bible Institute located in Dallas, Texas. In this way God has smiled and showered his blessings upon us. "Lord, now set us aflame for your glory!"

My wish for you today is as follows:

If you do not know a Savior *who can walk on water, one who can take all your wrongs and use them for his glory*, please give me the future honor of introducing you to my Jesus and a sinner's prayer of forgiveness.

Always live in such a way that at any moment's notice, you will be able to answer the call when the final bugle blows and Christ returns for his chosen people. Yes, with a huge smile and a bursting heart, I will joyfully meet and ecstatically greet you in heaven—*at our final home.*

Go with God in *all* you do…

Sincerely,
Dean Fulkerson

Have I not commanded you? Be strong and courageous! Do not tremble or be dismayed, for The Lord your God is with you wherever you go!

Joshua 1:9 (NASB95)

Resources on Post-Traumatic Stress Disorder

The PTSD Condition—
A Continuing Information Guide

My husband, Dean, had "a pronounced fear of being hurt." He had been emotionally abandoned as a child and again as a teenager and had determined to never be hurt again. His maternal grandmother was his salvation during a young life of aloneness and obscurity.

"The internal turmoil it creates makes them miserable, wanting to trust and feel connected, but not daring to out of fear of additional suffering."

After Vietnam, PTSD compounded the issue already at work:

> They will admit to wanting close emotional relationships but are comfortable living without them. If you betray or significantly wound them, they will simply write you off as "no longer existing."
> Banks, Jim. "*The Effects of Trauma and How To Deal With It.*" *House of Healing Ministries, 2011.*

The Veterans Administration's Motto—
Mission Statement:

"To care for him who shall have borne the battle, and for his widow and his orphan." Abraham Lincoln

It is a professionally documented fact:
There is no time limit for recovery from post-traumatic stress disorder; however, PTSD is treatable, and, if treatment occurs early, individuals can recover. In addition, prayer and trust in God's Word and promises will also promote and bring about recovery.

Post-Traumatic Stress Disorder: Why Is It That Not Everyone Develops PTSD?

The reason is probably a combination of factors. The two most obvious are: 1) the intensity, duration, and number of traumatic experiences, or 2) the person's mental interpretation of the experience.

Other Contributing Factors to PTSD

More exposures to recent horrific events; greater level of personal involvement in a traumatic event; current stressors—any lifetime major stress event; the individual's personality; a level of anxiety higher than average; history of severe traumatic events; reminders of overwhelming childhood traumas; strong feelings of personal responsibility for what happened; intense feelings of guilt; feeling as if one was "outside" his or her body or "in a movie" during a traumatic experience.

—The Vet Center
Government Veterans Affairs
Readjustment Counseling Service Guide

PTSD Conditions Focus on Survival

The brain interprets the original traumatic experience as extremely dangerous.

The brain generates powerful, intrusive memories and images of the traumatic event.

These intrusive thoughts discourage a person from going near that type of event again.

People with PTSD go to great lengths to avoid any stimuli, emotions or conditions that remind them of the trauma.

The brain also causes the entire system to go into a highly aroused state and to be "on the lookout" for even the slightest hint of a traumatic event similar to the one that produced the extreme stress reaction of PTSD in the first place.

Thus, "survival" is ultimately behind PTSD even if that survival comes with the cost of being in pain. (All too often this severe pain can include multiple marriages, the abandonment of children and the disconnection from immediate and extended family members.)

—The Vet Center
Government Veterans Affairs
Readjustment Counseling Service Guide

Stressor Determinations for Post-Traumatic Stress Disorder

What is post-traumatic stress disorder (PTSD?)

Post-traumatic stress disorder (PTSD) is a condition resulting from exposure to direct or indirect threat of death, serious injury or a physical threat. The events that can cause PTSD are called "stressors" and may include natural disasters, accidents or deliberate man-made events/disasters, including war.

Symptoms of PTSD can include recurrent thoughts of a traumatic event, reduced involvement in work or outside interests, emotional numbing, hyper-alertness, anxiety and irritability. The disorder can be more severe and longer lasting when the stress is a human initiated action (example: war, rape, terrorism).

Fact Sheet—New Regulations on PTSD Claims July 12, 2010 Department of Veterans Affairs Washington, DC

PTSD is the overwhelming of a soldier's ability to cope with the horrors of an event or events. Usually at least one person has died, and, therefore, intense fear is introduced into the warrior's system, causing an adrenaline rush—a "fight or flight" reaction. All bodily functions are directed toward the extremities to prepare for a survival mode.

However, in the combat soldier, this arousal system that causes a racing heart rhythm and stressed heavy breathing never shuts off, causing difficulties in his body, mind, and personal relationships.

War Zone Stress: For Active-Duty Military

Intense stress reactions in combat are very common.

Mentally and physically fit military personnel can have powerful stress reactions to horrific events.

The traumatic stress reactions are directly related to the event.

Traumatic stress symptoms do not indicate some internal weakness.

Intense stress reactions do not mean that you are going crazy.

The frequency and intensity of stress reactions often become less distressing as time passes.

Psychotherapy is not always necessary to recover from traumatic stress.

Intense or prolonged stress reactions may interfere with home life and the performance of normal military duties.

Intense and prolonged stress reactions may also interfere with unit cohesion and unit performance.

If distressing symptoms continue beyond three weeks, PTSD is more likely.

If one's ability to work, to perform tasks safely, and to take care of oneself and one's family is disrupted beyond three weeks, stress intervention and psychological treatment may help to restore the balance and get the person back to normal functions.

Effective treatments are available.

Military events that cause traumatic brain injury (TBI), typically bomb blasts, are extremely stressful to experience. TBI can be present along with PTSD, and the symptoms can overlap. Accurate diagnosis of TBI'S and PTSD and effective treatments are essential.

—The Vet Center
Government Veterans Affairs
Readjustment Counseling Service Guide

Post-Traumatic Stress Disorder

The common response to an uncommon event has been the same reaction shared among hundreds of thousands of veterans returning from the war zones throughout America's history and beyond.

"It is estimated that 400,000 Vietnam War vets suffer from PTSD—undiagnosed and untreated. Other estimates are as high as 1,000,000! Estimates state that only 23 percent of Iraq and Afghanistan military has sought help, thus far, for their mental health issues.

"We have a new generation of veterans struggling to adjust to a life interrupted and forever changed by war."

Readjusting to Postwar Society: Troubled Homecoming—by Thomas Childers, VFW Magazine; April, 2009

PTSD and War Veterans

"Most of us like to believe that we'll always be led by our own well-defined moral compass. Those who have been in war, or "warriors"—as the military may refer to them—have lost this sense of innocence or naiveté. They have seen firsthand that war is hell, and they know that soldiers do things they never believed they could possibly do—things that go against the kind of personal values and morals that may have led them to serve their country in the first place.

"But these soldiers became capable of doing such things because the military trained them to disregard their moral compasses. They were encouraged to adopt the mantra that you either kill or you'll get killed. Many realize later—sometimes months after they return home—that they're being plagued by flashbacks or nightmares filled with the faces of those they killed.

"Because of the nature of their trauma, these veterans will suffer more symptoms than most PTSD sufferers and may come to experience soul wounds.

"Dr. Edward Tick and Dr. Jonathan Shay, who have both been treating Vietnam War veterans for decades, strongly believe that soul wounds should be seen as an aspect of PTSD stemming from combat. They have heard many veterans speak with great emotional pain about how they felt their souls or fundamental selves slip away after killing someone for the first time. Drs. Tick and Shay also believe that if these veterans don't take action to bring their souls back, many will suffer an identity crisis so painful that it could lead to suicide.

"Perhaps you are seeing something akin to this in your own partner? While this is undoubtedly frightening for both of you, understand that the soul's drive is to create and preserve life. War is the antithesis of this. If your loved one marched forth into a war zone, he likely did so propelled beyond fear by the idea of doing something for a higher good—perhaps not only for the country, but for other people of this world, too.

"But once beyond the fury of battle, the people that he killed may no longer be seen as the enemy, but merely as people who were trying to defend their homes, families, and homeland. Now perceiving those killed as sharing his humanness, the agony of the veteran begins. Furthermore, your partner may be plagued by something called survivor's guilt—for living through the horrors of war when buddies did not.

"…many a war veteran returns to the civilian world with no real sense of who he is after breaking a personal ethical code. He is trapped in the emotional pain of a moral dilemma that seems irresolvable. Therefore, for true healing to occur, the veteran must confront painful questions. He must be able to tell highly personal stories saturated with raw emotion—emotion he has very likely been struggling to squelch instead.

"However, this emotion must be allowed to surface for the combat veteran to be healed. But because he believes this could prove emotionally overwhelming, he may turn to alcohol and drugs to keep the feelings at bay, ultimately exacerbating his problems.

"If you're the partner of a war veteran, you must try to help your partner engage in deeds that are creative rather than destructive—so your partner can come to realize that his soul is still there. Through this realization, your partner should discover profound healing."

England, Diane, PHD. The Post-Traumatic Stress Disorder Relationship—How to Support Your Partner and Keep Your Relationship Healthy. Pg. 10, 11, 12. Adams Media, 2009.

The Physiology & Psychology of PTSD

"One of God's top design priorities when He created us was that we be equipped to defend ourselves and survive in a wide variety of dangerous situations. To this end, He equipped us with an amazing set of response mechanisms in our brain.

"Our brain is divided into two halves. The left side is our analytical side. It scrutinizes incoming information logically, thinks rationally, explicitly and in concrete terms. It's on this side that practical information, our ability to speak, read, write, spell and do math is stored. This side remembers names and craves precision.

"If our left side is more like a 'computer,' our right side is more like a 'photo album.' This side remembers faces and craves rapport and relationship. It's our emotional side. It's intuitive, spontaneous, experience-oriented, artistic and creative. It stores emotions. We dream on this side of our brain. More importantly, this side is the 'alarm' side.

"Beneath these two halves is our 'lower brain' or brain stem. This part…controls all automatic life functions, such as our breathing, digestion and heartbeat. The lower brain trumps the two halves of our higher brain.

"When we encounter something that we feel threatens our life, a cascade of hormonal reactions is triggered. A nerve shoots a message to our adrenal glands to dump adrenaline into our bloodstream, causing our heart to beat faster, our lungs to pump harder, getting the rest of the body ready to either fight, fly or freeze. Our pupils dilate, giving us tunnel vision so we can focus on the threat and not be distracted by peripheral action. Thousands of small muscles in our arms and legs constrict, sending blood away from our skin and into our muscles for quick movement so that if our extremities are wounded, we won't bleed as badly. Our blood sugar and free fatty acids instantly ramp up, giving us more energy. Up to 70% of our brain-bound oxygen is quickly shunted into our muscles so we can run, kick or punch…Additional hormones give us uncommon strength and quickness.

"But something happens deep inside our brains, too. Our right-brain alarm goes off, and drowns out the logical analysis of our left brain. It screams, 'Less thinking, more action!' It also starts taking pictures…the noradrenalin heightens the emotional aspects of the situation making it more vivid and notable. Very strong and clear memories are being recorded, probably so we will remember this event and avoid it in the future.

"At this point, our lower brain takes over. It's live-or-die time. With this organ in control, nothing else matters. It automatically directs the rest of the body in very complex but focused ways to do whatever it takes to survive.

"Research has shown that your body will exhibit these built-in survival techniques no matter what your race or gender is, whether you come from a privileged background or the ghetto, whether you are mentally slow or highly intelligent, whether you come from a happy family or a broken one, whether you're a cheerful person or a total pessimist, whether you're young or old. But it's important to know two things:

"God gave us this reactive pathway so that we would be able to do whatever was necessary to survive. It kept your husband alive. God knows that when our lives are threatened this behavior needs to come out or we will die. No matter how hard your husband might have tried, he couldn't have stopped this reaction. We're unable to control ourselves when our brains have clicked into this mode."

Adsit, Chris; Adsit, Rahnella; Waddell, Marshele Carter, "When War Comes Home." Military Ministry Press 2008

The PTSD "Armored Man"

What other symptoms are common when a combat warrior suffers with post-traumatic stress disorder?

There Can Be Present:

- Lack of feelings/emotions
- Lack of trust/suspicious
- Stress and feeling helpless
- "Numbing"
- Frustration
- Poor self-esteem
- Intrusive memories/nightmares, depression, and apathy
- Loss of motivation
- Loss of interest

- Negative self-image
- Poor judgment
- Lack of communication
- Flashbacks
- Short-term memory loss
- Startle reflexes
- Anxiety
- Hyper-vigilance
- Poor concentration
- Insomnia
- Guilt/"survivor's" guilt
- Hyper-arousal/hyperactivity
- Isolation/withdrawal
- Anger/rage
- Severe sadness, grief
- Blaming of others
- Fear of recurrence
- Denial
- Conflicts/marital discord
- Loss of appetite
- Inability to sleep
- Fatigue

A PTSD-Impaired Household

"Children are <u>not</u> resilient. Have you been focusing your full attention on your partner, assuming that your children are resilient and able to deal with whatever life tosses their way? This may seem to be true if you're confusing surviving with thriving.

"Indeed, children do seem to be capable of surviving all sorts of horrific things simply because they have little choice but to do so. They develop defense mechanisms that help them get through difficult times, but not without repercussions.

"Furthermore, these defense mechanisms often get in the way once these children enter adulthood, keeping them from developing the desired type of relationship with a romantic partner or attaining closeness with their own children.

"In fact, rather than risk passing down a hurtful legacy, some will avoid marrying or having children—not because this is what they truly want, but because they feel that they are damaged goods. They believe that if they were to proceed and have families, they may be a cause of harm to their own children."

The Aftermath of Vietnam

"You may know that many children of Vietnam War veterans were impacted by growing up with fathers who had lost their capability to form intimate connections with their children and their wives. These soldiers were wounded by PTSD—although, remember, society did not know what PTSD was at the time. They often wanted to be left alone.

"Certainly, their children craved their love because it is normal and healthy to both want to receive as well as to give love, and they wanted the attention of these men who were emotionally crippled by PTSD. Unfortunately, rather than having this need met, these children often faced fathers who spewed forth anger due to PTSD's hyper-arousal symptom.

"These children felt painfully rejected, but they didn't understand what was happening. Like many children who face such painful things, they often blamed themselves for the problem. They believed that what happened had occurred because they were bad, which caused these children to come to harbor feelings of not being good enough.

"In fact, such children may have come to feel worthless and carried that feeling with them as they grew into adulthood. Fortunately, with the information that you're learning, your children (and grandchildren) don't have to suffer this type of experience."

England, Diane, PHD. "The Post-traumatic Stress Disorder Relationship—How to Support Your Partner and Keep Your Relationship Healthy. Pg. 212, 213. Adams Media 2009

Complications in the Managing of PTSD

The managing of PTSD is exacting and especially difficult when it is combined with any of the following entities:

- Numerous traumatic events as in frequent military combat missions.
- When military and personal trauma events are combined and occurring in the same amount of time.
- When there is alcohol and drug abuse.
- When there is a grief experience during the same timeline.
- When there is serious, substantial, and underlying, emotional depression.
- When there are physical disabilities.
- When there are memory and mental problems.
- When there are additional mental disorders.
- When there is an additional physical illness.

Dean suffered nonstop from post-traumatic stress disorder. For him all the many, many symptoms were intrusive, grueling, and challenging in so many areas.

However, the one that was the most problematic for him and our family was the consequences of his PTSD's anger and rage.

Please find below a breakdown and better interpersonal understanding of anger management and its consequences:

Anger Management: Interpersonal Effects for You or Your Loved One

Because of anger consequences:

- Others tend to avoid and distance themselves from you.
- You are less likely to have close friends and support systems.
- You are more likely to feel lonely and isolated.
- You are more sensitive to criticism.
- You are more likely to misread the intentions of others.
- Insults, screaming, yelling, and cursing can easily escalate into violent confrontations.
- Anger and appearing out of control can result in a loss of respect from loved ones.
- Overreactions to anger provide poor examples to children and others you may care about and want to influence.
- Anger closes out opportunities for looking at options to resolve problems and disagreements.
- Turning anger inwards and becoming quiet and withdrawn can lead to a "festering" anger that creates a negative and unpleasant atmosphere to be around.
- Ignoring, withdrawing, and/or acting cold toward someone you are upset with is hurtful and may make the situation even worse.

Which statements are true for you or your loved one?

- People tell me I have a bad temper.
- I have done things when I am angry that I later regret.
- My anger is sometimes out of proportion to the seriousness of the situation.

- My anger has gotten me into trouble.
- I have hurt others while I was angry.
- There are times I feel like I'm about to explode.
- My anger sometimes scares me.

Which additional statements are true for you or a family member or friend?

- I become quiet and withdrawn.
- I shut down and don't communicate.
- I am easily and often offended by what others say and do.
- I am not very aware of my anger.
- I only become aware of my anger after an incident.

The Quick Series Guide to Anger Management
The Vet Center—www.vetcenter.va.gov.

PTSD and Grieving

When PTSD is present, we enter a grieving process. In a previous chapter, I was grieving over what I had lost—what my faith and marriage had lost—to post-traumatic stress disorder!

Not only does the spouse grieve; the combat veteran also grieves over what has been taken from him and forever lost to PTSD, such as his youth and his childhood imaginings!

Hopes and dreams and innocence have been lost; relationships, the way we remember them, have been lost. We grieve because we do not want to let go of these components of our lives and our marriages—the history, the identity we love and cherish.

War and war trauma have stolen them. And it is different now—so different that it pains us unto death!

Some call it compassion fatigue! Showing compassion does not make you vulnerable, and when combined with fatigue, it shows the world the depth of your love for your partner.

Grief has been created in us in order for us to deal with life's losses and assimilate them into our faculties enabling us to become stronger, with more power and abilities.

You know the saying, "What doesn't kill us makes us stronger!" Grief is like that. When we are able and willing to work with it, grief can create in us powerhouses for life's journey, and as a result, we can tackle all life brings.

Yes, the man or woman, the combat soldier we saw leave for war never returned and will never return again. Nevertheless, at least someone came back in his/her place. We do have someone and something from which to build, if we choose to. Now, all we need is hope and compassionate people surrounding and supporting us.

Someone reading may state, "I didn't know my husband before the war. I married him after he came back. Now he won't include me in his pain because I wasn't around at that time and, therefore, must not understand."

I will suggest this answer for that statement: When there is present in a relationship, in a marriage, sufficient compassion, sensitivity, concern, caring, empathy, and abiding love—in addition to including the creation of a safe place for him/her to share his/her experiences, he or she will include you—and the family! (However, if they should not, then you have done for them everything in your power and at your disposal!)

This positive happened for us. Try it. Hopefully you, too, will experience positive results also!

PTSD: What Can Cause Combat Stress Responses?

The professionals in mental health have not discovered why some veterans have PTSD reactions to war trauma and other veterans do not.

Whether a veteran suffers with trauma or not does not say anything about his/her moral fiber or his/her inner makeup. Just because he/she develops PTSD does not mean that he/she is weaker and lacking in bravery or strength or aptitude; it is not saying that his/her fellow comrades have more strong points and are more fearless and daring and capable.

Also, the combat vet with post-traumatic stress disorder has not chosen to acquire this illness; it's not like he/she wants and is seeking to have PTSD.

The difference may have something to do with life's prior occurrences, such as having gone through a series of threatening experiences, perhaps encountering previous suffering and anguish, or there may be a definite lack of private and public assistance and encouragement.

Left untreated, PTSD can have a negative impact on the family as well and can progress into serious harmful habits.

If the combat soldier is self-medicating his/her stress, his/her nightmares, his/her flashbacks with alcohol, drugs, or isolation, he/she must be encouraged to seek treatment for his/her sake and those around him/her.

The longer he/she waits to seek help or the longer he/she remains undiagnosed, the lengthier will be his/her recovery.

Adsit, Rev. Chris, "The Combat Trauma Healing Manual." Military Ministry Press 2007

Adsit, Chris; Adsit, Rahnella; Waddell, Marshele Carter, "When War Comes Home." Military Ministry Press 2008

PTSD and Hope

Family members can develop secondary PTSD as a mechanism for surviving in a PTSD household. Existing with a combat warrior/veteran showing symptoms of post-traumatic stress can cause extreme anxiety and tension within the family and serious domestic upheaval.

Living within an impaired PTSD family unit has introduced us to adversity, tragedy, and crisis—sometimes our own and other times, it happens as we assist in our spouse's struggle. We must have H*O*P*E to not only persevere but to carry us into flourishing and growing our lives while we walk in a supportive role beside the lives of our partners.

There are four characteristics that people possess who have survived adversity:

1) To carry on, we must have a good friend—a friend who helps us cope with our terrifying fears. A friend who will listen and is nonjudgmental.
2) We must understand the magnitude of what we have lost—to enter the grieving process and to let the tears flow.
3) We must overcome guilt and regrets and concentrate on defining our good qualities.
4) To survive our difficult marriages, we must have a reason to live. We must allow ourselves to make future plans, to dream—to get beyond our past losses and grief.

H*O*P*E is something we seek after, we cherish and latch on to with a steel grip, because it is the motivation that propels our lives with reasons to grow, reasons to go on, to advance, to seek a life of abundance rather than to merely exist and function in limitation.

Because of being born in America, it seems that H*O*P*E is inbred in us. Presidents Washington and Lincoln often spoke of H*O*P*E. It is what motivates us, what fuels us to get up in the morning, to be of service to others, to be all we can be for family, friends, even strangers, and to do enjoyable, lasting things for ourselves, as well.

Webster states that the definition for the word hope is as follows: Hope is a feeling; we women are all about feelings. Therefore, hope is a feeling that what is wanted or needed will happen; it is a desire, accompanied by anticipation—to want very much, to look for, ; to be optimistic; to wish for.

When we hope against hope, it means we go on having hope though it seems to be baseless or foundationless.

To be hopeful is to be inspiring and giving hope.

To be hopeless is to arouse no hope, to despair, to be discouraged. Despondency implies the state of being in very low spirits due to a loss of hope and a sense of futility about continuing one's efforts.

Our greatest hope comes from God, who is our anchor in life. As we surround ourselves with understanding family and friends then our comfort zone, our outlook becomes healthier, more optimistic, more peaceful, and, therefore, more enjoyable.

In other words, Hope = helping overcome and provide encouragement; we must allow ourselves the "liberty, the permission" to overcome adversity (unfavorable circumstances) while providing encouragement for ourselves and others of us in need; to expand, develop, progress and evolve into well and whole participants in this life !

Recovery from PTSD

Recovery is not an instant cure.

Recovery is a daily, ongoing, and gradual process.

Recovery is not a complete elimination of all stress memories and symptoms.

Recovery means that a mature, healthy person maintains memories and emotions associated with the traumatic event and learns from them.

Healing means fewer, less disturbing symptoms and greater confidence in your ability to manage them.

PTSD: Spiritual Symptoms

- World is unjust or unfair
- Loss of belief in God
- Lack of order and congruence in life
- Not feeling spiritual
- Shattered self-esteem and self-efficacy
- Hopelessness
- World is unpredictable and unsafe
- No trust of others
- Feeling abandoned by God
- Finding it hard to pray
- No spirit of thankfulness
- Seeing no value in Scripture

A crisis of faith is a condition in which a person's normal, established relationship with God or one's spiritual worldviews are violated and appear helpless or useless. A crisis of faith is characterized by:

- Cessation from practice of faith
- Religious obsessions
- Religious compulsions
- Religious hallucinations or delusions

Symptoms Requiring Immediate Corrective Action

- Chest pain or difficulty breathing
- Excessive blood pressure
- Collapse from exhaustion
- Unusual cardiac patterns
- Mental confusion, disorientation to place, time, and person
- Hallucinations, delusions, disordered, and racing thoughts

- Severe fear and panic attacks
- Numb, shock-like state
- Exaggerated emotions
- Uncontrolled rage
- Slurred, unintelligible, extremely slow or rapid speech
- Violent outbursts
- Suicidal actions
- Continuous rocking motions, facial tremors or body shakes
- Flashbacks (Flashbacks are extremely vivid images that cause a person to feel as though the event is happening again. Flashbacks are actually hallucinations and serious signals of distress. Professional intervention is indicated.)

The Vet Center –"PTSD" 2006-2009 quick series
"Traumatic Stress" 2008—2009 quick series www.vetcenter.va.gov

PTSD: "Coping Measures That Do Not Work"

Avoid these behaviors:

- Alcohol or drug use to sleep, relax, lower anxiety, or block thoughts and images about combat. Substances cannot cure PTSD.
- Social isolation. Avoiding people cuts back on friendships, social support, and emotional closeness. It also means that the veteran has more time to worry, be lonely, and feel helpless.
- Dropping out of pleasurable or recreational activities. This means fewer opportunities to feel good about one self and to develop a sense of achievement.
- Anger keeps people away and blocks positive connections and support from people who care about you.
- Turning off people, places, thoughts, or situations that remind you of the traumatic event. It does not control distress, and it prevents you from progressing in recovery.

- Constant work. Work addiction is no solution. It deepens isolation and eliminates many of life's positive experiences.

"Measures That Help"

Do not leave your recovery up to others. They can certainly help, but you have to do most of the work. You are the most important person in your recovery.

Coping measures that help:

- Participate in crisis and stress management programs.
- Obtain a psychological evaluation to confirm PTSD.
- Learn about PTSD. Read books. Take a class.
- Accept appropriate help.
- Remember that most people recover from PTSD.

The Vet Center "PTSD" 2006 - 2009 Quick Series - www.vetcenter.va.gov

Spiritual Measures for Recovery

- Begin your new life with Christ.
- Daily prayers: create a close relationship with God.
- Hide God's Word (Bible) in your heart.
- Seek God's plan, his will, for your life.
- Believe and trust in God's ability and willingness to create miracles in the recovery of PTSD.